ENHANCING TEACHER EDUCATION, DEVELOPMENT, AND EVALUATION

Enhancing Teacher Education, Development, and Evaluation examines the complex role that recent educational reforms have played in the teaching profession. The failure of programs like Race to the Top to benefit teaching and learning outcomes has yielded many questions about what went wrong and how a research-based plan for true systemic progress could actually work. Covering inaccurate narratives about schools and student achievement, evidence for teacher effectiveness, and the history and repercussions of Race to the Top, this book culminates with a proposal for future research and policy initiatives that more accurately and more equitably prioritize the measurement and improvement of teaching and learning. Five concise yet comprehensive chapters invite teacher and principal educators, teachers and school leaders in training, district administrators, policymakers, and other stakeholders to better understand the implications of and possible paths beyond misguided reform efforts. An overview of the recent past and an inspiration for the immediate future, this definitive analysis offers insights into how more reasonable, empirically derived strategies will ultimately foster more successful schools.

Alyson L. Lavigne is Assistant Professor of Instructional Leadership at Utah State University, USA.

Thomas L. Good is Professor Emeritus (and former Chair) of the Department of Educational Psychology at the University of Arizona, USA.

ENHANCING TEACHER EDUCATION, DEVELOPMENT, AND EVALUATION

Lessons Learned from Educational Reform

Alyson L. Lavigne and
Thomas L. Good

Routledge
Taylor & Francis Group

NEW YORK AND LONDON

First published 2019
by Routledge
52 Vanderbilt Avenue, New York, NY 10017

and by Routledge
2 Park Square, Milton Park, Abingdon, Oxon OX14 4RN

Routledge is an imprint of the Taylor & Francis Group, an informa business

© 2019 Taylor & Francis

Library of Congress Cataloging-in-Publication Data
Names: Lavigne, Alyson Leah, author. | Good, Thomas L., 1943- author.
Title: Enhancing teacher education, development, and
evaluation : lessons learned from educational
reform / Alyson L. Lavigne and Thomas L. Good.
Description: New York, NY : Routledge, 2019. |
Includes bibliographical references and index.
Identifiers: LCCN 2018057369| ISBN 9781138640887
(hardback : alk. paper) | ISBN 9781138640894 (pbk. : alk. paper) |
ISBN 9781315630892 (ebook)
Subjects: LCSH: Teachers--Training of--United States. |
Teacher effectiveness--United States. | Educational change--United States.
Classification: LCC LB1715 .L34 2019 | DDC 370.71/1--dc23
LC record available at https://lccn.loc.gov/2018057369

ISBN: 978-1-138-64088-7 (hbk)
ISBN: 978-1-138-64089-4 (pbk)
ISBN: 978-1-315-63089-2 (ebk)

Typeset in Sabon
by Taylor & Francis Books

CONTENTS

ILLUSTRATIONS

Figure

Tables

ABOUT THE AUTHORS

Alyson L. Lavigne is Assistant Professor of Instructional Leadership at Utah State University. Using her training as an educational psychologist and classroom researcher, Lavigne has conducted research on teacher retention, teachers' beliefs, teacher supervision and evaluation, and Latinx students' experiences. Her work has been featured in *Teaching and Teacher Education, Teachers College Record, Journal of Teacher Education, Education Policy Analysis Archives, and Humanity & Society*, and in three recent books co-authored with Thomas Good, *Looking in Classrooms* (11th ed.), *Improving Teaching through Observation and Feedback: Going Beyond State and Federal Mandates*, and *Teacher and Student Evaluation: Moving Beyond the Failure of School Reform*. Most recently, she has merged her interest in educational policy, specifically teacher evaluation, and teaching and motivation in schools that serve Latinx students, in order to focus on instructional practices and leadership in schools that serve diverse youth and dual language learners.

Thomas L. Good is Professor Emeritus (and former Chair) of the Department of Educational Psychology at the University of Arizona. Previously he has taught at the University of Texas, Austin and at the University of Missouri, Columbia. His long-term interests include the improvement of teaching and classroom learning. This work, focused on research on teacher expectations and teacher effectiveness, has been supported by many agencies including the National Institute of Health, the National Science Foundation, the National Institute of Education, the Carnegie Foundation, the Spencer Foundation, and the U.S. Department of Education. His books have been translated into several languages including Chinese, Japanese, German, and Spanish. He also has broad interests in policy issues such as proactive youth development. And, in recent collaboration with Alyson Lavigne, he has written two books that systematically explored educational policies focusing on teacher evaluation: *Improving Teaching through Observation and Feedback: Going Beyond State and Federal Mandates*, and *Teacher and*

Student Evaluation: Moving Beyond the Failure of School Reform. Also, they reviewed extant research on theoretical conceptions of various educational topics, their research base, and their collective value for informing teacher practice in the recent revision of the textbook *Looking in Classrooms* (2018).

PREFACE

This is an ambitious and, we hope, influential book about school reform, our third volume on this complex topic. Our last two books explored the rise of contemporary accountability programs and suggested best practices for working through these demanding evaluation guidelines. Here we capture *why* these school reforms have failed even though they have consumed vast resources, including time and money. Further, our various analyses of reform movements have provided us insight into *how* better planning can lead to more reasonable reform strategies and ultimately more successful schools.

Our book pays careful attention to Race to the Top (RTTT). Our review of RTTT (a federal reform mandating high-stakes teacher evaluation) considers its intent, its selection and funding of winners, its methodology, and its measures of success—improvements to teaching and learning. Our results describe principals' performance in providing teacher feedback, teachers' classroom practices, and student achievement. We combine our knowledge of past reforms, the results of RTTT, what others have written about RTTT and past reforms, and our own extensive experiences in classrooms to describe coherent strategies for improving schools. Our suggestions build on past knowledge but also offer bold and productive new pathways.

In Chapter 1, we provide a context for our book by presenting a paradox that reflects the climate that surrounded RTTT (and still exists today): Teachers are highly valued, yet starkly underpaid. What factors explain this paradox? In Chapter 1, we suggest that this paradox exists in part because the media and policymakers project negative and inaccurate narratives of schools, teachers, and students—blaming teachers for students' low achievement. We note the more recent sympathetic coverage by the media and, with it, the possibility of improving educational resources and productivity. Whether these trends—positive public and media support for teachers—will continue remains to be seen.

Chapter 2 shows the evidence that teachers matter (as noted in Chapter 1). Unfortunately, policymakers used this research knowledge to erroneously conclude that high-stakes teacher evaluation was necessary if schools were to be transformed. Policymakers capitalized upon the research on teachers' effects and combined it with the mistaken belief that teachers *caused* low achievement. Here we explore questions such as: How much do teachers matter? Do some teachers matter more than others? What teaching practices consistently relate to student achievement outcomes? Is teacher effectiveness stable? We close by noting that available research on teacher effects had rich potential to inform RTTT. This chapter establishes what is known and not known about effective teaching and it creates realistic expectations about what teachers can do alone to overcome the effects of poverty.

In Chapter 3, we provide a brief history of the last 40 years of education reform leading up to RTTT. Then we broadly describe RTTT. We address: How did RTTT emerge? What did RTTT entail? What were the intended independent and dependent variables? What did RTTT assume about teaching and learning? We note that in addition to improving the overall effectiveness of the teacher pool through more rigorous evaluations, RTTT sought to improve education by requiring principals to spend more time in classrooms and providing teachers with more feedback. We also consider: How were RTTT applicants scored? Who won RTTT dollars? Why? Was the evaluation fair?

In Chapter 4, we analyze the effects of RTTT. We ask: Did it change how principals enacted teacher evaluation and supervision? In addressing this issue, we provide a specific analysis of principal practices before and after RTTT. How good were the measures used to evaluate teachers? We include findings from major projects that explored the effects of RTTT policies and practices on teaching and learning outcomes. We report the effects of RTTT on student achievement (generally and for specific subgroups of students). Finally, we ask and answer: Did RTTT improve teaching and learning through observation and feedback or the overall composition of teacher effectiveness through more rigorous teacher evaluations? Our answer is no, and we present evidence that teachers and principals agree.

In Chapter 5 we explore: What went wrong? Why did RTTT fail? In our analysis, we discuss policymakers' failure to account for various factors, including: the preparation of principals to be instructional leaders, the complexity of teaching, and the existing knowledge on teacher effects. Following our assessment, we address: What now? We provide suggestions for future education reform. We discuss how teacher and principal-preparation programs can prioritize improving teaching and learning. We provide principals with strategies for observing and enhancing teacher growth and development. We suggest ways for classroom research to inform decision-making and improve teaching and learning. Finally, we note how schools and society can support these efforts, and we underscore that society and policymakers need to recognize that teachers can only do so much.

In this book, we thoroughly document that RTTT failed. Once again, we find policymakers enacting expensive and sweeping reform that ignores both school context and existing research. We gather insights from this failed reform and combine them with research knowledge to provide suggestions for improving practice.

Toward the future: teachers are important to students, and to society. As in any profession, teaching can be improved. And, as in any institution, some individuals perform better than others, and there is ample room for any of us to improve over time. Although it must be an important part of any district's improvement portfolio, too much emphasis has been placed on individual improvement, rather than allowing teacher teams (e.g., grade level) to cooperatively devise and implement reform. We believe that it is time for fundamental reform strategies to shift from external to internal control. Years of reform and tons of research has illustrated that mandated top-down reform fails. It is time to trust and to allow teachers, principals, superintendents, and school-board members to assume the responsibility for enhancing schools. Beyond this, citizens need to stop policymakers from implementing expensive, sweeping, and unrealistic reforms that are not supported by research evidence. Instead, citizens need to demand that policymakers fund schools with the resources that they need—and, if they do this, they can expect that educational performance will improve. Tomorrow's enhancements depend more upon additional resources than they do on increased evaluation.

ACKNOWLEDGMENTS

We acknowledge the helpful and extensive work by Natasha Sterzinger and Shouqing Si who assisted with typing drafts of chapters, preparing tables, checking and formatting references, and tracking down relevant literature. Finally, we would like to thank our dedicated editor, Dan Schwartz, who was with us from start to finish.

1

TEACHING IN AMERICA
A Paradox—Highly Valued but Lowly Paid

Introduction

This chapter raises a paradox. Given that we know A) that teachers are important determinants of student learning, and B) that society values student achievement, then C) why are teachers underpaid? Before discussing this paradox, we present a very brief review of research on *effective teaching* to support our claim that teachers have important effects on student learning. We do this because some citizens question teachers' importance. At one time (as recently as the early 1970s) many social scientists believed that teachers made little difference to student learning, as it was commonly believed that student learning was due primarily to social class and inherited intelligence. In time, research established that teachers can make a difference to student learning.

We begin the chapter by firmly asserting that teachers have important effects on student achievement. Today we know that teachers are important and we cite numerous scholars who have concluded that teachers impact student achievement. Later, in Chapter 2, we illustrate how this knowledge was obtained and discuss its implications for teaching practice and evaluation.

After clearly establishing that teachers are important, we discuss the central issue of this chapter—that teachers are highly valued but underpaid. As we document that teachers are underpaid, we also show that fewer teacher candidates are now entering teacher-education programs than before, that we have a teaching shortage in many places, and that teacher morale and salaries continue to decrease. Despite these conditions, parents value teachers and schools, especially the ones their children attend. Parents and citizens are increasingly reporting that teachers deserve more pay, and yet teachers remain poorly paid. How can this paradox be explained?

This chapter also addresses the media's influence on public education. We document that, historically, the media have depicted teachers and schools negatively. We discuss why that has occurred. In marked contrast, we report that the media have become more supportive of teachers, perhaps because of the recent and highly salient teacher strikes that made the media (and the public) more aware of teaching conditions and the difficult problems that teachers face. Yet criticism of public education exists (and may increase). Whether favorable media attention for teachers will continue remains to be seen.

Until recently, educators have not been able to make the case to the media that teachers are important. As we discuss later in the chapter (pp. 26–27), a particular reason why educators have not been heard is because of the publication of government reports such as "A Nation At Risk," "No Child Left Behind," and "Goals 2000." These reports have lamented the crises of schools and the fact that many of our teachers and schools are failing. In this chapter, we refute these reports and reach more favorable conclusions about teachers and student learning. We argue that there is increasing evidence—including low pay for teachers, below-par working conditions, and the shortage of teachers—to justify the need for more resources for public schools, their teachers, and students. However, it remains to be seen whether or not citizens, policymakers, and the media will support increased funding for schools. We end by noting that some 'pushback' has been directed toward recent gains in media and public support for teachers.

A Brief Comment on the Research on Teaching: Then and Now

Then: Little Was Known About Teacher Effectiveness

The search to identify teacher actions that influence student achievement has had a long history. At one point, little was known about the relationship between teacher actions and student achievement. This lack of knowledge is demonstrated in the two quotes that appear below:

> The simple fact of the matter is that, after 40 years of research on teacher effectiveness during which a vast number of studies have been carried out, one can point to few outcomes that a superintendent of schools can safely employ in hiring a teacher or granting him tenure, that an agency can employ in certifying teachers, or that a teacher-education faculty can employ in planning or improving teacher-education programs.
>
> (Barr et al., 1953, p. 657)[1]

> This review is an admission that we know very little about the relationship between classroom behavior and student gains. It is a plea for more research on teaching. It is also a plea to educational researchers and to teacher educators to devote more time and money to the study of classroom teaching.
>
> (Rosenshine & Furst, 1971, p. 37)[2]

2

Now: Much Is Known About Teacher Effectiveness

Today, we know that teachers are important determinants of students' learning. And we have known this for roughly 45 years (Good, Biddle, & Brophy, 1975). Students enter the classroom with widely different levels of knowledge and life experience. However, beyond those differences, future learning progress depends greatly on classroom teachers. Teachers have greater impact on students' academic learning than any other school factor—including textbooks, the quality of the library, technology, or the science laboratory. The importance of teacher effects on student achievement is widely acknowledged (Aaronson, Barrow, & Sanders, 2007; Berliner & Tikunoff, 1976; Brophy & Good, 1986; Cohen, Ruzek, & Sandilos, 2018; Fisher et al., 1981; Goldhaber, 2016; Goldhaber & Brewer, 1999; Good & Grouws, 1979; Good, Grouws, & Ebmeier, 1981; Hanushek, 2011; Hanushek, 2016; Hanushek, Kain, & Rivkin, 1998; Konstantopoulus, 2014; Rubie-Davies, 2014). In Chapter 2 we will explicate this assertion—that teachers are important—by illustrating how this knowledge was obtained and its importance for practice and policy.

A Paradox: Teachers Are Valued but Underpaid

Teachers are important but underpaid. Within this paradox there are conflicting riptides of opinions. Some say that teachers have easy jobs, they have their summers "off," and they are protected by strong unions, meaning that ineffective teachers remain and consequently our students achieve less. Further, these critics often assert that schools are dangerous places and that teachers do not do enough to protect students. In contrast, other voices contend that teaching is complex and that teachers perform admirably, especially when considering the conditions they face (e.g., teaching students who speak multiple languages or dealing with the pernicious effects of poverty). Given these clashing opinions, how can society make conclusions about the quality of teachers and the remuneration they deserve? We now address these conflicting opinions.

Teachers Are Acclaimed by Famous Athletes, Actors, and Actresses

Teachers are often remembered fondly by their students. Although adults may not have liked all their teachers, almost everyone can identify at least a handful of teachers that impacted their lives. Famous athletes like Magic Johnson—a former basketball All American at Michigan State University and NBA star for the Los Angeles Lakers, and now a part-owner of the Los Angeles Dodgers as well as a chain of movie theaters and other businesses—has frequently expressed the importance of his fourth-grade teacher. Many actors and actresses have also paid tribute to the important teachers in their lives (including Freddie Prinze Jr., actor and author of *Back to the Kitchen*; Carrie Preston, star of *Claws*; Scott Foley, star of *Scandal*; Katherine

McNamara, star of *Shadowhunters*; Lea Michele, star of *The Mayor*; Darby Stanchfield, star of *Scandal*; Erika Christensen, star of *Ten Days in the Valley*; see Brown West-Rosenthal, 2017).

Similarly, literary works, films, and TV shows, often focus on the positive impact of teachers. Consider just a few movies reflecting the importance of teachers: Mr. Keating in *Dead Poets Society*, Jaime Escalante in *Stand and Deliver*, Mrs. Johnson in *Dangerous Minds*, Walter White in *Breaking Bad*, Jane Eyre in *Jane Eyre*, Mark Thackeray in *To Sir, With Love*, Sue Sylvester and Will Schuester from *Glee*, Glen Holland from *Mr. Holland's Opus*, Mr. Garrison from *South Park*, Lydya Grant from *Fame*, Miss Honey from *Matilda*, Dewey Finn from *School of Rock*, Albus Dumbledore from *Harry Potter*, and Mr. Chips from *Goodbye Mr. Chips*.

Most Americans Support Teachers

Table 1.1 illustrates that Americans show significant support for public schools and their teachers. Most public-school parents have consistently rated their local schools as doing well—often with an A or B—and they have done so consistently since 1984 (PDK, 2016). This stable parent report fails to support the notion that schools are *in crisis*. Together, data from these polls suggest that the greater the interaction an individual has with schools, the more favorably they rate the schools. The average American (especially those without children in school) is less positive than the average American parent about American schools and the parents are more supportive of the schools that they know best—the ones that their children attend. Later, we will discuss more fully this discrepancy between Americans who have children in school and those who do not (p. 5, 8). Further, we discuss the sharply different ratings in how local schools are rated versus schools nationally (p. 5, 8).

The Teaching Profession Is Valued

Not only are individual teachers affirmed but the field of teaching itself is also considered important to society. In 2013 the Pew Research Center (2013) (Religion & Public Life) surveyed citizens about those professions that make a significant contribution to society. The military ranked first—as 78% of respondents reported that the armed services contributed a great deal to society's wellbeing. The next highest rating was for teachers (72%), followed by medical doctors (66%), and scientists (65%). Subsequently, along these same lines, the Pew Research Center (2017) reported that education was the third biggest issue that citizens thought that Congress and the president should address. Only terrorism and the economy drew more concerns from the public.[3]

Table 1.1 Selected Results from the *Phi Delta Kappan* Survey on American Education

Phi Delta Kappan (PDK) Survey on Grading the Schools: Key Findings from the Public's Attitudes Toward the Public Schools Annual Survey

Year/ Annual Poll #	Key Findings from the Responses of American Citizens and Public-School Parents *(Parents' responses reflect the schools attended by their oldest child)*:
2018 (50th Poll)	• 70% of public-school parents give their local schools an A or B. • 43% of Americans rate their local schools as either A or B. • 19% of Americans rate public schools *nationally* with an A or B. • 66% of Americans state that teachers are underpaid. • 78% of public-school parents and 73% of Americans (including 6 in 10 identifying as republicans) would support teachers in their community if there went on strike for more pay.
2017 (49th Poll)	• 62% of public-school parents give their local schools an A or B. • 49% of Americans give their local schools an A or B grade, matching its average since 1999. • 24% of Americans give public schools *nationally* an A or B grade. • In terms of just As, 15% of public-school parents give their local schools an A (which has increased from 9% a decade ago). This figure has only been surpassed once, in 1974.
2016 (48th Poll)	• 67% of public-school parents give their local school an A or B. • 48% of Americans give their local schools an A or B. • 24% of Americans give public schools *nationally* an A or B grade. • The share of Americans giving positive grades to the nation's public schools is up 7% since 2014, yet grades for local public schools have remained steady … This gap is its smallest since 2008.
2015 (47th Poll)	• 70% of public-school parents gave their local schools (attended by their oldest child) with either an A or B. • 51% of Americans gave their local schools either an A or B. • 21% of Americans gave schools *nationally* an A or B (which is consistent, given that over the past decade this has ranged between 16% and 22%). • 19% of public-school parents give schools *nationally* an A or B. • Biggest problem their local schools are facing: Financial support (has been top of list for a decade).

Phi Delta Kappan. (2017). The 49th PDK poll of the public's attitudes toward the public schools. Retrieved from https://journals.sagepub.com/doi/pdf/10.1177/0031721717728274. Phi Delta Kappan. (2018). The 50th PDKPoll of the public's attitudes toward thhe public schools. Retrieved from http://pdkpoll.org/assets/downloads/pdkpoll50_2018.pdf. Phi Delta Kappan. (2016). Why school? The 48th Annual PDK Poll of the Public's Attitudes Toward the Public Schools. *Phi Delta Kappan*, 98(1), NP1–NP32. https://doi.org/10.1177/0031721716666049. Phi Delta Kappan. (2015). The 47th PDK/Gallup poll of the public's attitudes toward the public schools. *Phi Delta Kappan*, 97(2), 52–57.

Given the perception that teaching addresses an important societal role and that society, and parents in particular, think that schools are doing an adequate job, it would seem that teachers should be adequately compensated. But they are not. If we were to express the value of teaching to society, the equation would seemingly be: good teaching = good salary. As we know from our study of algebra, one side of the equation should balance the other side. Unfortunately, the accurate equation in 2018 is that good teaching = inadequate salary.

Teachers Are Not Paid Well

In 2016–2017, the estimated average salary for K-12 teachers was approximately $58,950 (National Center for Education Statistics, 2017). The median pay for high-school teachers was $59,170 and the median pay for kindergarten teachers was $56,900. To put these figures in perspective, Fottrell (2018) noted that the average pay for an accountant was $69,350 and the current pay for a health service manager was $98,350. All these jobs (i.e., teachers, accountants, and health service managers) require a bachelor's degree, but clearly the average pay across these professions varies substantially.

How about beginning teachers' salaries as opposed to those of experienced teachers? In the 2016–2017 school year, a new teacher's starting salary was $38,617 on average. Starting salaries vary notably across states, with the District of Columbia boasting the highest at $51,359 and Montana having the lowest at $30,036 (National Education Association, 2017). (For detailed information see the Bureau of Labor Statistics at www.bls.gov.[4]) How do these compare to beginning wages in other professions? Not well. The average starting salary for teachers in California is $44,782 (National Education Association, 2017). The average starting base salary of a correctional officer in California is $53,256 and many make much more because of overtime and bonus payments (California Department of Corrections and Rehabilitation, 2018). And the differences in the amount of money to incarcerate a prisoner in California in 2016–2017 were roughly $71,000/year (California—Legislative Analyst's Office, 2016). In contrast, the expenditure per student for the 2014–2015 school year was $10,449/year (NCES, 2018).[5,6]

Typically, teachers do not get paid for overtime, nor do they receive bonuses, unlike some other professions. Consider that in 2017 the average *bonus* on Wall Street was $184,200, which was a 17% increase over the previous year. Importantly, this one-year bonus is almost five times greater than the annual salary of beginning teachers. Consider that the average salary paid to Wall Street workers was $422,000 (Dugan, 2018). Despite the fact that teachers are ranked of high importance and Wall Street workers are not (Pew Research Center, 2013), teacher pay is dwarfed in comparison to the remuneration of Wall Street workers.

Other countries

American teachers are paid considerably less than teachers in European countries such as Denmark, Germany, and Norway (Noack, 2018). In contrast to the United States, in almost all other countries that are members of the Organisation for Economic Cooperation and Development (OECD) (there are over 30), teachers' salaries have increased since 2005 according to an OECD 2018 report that compares teacher wages between 2005 and 2017.

Further, in Europe, teachers are often top earners and sometimes make more money than, for example, web developers or entry-level doctors (Noack, 2018). No other developed country has such a large pay discrepancy as does the US between teachers and other professionals with similar degrees.

What accounts for the gap between the importance of teaching and the rewards that American policymakers provide? Surely there must be some reason to explain why politicians pass budgets that compensate teachers so inadequately. What charges have been made against teachers? Why are teachers (and in our judgment, wrongly) short-changed?

The Charges Against Teachers

Disparaging negative claims are frequently made about teachers and teaching. Consider these claims:

- Teaching is an easy job and anybody can do it.
- Student achievement is exceedingly low and teachers are responsible.
- Students' poor achievement places our country at economic risk.
- Low graduation rates are due to inadequate teaching.
- Inadequate teaching occurs because teachers make too little effort.
- Lack of teacher effort is because strong teacher unions protect inadequate teachers.
- In school districts that do not have teacher unions, principals support poor teachers by rating them as effective—thereby refusing to identify incompetent teachers.
- The low quality of the present teaching force discourages young adults or established professionals in other fields to consider teaching as a career.
- If somehow we were to encourage potentially good teachers to enter teacher-education programs, these programs are so bereft of quality that such a candidates' potential would not be realized.
- We know what good teaching is, if only teacher-education programs would prepare teachers rather than complaining about social justice and inequality.

Media Reports Frequently Depict Schools as Failing and Teachers as Inadequate

However, despite considerable evidence that the critics charge against teachers is problematic—the criticism has "stuck" and thus these critics (including government reports[7]) have had considerable impact on the media. We have all seen pejorative headlines aimed at teachers, but admittedly it is difficult to determine how those headlines impact citizens and policy makers' beliefs about schools and teachers—and the level of compensation they deserve. Yet, negativity of media coverage undoubtedly lowers expectations about the quality of teachers for some, if not many readers. Consider the examples of negative depictions of teachers and schools that appear below in Table 1.2.

If you were a teacher reading these and many other headlines, would you feel supported and/or valued? Probably not. If you were a prospective teacher, would this information inspire you to teach? Probably not. On a national level, teachers rarely receive support from media outlets, but some teachers do receive positive support from students and parents in their local schools (and this may reduce the sting of media attacks on them to some extent). Still, it seems safe to conclude that these negative media accounts of teaching would not contribute to teachers' interest to stay in the field, nor would they encourage prospective teachers to join the field. Additionally, these negative reports would not encourage citizens to invest in education, especially those who do not have children at school. We now discuss the possible media effects on citizens who have more or less knowledge of schools.

Media Negativity Impacts Some Citizens More Than Others

Citizens with children in local schools possess personal knowledge of how teachers perform, and they often meet with teachers and receive classroom and school newsletters. Thus, their opinions about the quality of teachers are less dependent upon media depictions of schools. In contrast, the roughly 66% of citizens who do not have children in school are unlikely to have personal knowledge of what occurs in schools. Hence, they are highly dependent upon media coverage in forming opinions about the quality of schools. However, public-school parents may also be impacted by media because, as noted in Table 1.2, most parents rate their local schools extremely well, and yet only few would say the same nationally. For example, in 2017, 62% of public-school parents gave local schools an A or B, whereas only 24% gave schools nationally an A or B.

Thus, many citizens are potentially impacted by the negative media reports about schooling in America. Not only do teachers and parents read these headlines, they are also read by policymakers. Given the continual deluge of negative headlines, it would seem reasonable to conclude that this coverage would not encourage them (nor the 66% of taxpayers who are not parents) to increase teacher pay or to add other resources to education. Further, consider that much media coverage of schooling has been harsh. For example, Coe and Kuttner (2018) provided an authoritative 35-year review of educational coverage in television news, and concluded that these reports typically stressed school failure, often lampooned teachers as caring but ineffective, and unions as self-serving.

An Especially Egregious Media Example of Teacher-Bashing

The media coverage of 'bad teaching' is sometimes vicious. Consider the November 3, 2014 *Time Magazine* cover, which graphically depicts a judge's

Table 1.2 Examples of Negative Media Reports about Teachers and Schools

Date	News Source	Title	Link
Oct. 13, 2017	*New York Times*	Caught Sleeping or Worse, Troubled Teachers Will Return to New York Classrooms	https://www.nytimes.com/2017/10/13/nyregion/troubled-teachers-back-in-classrooms-new-york.html
Sep. 7, 2017	*New York Times*	New York's Bad Teachers, Back on the Job	https://www.nytimes.com/2017/09/07/opinion/new-york-bad-teachers.html
Apr. 27, 2017	*HuffPost*	Elementary School Teachers Accused of Bullying Students, Forcing them to Fight	https://www.huffingtonpost.com/entry/teachers-bullying-students_us_590248d4e4b0bb2d086c22b3
Aug. 15, 2016	Fox News	If Your Child's School Is Failing, Thank a Union	https://www.foxnews.com/opinion/if-your-childs-school-is-failing-thank-a-union
June 29, 2016	*The Atlantic*	Firing Bad Teachers: A Superintendent and a Teacher's Union Official Debate: Can due process for educators coexist with the ability to terminate abusive or unqualified individuals?	https://www.theatlantic.com/education/archive/2014/06/firing-bad-teachers-a-superintendent-and-a-teachers-union-official-debate/373651/
Apr. 1, 2016	*HuffPost*	All Teachers Suck. And Should Be Fired. And Stoned to Death.	https://www.huffingtonpost.com/eileen-oconnor/all-teachers-suck-and-sho_b_9587508.html
Apr. 1, 2015	*New York Times*	Atlanta Educators Convicted in School Cheating Scandal	https://www.nytimes.com/2015/04/02/us/verdict-reached-in-atlanta-school-testing-trial.html
Nov. 14 2014	CNN	Texas Teacher Fired After Ferguson Tweets	https://www.cnn.com/2014/11/14/us/texas-teacher-fired-ferguson-tweet/index.html
Nov. 3, 2014	*Time Magazine* Cover	Rotten Apples: It's Nearly Impossible to Fire A Bad Teacher	http://time.com/3533615/in-the-latest-issue-11/
June 16, 2014	Hechinger Report	How Many Bad Teachers Are There?	https://hechingerreport.org/many-bad-teachers/

(Continued)

Date	News Source	Title	Link
June 13, 2014	CNN	Will California Teacher Tenure Ruling Be a Lesson for Other States?	https://www.cnn.com/2014/06/13/us/teacher-tenure/index.html
Oct. 24 2013	Forbes	A Key Reason Why American Students Do Poorly	https://www.forbes.com/sites/georgeleef/2013/10/24/a-key-reason-why-american-students-do-poorly/#24572c7b2349
Mar. 29, 2013	National Public Radio	Grand Jury Indicts Dozens of Atlanta Educators over Cheating Scandal	https://www.npr.org/sections/thetwo-way/2013/03/29/175728192/grand-jury-indicts-dozens-of-atlanta-educators-over-cheating-scandal
Nov. 16, 2012	*The Atlantic*	Why Do So Many Teachers Quit Their Jobs? Because They Hate Their Bosses	https://www.theatlantic.com/national/archive/2012/11/why-do-so-many-teachers-quit-their-jobs-because-they-hate-their-bosses/265310/
Jan. 11, 2012	*New York Times*	The Value of Teachers	https://www.nytimes.com/2012/01/12/opinion/kristof-the-value-of-teachers.html
July 7, 2011	*Washington Post*	Shocking Details of Atlanta Cheating Scandal	https://www.washingtonpost.com/blogs/answer-sheet/post/shocking-details-of-atlanta-cheating-scandal/2011/07/06/gIQAQPhY2H_blog.html
June 24, 2011	*The Atlantic*	"Bad Teacher," the Answer to Sappy, Useless Good-Teacher Flicks: Finally, a film that takes down the destructive myth of the hero instructor	https://www.theatlantic.com/entertainment/archive/2011/06/bad-teacher-the-answer-to-sappy-useless-good-teacher-flicks/240949/
Sep. 20, 2010	*Time Magazine* Cover	What Makes a School Great: It all starts with the teachers … and why it's so hard to find good ones	http://content.time.com/time/covers/0,16641,20100920,00.html
Mar. 23, 2010	National Public Radio	Are Teachers Unions to Blame for Failing Schools?	https://www.npr.org/templates/story/story.php?storyId=125019386

(Continued)

Date	News Source	Title	Link
Mar. 10, 2010	Center for American Progress	Removing Chronically Ineffective Teachers	https://www.americanprogress.org/issues/education-k-12/reports/2010/03/10/7525/removing-chronically-ineffective-teachers/
Feb. 24, 2010	CNN	All Teachers Fired at Rhode Island School	http://www.cnn.com/2010/US/02/24/rhode.island.teachers/index.html
Feb. 5, 2010	Newsweek	Why We Must Fire Bad Teachers	https://www.newsweek.com/why-we-must-fire-bad-teachers-69467
May 4, 2009	US News	Urban Schools Need Better Teachers, Not Excuses, to Close the Education Gap	https://www.usnews.com/opinion/articles/2009/05/04/urban-schools-need-better-teachers-not-excuses-to-close-the-education-gap
May 6, 2008	*Guardian*	Poor Teachers Affecting Pupils' Grades, Study Shows	https://www.theguardian.com/education/2008/may/06/schools.uk5
Dec. 8, 2008	*Time Magazine* Cover	How to Fix America's Schools	http://content.time.com/time/covers/0,16641,20081208,00.html
Nov. 21, 2005	*New York Times*	Why the United States Should Look to Japan for Better Schools	https://www.nytimes.com/2005/11/21/opinion/why-the-united-states-should-look-to-japan-for-better-schools.html

gavel about to crush a bright red apple (*Time Magazine*, 2014). However, its attack on teachers does not end there. Internally, the cover story has the caption "It's really difficult to fire a BAD TEACHER." This is accompanied by a picture of four apples—in which one is rotten. To many readers this would suggest that 25% of our teachers are rotten and that they harm students. Understandably, many teachers and citizens were outraged by *Time Magazine*'s claim that many teachers were nothing more than bad apples.

The cover, editorial, and article consistently derided the teaching field by suggesting that it contains many incompetent teachers who cannot be fired, and that our students perform poorly in comparison to their international peers because of inadequate instruction. The magazine is replete with negative statements about teachers. For example, the comment that even students in Estonia outperformed those in America was "damning" and presumably chosen by both the editor and author to lampoon American teachers. As we will see later (p. 12, 14), Good (2014)[8,9] contended that there are compelling reasons why students in Estonia achieved well. And, now in 2018, it is clear that students in Estonia continue to do well.[10]

The Case for Teachers

Good (2014) wrote a letter criticizing the negative depiction of teachers in the 3 November edition of *Time Magazine*. His letter was not published by *Time Magazine*, however it was adopted by Division 15 (Educational Psychology) of the American Psychological Association as an official protest of the magazine cover and article. Interested readers can examine the letter at https://cloakinginequity.com/2014/10/31/teachers-matter-the-letter-defending-educators-time-wouldnt-print-timeapologize-timefail/.

Good (2014) noted that the explanations for the poor achievement in American schools were about things that were outside teachers' control. He referred to a report from the Stanford Center on Poverty and Inequality (a bipartisan research center, funded by various sources including the U.S. Department of Education) State of the Union Report (2014). This report had analyzed data from many viewpoints including labor markets, education, poverty, income, and health inequality, and documented the serious and growing problems of poverty and inequity including:

- Income inequality shows a relentless growth over 30 years.
- Economic and racial disparities in health outcomes are substantial.
- The consequences of these inequalities include producing "too many children poorly prepared for school."
- The number of children living in extreme poverty continue to increase.
- The relative wealth of those under 35 (those with more school-age children) has declined in comparison to that of older Americans.

Like those criticisms of teaching we presented earlier in the chapter, David Berliner, Gene Glass, and their colleagues (Berliner & Glass, 2014) identified 50 charges that are often made against teachers and schools. They called these charges "myths" and presented data to show that these charges were blatantly false. They noted that although these claims were frequently made in major media outlets, they were not true.

- International tests prove that the US is a second-rate educational system.
- Merit pay is a good way to increase the performance of teachers.
- Subject-matter knowledge is the most important asset a teacher can possess (see below).
- Standards in American education are being dumbed down.
- The money available to schools is distributed equally across schools (see below).
- Education will lift the poor out of poverty and enrich our entire nation.

The Charge Against Teachers Has Been Challenged

Berliner, Glass, and colleagues were responding to the onslaught of negative reporting frequently found in media sources. In the list that Berliner and Glass (2014) present, the intent of the criticism directed toward teachers and schools is generally clear. However, we amplify a couple of points to make the putative charge against teachers salient.

First, the comment about subject-matter knowledge may confuse some readers, but the message here is that society wastes too much money on teacher education, and instead we should hire arts and science graduates who *know* mathematics or science. Simply put, the belief is that subject-matter knowledge alone is sufficient to effectively teach in public schools. Why waste money on teacher education? However, data show that subject-matter knowledge is less important than various other skills and knowledge that teachers possess. There is ample evidence to show that knowledge of differential equations does not make a teacher better in teaching math to fourth-grade students. Presenting mathematics in ways to communicate effectively with young learners is exceedingly difficult, and demands more than subject-matter knowledge alone, as important as that is (Good & Lavigne, 2018; Hill, Umland, Litke, & Kapitula, 2012).

The second point, the comment about money being equally distributed across schools, may also benefit from amplification. The implied "meaning" in this myth is that all American students are supported equally with educational funds. This is not true because federal expenditures on education represent but a small part of school budgets and disparities in state and community funding are notable. This results in unequal funding and means that typically schools that instruct students from low-income homes receive notably less funding than schools that serve students from high-income homes (more on this later, p. 14). Thus, the "illusionary claim" that funds are equitably distributed obscures the fact that teachers who teach in schools serving students from low-income homes typically have fewer resources than those in more affluent schools. The implication by those critical of teaching is that it is ineffective teachers that cause low achievement and not inadequate funding.

School Critics Ignore the Wide Variation in School Conditions and Outcomes

Both the media and policymakers make egregious errors when they talk about schools in general terms. This is because generalizing about the effects of teachers and schools on student achievement is difficult unless the varied conditions in which American education unfolds are taken into account. (Schools vary in the level of resources that they receive, and in many other ways; some schools have homogenous student populations, whereas other schools have student populations that vary notably in socioeconomic status, ethnicity, and race.) Thus, it is not surprising that achievement varies widely from school to school. Bracey (1997) reported that the US leads the world both in terms of the number of high performers *and* low performers on international tests. These differences can be huge. Consider that in the same year students in Naperville, Illinois led the *world* in mathematics performance, whereas children in Dade County, Florida provided the *lowest* scores.

Good (2014) also suggested that data collected in the Programme for International Student Assessment (PISA) International Testing program showed that high-performing countries (including Estonia) allocated resources more equitably among income-advantaged schools and income-disadvantaged schools. However, in the US, high-poverty districts spend 15.6% less per student than more affluent districts do (U.S. Department of Education, 2015). In some states, such as Pennsylvania, high-poverty districts spend 33% less. These patterns replicate when examining district spending by percentage of minority students served. In Nevada, the highest-minority districts spend 30% less on students than the lowest-minority districts (U.S. Department of Education, 2015). Differences in resource and spending allocations have real effects. In the US, for example, the average White 13-year-old reads at a higher level and performs better in math than the average Black or Latino 17-year-old (Carter & Welner, 2013).[11]

As noted, data collected in the PISA make it clear that high-performing countries allocate resources more equitably among income-advantaged schools and income-disadvantaged schools. Thus, Estonia and most industrialized counties distribute money more equally to schools than is done in the US and thereby provide a playing field that is more level for all participants. Further, more equitable countries also provide better nutrition and healthcare for their citizens, especially children. The modest U.S. national achievement average is reasonably attributed to a child poverty rate (household income below half the national mean) that exceeds 20%, and is considerably higher than in comparable countries (e.g., Finland has a child poverty rate of less than 5%). Given these figures, it is clear that teachers in the US deal with more students living in poverty than do teachers in other advanced countries. Later we return to this issue to explicitly relate poverty to student achievement (p. 17).

Since the data linking fewer resources to lower achievement are correlational, they do not allow for causality claims. We know that poverty is closely associated with poor achievement, but does it cause it? We cannot claim causality, but we can acknowledge that there is a logical relationship between poverty, equity, equal opportunities to learn, and achievement. The following quote captures exceedingly well the logical argument between poverty and achievement. And, illustrates that the playing field for American students is not level:

> To visualize how unfair this system has become, imagine two children asked to race to the top of a stairway. One child is well nourished, well

trained, and well equipped; the other lacks all these basic resources. But, instead of designing a system around the needs of this second child, her stairway (akin to the minimal opportunities and resources available at her school) is steep and slippery. Meanwhile, the first child's stairway is replaced with an escalator. Holding these two children to the same standards may allow for a comforting "no excuses" sound bite, but it does nothing to help that second child achieve.

(Carter & Welner, 2013, p. 9)

The Destructive Effect of Poverty on Education Has Long Been Noted

In 1996, Natriello stated that poverty reduces educational performance,

the simple problem of US education at the end of the 20th Century is not the lack of standards or the barriers to implementing technology ... the central problem of U.S. education is the insufficient and unequal distribution of educational and economic opportunities, and in the development of this problem, both the corporate sector and the governmental sector have played major roles that the leaders of both sectors seem to forget.

(Natriello, 1996, p. 7)[12]

Despite this warning (and others that followed, e.g., Pallas, Natriello, & McDill, 1989), little has been done, and we have observed increased poverty levels and increased inequities. Currently the US is one of the richest countries in the world and one of the most inequitable. And, this inequity continues to grow. Notably, the wealth held by the top 1% has skyrocketed in the US but less so in other developed countries (Alvaredo, Atkinson, Piketty, & Saez, 2013). Earlier, when we discussed Berliner and colleagues' (Berliner & Glass, 2014) analysis of the charges against American education (p. 12), we noted that some critics of education have attempted to create the illusion that funds are distributed equally to schools. Their motivation is to distract from the very real situation—that, in fact, fewer resources are given to schools attended by students from low-income homes.

Teachers Alone Cannot Compensate for the Effects of Poverty on Students

While it is true that teachers are the single most important educational variable that can be directly influenced by policy action, teachers—in the *best* of circumstances—account for roughly 21% of the variance in student-achievement outcomes (Konstantopoulos, 2014; Nye, Konstantopoulos, & Hedges, 2004). Nearly 80–90% of a student's achievement outcome is attributable to other factors, and the effects of poverty on education are huge and emerge early. Despite the growth in publicly-funded preschool programs, only 41% of children from low-income homes are enrolled in preschool compared with 61% in more affluent families (U.S. Department of Education, 2015). How are teachers expected to make up for the effects of limited preschool experiences with fewer resources? How can teachers alone ameliorate the destructive effects of poverty? We suspect that they cannot, without being given more societal resources, as in Finland and Estonia.

It is hard to overstate the effects of poverty on education. Berliner, in a letter published by the *Washington Post* (Strauss, 2018), made these effects visible:

> research demonstrates that if you know the average income, the average level of parental education, and the percentage of single-parent households in a community—just these three variables—you can predict with great accuracy the performance on the standardized test scores used by that community to judge its schools ... it's not the quality of our teachers or curriculum that allows such remarkably accurate predictions: Demographics allow for that.

Berliner (2018) was not suggesting that teachers and students in high-poverty schools did not make progress, as some students and teachers do function relatively well in these circumstances. Understand that Berliner's statistics relating poverty and other variables to educational outcomes were based on predictions for low-income schools in general and not predictions for all teachers and schools. Some students beat the odds and achieve well with the support of teachers and significant others. We make two points. First, poverty and related variables markedly lower the performance of many of our students. Still, we stress that teachers in some schools work diligently and have positive effects on students' achievements. But it is equally important to acknowledge that teachers do not accomplish as much as they could have if students had preschool experience together with those life opportunities that are afforded to children who live in more affluent circumstances (see McCaslin & Good, 2008; Owens, Reardon, & Jencks, 2016; Reardon, 2016).[13,14]

The Media's Neglect of Poverty

As we have seen, researchers spend a lot of time noting the negative effects of poverty on educational aspirations and attainments, including conducting research to actually describe and understand what happens in those schools and classrooms that serve students from low-income homes. In contrast, the issues of poverty and its effects on educational progress (and teachers' success despite these conditions) are rarely highlighted in media reports. Regrettably, media reports that assail low student-achievement scores typically give the impression that teachers and schools have failed students, and rarely suggest that societal support and low levels of funding are also part of this problem. (Later we document this misleading reporting by the media (p. 16–18).)

Teachers' Limited Control

Media accounts and policymakers often do not understand or acknowledge that there are many things that teachers cannot control. Teachers teach the students assigned to them: they cannot pick their students. Additionally, many of their students live in poverty (or near poverty) and do not have the rich educational resources that other children have. Beyond poverty, there are other things that dampen student achievement that teachers do not control. For instance, teachers cannot guarantee attendance, and they cannot increase achievement if students are absent. There is much evidence that some students are frequently absent. Balfanz and Brynes (2012) reported that 10–15% of students (5 million to 7.5 million students) are chronically absent, missing 15 days of school or more in a single year. Such frequent absenteeism lowers student achievement. García and Weiss (2018) showed the negative relationship between absence and achievement. They noted that during the month before testing, students who missed three or more days scored 0.3–0.6 standard deviations lower on the 2015 NAEP mathematics test than did students who did not miss school. And, unfortunately, the students who miss school the most came from low-income homes. Indeed, students living in poverty (defined by income status) missed more school than those associated with race/ethnicity, and language status.

Just as student absences are outside of a teacher's control, so are the speed with which and extent to which teacher vacancies are filled. Teacher shortages continue to exist across the nation, especially in certain subject areas (math, special education, science, foreign language, and English as a Second Language) (U.S. Department of Education, 2017). At the start of 2018, there were 116,000 fewer public-education jobs than when the recession began in 2007. Further, due to the increasing number of students, 389,000 teacher jobs would have to be added to keep the teacher/student ratio the same in 2018 as it was in 2007 (see Gould, 2018). Fewer classroom teachers means that those teachers who remain teach larger classes.

The Role of the Media in Influencing American Education

The media have an important role in framing public attitudes and this is as true for educational policy as it is elsewhere. This conclusion is commonly reached, although the evidence about how it occurs is relatively sparse. We do know that the coverage of education is narrow and various individuals have called attention both to this general neglect of educational coverage and have lamented the fact that when education is covered it is likely to be negative (Coe & Kuttner, 2018; Keogh & Garrick, 2011; Ulmer, 2016).

Coe and Kuttner (2018), in a 35-year review of education coverage on television news, found that education received primarily negative reports. What was that television coverage based on? To answer that question the authors created a typology of news coverage so that they could identify the major themes that were featured. Those topics that received the most news coverage were: *teaching and learning* (what is taught, why it is taught, and how well do students learn); *structures of schooling* (how teachers are recruited, small schools, school choice, and teacher pay); *climate, health, and safety* (students' safety and wellbeing in schools as well as the schools' capacity for addressing health issues, such as unsafe sex, obesity, and drug use); and *equity and diversity* (inequities in funding, efforts to promote equity, and stories about racial-achievement gaps).

What topics got most coverage? Coe and Kuttner (2018) found that *teaching and learning* was the topic most covered and represented 34% of the total coverage. *Structures of schooling* received 29% and *climate, health, and safety* received but 23%. The least covered topic was equity and diversity, which attracted 13% of the coverage. These data suggest that media coverage focused more on the *problems* of schooling than the *conditions* of schooling. As noted above, poverty is an important issue, not only in its own right, but also because it affects the educational progress of students. Although educational researchers write frequently about issues of poverty, the media provide relatively little coverage.

The authors also noted that negative stories stressing the failures of schools and teachers occur much more frequently than success stories:

> That is, discussions of standards and school quality more often stressed the failures than the successes of education in the United States. What is more, those stories that were positive often focused on specific cases—for instance, a single school or teacher implementing an innovative program.
>
> (Coe & Kuttner, 2018, p. 8)

In contrast, they noted that when reporting negative trends, the focus was on schools in general. This suggests that good news was presented as an exception, whereas bad news was conveyed as typical or normative.

Does the Negativity of the Media and the Policymakers Harm Teaching?

Inaccurate media characterizations and policymakers' assertions that schools are *in crisis* contribute to lower teacher pay and poor perceptions of the profession, and arguably to the teacher shortage. As demonstrated, American media headlines *infrequently* describe the difficulties of teaching and the inadequate funding of schools—especially when it comes to schools serving students from low-income homes. In contrast, they *frequently* report that schools are failing, have declining levels of achievement, and are replete with rampant absenteeism and uncontrolled school violence. Indeed, some have noted that the media portrays schools as being in a state of constant crisis (e.g., Cohen, 2010; Gerstel-Pepin, 2002; O'Neil, 2012), and their unions are frequently a target of derision (Tamir & Davidson, 2011; Thomas, 2011; Ulmer, 2016). Does the parade of pejorative media reports about poor teachers erode society's willingness to pay their teachers? Has the lack of positive reporting led legislatures to give low pay to teachers? Has awareness of this poor pay reduced the number of individuals who want to teach? Teachers have been attacked by policymakers who argue the need for stringent teacher evaluations and the 'need to weed' out those who are incompetent. But is it plausible to claim that these attacks on schools (and teachers) have actually impacted enrolments in teacher-education programs? Similarly, have these negative descriptions of teachers led to the visible teacher shortage? We explore this possibility now.

The Pay Gap for Teachers Is Increasing

Teachers make much less than those in other occupations with similar training and geographical location. Given this pay gap, it seems possible to argue that policymakers (and media reports) *have created such a large pay gap* that citizens are not simply aware of the discrepancy between what teachers do and what teachers earn but they have become alarmed about it. In the Phi Delta Kappan Poll (2018), *66% of parents reported that teachers are underpaid* and only 6% reported that teachers were overpaid. Importantly, 73% would support teachers if they went on strike for more pay. Similar results were reported in a poll conducted in 2018 by the journal *Education Next* (Cheng, Henderson, Peterson, & West, 2019). In that poll, respondents were provided information on the average teacher salaries in their state. Given this information, 49% indicated that pay for teachers in their state should increase. This was a 13% jump from the previous year for those supporting increased teacher pay. Interestingly, 63% of respondents in the states that had experienced teacher strikes in early 2018 wanted to increase teacher pay as compared to 47% elsewhere (the teacher strike of spring 2018 will be described below, p. 22–23.) This suggests that the teacher strike impacted public opinion.

Teacher Pay Has Decreased in Comparison to Other Workers[15]

The gap between teacher value and their pay has widened. Allegretto and Mishel (2018)[16] showed this gap by calculating, in percentage terms, how much teachers make in comparison to those with comparable education, experience, and age. Teachers on average earned 18.7% less than other workers, and in some states the gap is very much greater 36%. And, there is no state where teacher pay is equal to or higher than that of other college graduates. These are striking data, especially when it is considered that in 1979 teachers (after adjusting for age, education, race, geographical location, and other factors) were paid only 5.5% less than their peers. (Further, recall that teachers are paid less than their international peers and that this gap has been increasing since at least 2005.)

What accounts for this pay gap between teachers and other professions and the fact that it continues to increase? Is it because states do not have the money to compensate teachers fairly? Allegretto and Mishel (2018) disregard this argument and assert that scarcity of funds is not the explanation. They contend that deteriorating teacher salaries are not because of weak budgets but because state legislators have preferred to give tax cuts to the wealthy and to corporations.

Desirability of Teaching Declines

In addition to their beliefs that teachers are underpaid, a majority of parents also do not want their children to be teachers. Significantly, 54% of parents reported that they don't want their children to be teachers (Phi Delta Kappan, 2018). The question about children becoming teachers has been asked to parents since 1969 and this is the first time that a majority of parents have not wanted their children to be a teacher. Why not? Parents say that pay and benefits are inadequate.

Apparently, many children are listening to their parents, as it is the case that applications and enrolments to teacher-education preparation programs are declining. Various sources show that students planning to attend college are less interested in a teaching career than before. Twenty years ago, 9% of students planned a career in education. In 2010, 7% of high school students taking the ACT test planned on becoming a teacher (ACT, 2016). High school graduates' interest in a teaching career dropped to 5% in 2014 and to 4% in 2015. Researchers at UCLA (Eagen et al., 2017) reported that currently only 4.6% of college freshmen plan to major in education. In addition to a declining interest in becoming a teacher, those who do express an interest in education careers have lower than average ACT scores and are notably weak in math and science. Once in college, these trends continue. In 1975, 22% of college students majored in education, by 2015, this number declined to 1 in 10 (Passy, 2018).

This has resulted in all-time low levels for teacher-education preparation program candidates and graduates (Flannery, 2016). According to the American Association of Colleges for Teacher Education (2018), between 2007–2008 and 2015–2016 school years there was a 23% drop in the number of students who completed teacher-education programs. In 2016, Colorado recorded a record sixth straight year decline in students completing traditional teacher-education preparation programs—down a whopping 24.4% since 2010 (Colorado Department of Higher Education, 2016).

TEACHER SHORTAGE

The decreasing number of those seeking a teaching career, coupled with those who are leaving, has created a teacher shortage. This shortage varies by state but recent evidence makes it clear that there is a national shortage of teachers (U.S. Department of Education, 2017).[17]

According to a report prepared for the Education Department's National Center for Education Statistics (Malkus, Mulvaney Hoyer, & Sparks, 2015), in 2011–2012, 68% of public schools in the US had at least one vacancy and 15% of schools reported that those openings were either "very difficult" or nearly impossible to fill. While that marks an improvement from the late 1990s and early 2000s, when 83% of schools had vacancies, and 36% reported difficulties filling them, it's still hardly hopeful. And, as previously noted, the need for teachers will likely increase because more teachers will be needed for the increased number of K-12 students—who are expected to increase to 51.4 million by 2025. In order to maintain class size, many more teachers will be needed in addition to filling the gaps from the current shortage (Gould, 2018). Gould (2018) also reported that the Economic Policy (EPI) spelled out consequences other than larger class size and noted that fewer teachers also meant fewer extracurricular activities, less time for curriculum planning, or innovation, and fewer teacher aids.

MAKING THE CASE

In summary, a case that the media and the policymakers have had deleterious effects on the teaching field is based upon the evidence that teacher pay, teacher morale, the conditions of teaching, and applications for teacher programs are all decreasing, as is the number of parents who want their children to become teachers. The impact of all of this is that more teachers are leaving teaching for reasons other than retirement than ever before (Ingersoll, Merrill, Stuckey, & Collins, 2018).[18] We struggle to attract students to teaching and once we do persuade them to become teachers, we struggle to keep them in classrooms. Ingersoll (2016) notes that nearly 25% of the teacher workforce is in transition. Clearly a lot of teachers enter or exit the profession every year. We have argued that the media's constant depiction of schools and teachers as failing and falling far short of their international peers on standardized tests has had a damaging effect. Certainly, this is plausible. But again we caution correlational evidence does not allow for anyone to argue that there is a cause-and-effect relationship.[19]

Teachers Advocate for Themselves: Teachers Strike

In the spring of 2018 teachers in several states—Arizona, Colorado, Kentucky, Oklahoma, and West Virginia—advocated for themselves by going on strike for better compensation as part of the #RedforEd movement—a collective effort made by millions to advocate for better working conditions and funding for public education (http://neatoday.org/redfored/). In addition to striking, teachers also explained their case and needs via social media outlets. The strikes drew tremendous support from parents and citizens and garnered better pay in several states (for more information about the strikes and the concessions gained see: Hess, 2018; Hess & Martin, 2018; Karp & Sanchez, 2018; Mosle, 2018; Page, Nzanga, & Simon, 2018). In addition to gaining state legislators' attention and, in a few states, their support, teachers also received considerable media support during and after the strike. And, as noted earlier, the 2018 PDK poll of citizens' attitudes about schools was very supportive of both the effectiveness of teachers and their need for higher wages. We have a chicken-or-egg issue (which came first?) here, because public opinion was also notably supportive in 2017 before the strike.

However, the data that exist show the plausibility and immediate effects. Cheng et al.'s 2019 report indicated that 63% of respondents in the states that had experienced teacher strikes in early 2018 wanted to increase teacher pay, as compared to 47% elsewhere (Cheng et al., 2019). Further media coverage of the strike was fair and often very favorable toward teachers. For example, Hess (2018) analyzed how five major newspapers covered the strikes. He noted that the general framing of the walkout was fairly impartial with 56/59 article headlines providing no noticeable support for or against the strike. However, within the articles (if citizens read them), 80% of the quotes from students, parents, and teachers supported the strikes—whether teacher strikes were solely because of changing media coverage is not certain, but clearly teachers advocating for themselves and their students was important.

This uprising led to more teachers running for office in the most recent midterms than ever before. According to the November 21, 2018 update by *Education Week* (Riser-Kositsky, Will, & Burnette, 2018), 177 teachers ran for political office, 41 of whom won their primaries (67 ran unopposed and 5 were written in). In Kentucky and Oklahoma, where there were notable teacher strikes, 34 and 55, respectively, current or former teachers ran (Thompson, 2018). (For a list of teacher candidates see https://www.edweek.org/ew/section/multimedia/teachers-running-for-state-office.html.)

Although the sheer number of actual teachers (i.e., those currently holding a teaching job) was a highly significant point, interestingly some news sources exaggerated the number of teachers who ran for office. Ironically, this illustrates that the media can overreport good educational news just as they have historically underreported good news. For example, Wong (2018) reported that various sources, including the Christian Science Monitor, the Associated Press, and Vox, reported on the unprecedented number of educators seeking political office. Vox noted that 1,000 teachers would be on the ballot and *USA Today* contended in a bold headline "'We're Just Fed Up': Teachers Running for Office in Record Numbers, Motivated by Low Pay and Education Cuts" (Schnell, 2018). Indeed, the NEA claimed that 1,800 were running for election (Wong, 2018). Part of the issue here is how 'educator' is defined, as the NEA uses the term literally including anyone that works in an education-related job.

Others have cautioned that the significance of many teachers running for office may have been overhyped. Hansen, Levesque, and Valant (2018), writing for the Brookings Institution (Brown Center Chalkboard) reported:

> today, it appears that any swell in support for education may have subsided with the teacher actions earlier this year. Ballot initiatives across the country to increase educational funding or its use had a middling success rate, and ironically, were less successful in states where education spending is low, like Oklahoma and Utah. (para 11)

However, we believe that, regardless of the number of teachers who won, the political activity of teachers in running for office (and, of course, #RedforEd demonstrations across the country) displayed teachers' political muscle. By striking and by running for political office, teachers successfully gained the public's attention and forcefully conveyed to citizens the reality of educational problems that teachers face. Importantly, teachers not only made citizens aware but also garnered new public support and positive media coverage. These collective actions likely will have continuing impact in the future as candidates (no matter what their political identification) will be more cognizant of educational interests.

Are the Media Becoming More Supportive of Teachers: Has the Pancake Flipped?

The media coverage of the teacher strikes was positive. For example, consider *Time Magazine*'s cover from September 13, 2018, which placed in bold letters "I have a master's degree, 16 years of experience, work two extra jobs, and donate blood plasma to pay the bills. I'm a teacher in America." And a recent *New York Times Magazine* issue (September 9, 2018) included a special section (The Education Issue) entitled "Teachers are Under Increasing Pressure—from standardized tests and school shooting to slashed budgets and speech in the classroom. As America's hardest job gets harder, they are also becoming a political force" (p. 33). Articles in the special issue included: 1) "How Do You Walk Back into a Classroom Again? Teaching in the age of school shootings" by Interlandi and Mitchell; and 2) "The Second

Shift: What Teachers Do to Pay Their Bills" by Lowe and Ulrich. Unlike past media coverage, current stories are emphasizing the context of teaching and illustrating that teachers often face complex issues.

Although public media are currently more sympathetic to teachers and teaching (and we hope this continues ... but, as we know so well, it is possible that the next round of low student scores or a new national report may dissipate this current support for teachers), time will tell if this attitude shift does indeed continue. Given this decade-long attack on schools, and the explicit message that teachers are responsible for students' low achievements, it may be difficult to overcome these impressions. After all, today's high school students are expressing less interest in teaching, and accordingly fewer students are entering teacher-education programs. And, although we have argued that famous Americans remember the importance of a teacher, it should also be noted that personal stories reporting the value of a teacher are simply that ... about a teacher.[20]

After the strikes, many people have contended that it was a watershed moment and that positive media coverage has increased and likely will continue to do so. For example, Karp and Sanchez (2018) argued that support for teachers would continue and spread to other areas as well. They reported that, "the wave of struggles sweeping through the United States are more than 'red state' revolts. They are rebellions against the austerity and privatization that has been driving federal and states economic policy for decades" (p. 4). Others have also pointed to several recent media reports as examples of a changed attitude toward teachers. Strauss (2018) noted that three covers of *Time Magazine* characterized the changing media position on teachers. The first of these is a 2008 *Time Magazine* cover that shows Michelle Rhee, then the DC Public Schools Chancellor, holding a broom with the title "How to Fix American Schools." The issue held a feature article by Amanda Ripley entitled "Michelle Rhee is the Head of Washington DC Schools. Her battle against bad teachers had earned her admirers and enemies—and could transform public education." The second is the November 3, 2014, cover discussed earlier, "Rotten Apples: It's Nearly Impossible to Fire a Bad Teacher," see p. 8, 9 in this chapter. And the third is a September 24, 2018, issue: the cover shows a picture of a concerned teacher and the issue has a featured article by Katie Reilly entitled "My child and I share a bed in a small apartment. I spend $1,000 on supplies and I've been laid off three times due to budget cuts. I'm a teacher in America." The issue also included two other teachers and supportive comments ... the *Time Magazine* featured three unique covers.

Counter Attacks

Other forces are already at work expressing differences of opinions about teachers ... public school teachers have competitors and have to deal with groups that oppose them on philosophical grounds. The counterattack against teachers' salaries and the bargaining of rights of teachers' unions continue. The Supreme Court decision in Janus, at least temporarily, has reduced union influence and finances by prohibiting unions from charging "agency fees" to employees who decline to join the union as full members. Will (2018a) reports that teachers' unions in several states have been hit with lawsuits and that more are expected to follow. Membership in teachers' unions appears to be declining. Will (2018b) notes that, since April 2017, the National Education Association (NEA) has lost roughly 17,000 members. And an editorial in the *Wall Street Journal*, entitled "Unions Get An Economics Lesson," noted in October 2018 that since the *Janus* decision the NEA had lost 87,000 paying members, resulting in the need to cut $50 million from their budget. The goals of these lawsuits are to divert the attention and the resources of the union from increasing public awareness of educational needs to spending time and scarce resources to fight lawsuits. Some feel that the ultimate goal is to get to the Supreme Court where support for bargaining appears to have diminished.

Even Harvard University is blaming teachers (Lockhart, 2018). For example, in the recent lawsuit addressing the possible discrimination against Asian students, a Harvard admission officer noted that these students are less likely to be admitted because their personal ratings are lower than those of other applicants. Personal ratings include teacher recommendations, alumni statements, and student's personal statements. In the trial, teachers have been noted as providing less supportive letters for Asian students. Further, Asian students have been characterized as less courageous and less likable. It is hard to believe that teachers are writing recommendations noting the student is not courageous or not likable, thus these assertions appear to be inferences made by Harvard officials.

We applaud the possibility that the tides of media support are turning positively, but we also note that negative depictions of teaching may continue. Those who believe that teaching is easy (and, ironically, still done poorly) may have difficulty in changing their opinion. This is distinctly the case because there is considerable evidence that "bad is stronger than good." Baumeister, Bratslavsky, Finkenauer, and Vohs (2001) review a large body of research to show that, in terms of cognitive load, bad events, outcomes and memories swamp positive ones. Bad impressions and stereotypes are formed more quickly than good ones and are more resistant to change. Bad information is processed more thoroughly— individuals spend more time thinking about bad events or bad pictures, and are more likely to remember them as opposed to good ones. Perhaps most notable is that bad feedback (e.g., news headlines) are so vivid that they swamp positive ones—so much so that it takes about *seven* positive outcomes to mediate the effects of *one* negative comment. Given that we have documented the bad rap teachers and schools get in the media (Coe & Kuttner, 2018), overcoming these negative perceptions will be a hefty task.

Government Influence on the Media

Obviously, government reports on schools and the validity of their accomplishments influence, and will continue to influence, media reports, and consequently will continue to affect the 66% of Americans who do not have children. As we have suggested, the media, arguably, have had an impact, possibly a substantial impact, on public perceptions. These negative media reports do not come out of "thin air" and we explore the possibility that government reports (and, to a lesser extent, foundation reports) that assert the failure of public schools have impacted media coverage.

During the past several decades federal commissions and laws (e.g., "A Nation at Risk," "No Child Left Behind") have reached serious negative conclusions about the quality of our schools, the ability of teachers, and even students' efforts. These negative judgments stem from many sources but undoubtedly of the two biggest are: 1) students' poor performance in international tests; and 2) complaints from the business community that students are not sufficiently qualified for many jobs.

The claim that students are not prepared for many jobs is hard to verify. In contrast, students' scores on international tests are public information and easily obtained. These concerns about our students' poor performances are announced in local newspapers and in the national media ... and this coverage of inadequate student performance leads to concerns not only about the students but also about the teachers and schools (especially for the 66% of citizens who do not have children in school).

Using international data as definitive information about American schools is flawed, as many scholars have reported (Berliner & Biddle, 1995; Bracey, 1997; Good & Braden, 2000). Yes, it is true that many American students score lower than students elsewhere. Unfortunately, American policymakers and the media pay too much attention to *average* student performance. These average descriptions of American schools are highly misleading because our schools are so varied. On average American students performed lower than students from many other developed countries, but it is also true that many American students also scored at the very highest levels (and sadly some at the very lowest levels). In addition to this wide range of student performance, it is the case that international tests have aspects that make these comparisons difficult.[21] Still, even if the validity of the tests is accepted at face value, we know that there are critical societal differences in resources afforded to education between the US and other high-performing countries.

What is the effect of exaggerated claims about our students' educational failure? Typically these reports documenting students' poor performance lead to new commissions, and sometimes laws, to solve the educational problem—and to solve it quickly. Simple solutions are proposed, even though only *some* students achieved at low levels. The inflated nature of the problem and the rush to solve it guarantee that reform solutions are so poorly conceived that they are incapable of solving the problems that they should be addressing. Some reform plans set forth outrageous, unrealistic, and, indeed, unattainable outcomes (e.g., Goals 2000[22]). And then, when these goals are not achieved, they produce new waves of concern and new demands for new reforms. The cycle repeats itself.

Like any other institutions, schools *can* be improved. There are correctable problems in schools, even though public schools are not *in crisis*. Unfortunately, the assertion that schools are in crisis and the inevitable search for miracles to solve ill-defined problems have prevented a reasonable assessment of our schools and how they can be improved.

Thus, policymakers and the media have used unfair comparisons to negatively present the quality of American education. Simply put, their framing is inadequate, unfair, and prevents a realistic assessment of where our schools are and how they can be improved.

Paradox Revisited

As noted, teacher pay and teacher importance are not aligned. Recent political activity, by teachers themselves, has drawn attention to the issue of low pay. However there is still no federal policy addressing issues such as low teacher pay, teacher burnout, and the general loss of interest in teaching as a career; and, thus, if these issues are not addressed, in time more teachers lacking qualifications may enter the classroom. In some countries, where student performance is notably high, there has been a long tradition of investing in teachers (e.g., Finland, Singapore); other countries, including Estonia, the Netherlands, British Columbia, and China, are now taking active steps to increase teacher pay and to make teaching more attractive as a career (Aristorenas, 2018).

It is clear that teachers should be supported with appropriate remuneration and good working conditions. But many policymakers do not agree. Our best hypothesis for explaining this paradox is that the constant reminders of failing schools, inadequate teachers, and underachieving students (coupled with "the golden promises" of reforms promising magical solutions) have blurred reasonable expectations of what teachers can accomplish. Reform proposals often implicitly suggest that teachers can overcome the effects of poverty: thereby leaving teachers in an untenable position. That is, no matter how hard and well teachers work, what they achieve is diminished by what they have *not* achieved, and indeed, in many cases, what they *cannot* achieve.

Historically policymakers and the media have created unfair expectations of what teachers and schools can accomplish. These actions have contributed to the paradox we face today: valued but poorly paid teachers. However, if the issues of poor pay and below-par working conditions are allowed to continue, we may see a decrease in both the quality of teaching and amount of learning. This decline can be reversed, but to do so will require increased financial, societal, and political support. We return to this possibility in Chapter 5.

Conclusion

This chapter presented a paradox. Teachers are respected and valued by many, and especially by parents, but in sharp contradiction they are poorly paid. We cannot fully explain this paradox, but we have offered a possible reason as to why teachers are inadequately compensated. Our analysis illustrates that negative and inaccurate criticisms of teachers by policymakers and the media often focus on educational failures, while ignoring educational successes, thus fuelling the conditions that lead to low pay and a declining interest in teaching. These harmful actions of the policymakers and the media may not be intentional, but they have real and often negative effects regardless of intention.

Whatever the cause of the paradox, we argue that it is time to balance the equation between worth and compensation so that good teaching = good pay. Our call for action stems from evidence revealing growing teacher shortages, declining working conditions and teacher pay, decreasing numbers of teachers in training programs, and the fact that parents, increasingly, do not want their children to be teachers. Collectively these factors suggest that the quality of American education may have reached a tipping point. The quality of American teachers—a profession that most American citizens believe makes an important contribution to society—may deteriorate markedly if these trends are not reversed.

However, the tides may be turning. We considered the possibility that media expressions of support for teaching may be strengthening for two reasons: 1) the teacher strike of 2018 (teachers took their case to the American people); and 2) public concern (teachers' poor pay and working conditions became so acute that they alarmed citizens). For whatever reason, it is clear that media support for teachers is greater than perhaps it has been than before the publication of "A Nation at Risk" in 1983. Although media support may be new, parents' support for teachers has never wavered. Both the community and parents have consistently rated local schools higher than they have rated schools nationally. And of course, parents (who likely know schools the best) rate, and continue to rate, the school that their oldest child attends as very good.

Will favorable media support continue for teachers? Will parent support for teachers continue? Will these two factors and others (e.g., teacher strikes) combine in ways that will result in better pay and working conditions for teachers? Counterattacks on unions and their teachers have increased and, unfortunately, these battles will expend resources that otherwise could have been used for increasing the public's knowledge and understanding of effective teaching. The resolution of these competing conceptions of teaching (i.e., teachers play an important role versus the field is rampant with "bad apples") remains to be determined. Time will tell, but it is clear that unless policymakers acknowledge teaching as a critical and worthwhile profession, schools will struggle to attract and retain their teachers. Unfortunately students—and society at large—will pay the price.

Also, policy leaders, citizens, and the media need to better understand the current research base surrounding effective teaching (and invest in expanding this research knowledge). Understanding this research base will provide a delineation of what teachers can and cannot accomplish with current resources. Further, if citizens are to have informed discussions, it is important that they understand the complexity of teaching in today's schools and that they realize that teachers cannot make up for all the inequities of society—especially poverty. Discussions surrounding meaningful school improvement would help to negate the notion that schools are *in crisis* and allow for productive reform, focusing on what is possible with additional or other resources and more coherent reform plans. Beyond this, it is imperative that federal and state educational policies change from "top-down mandates" and "sweeping reforms" to more carefully controlled *local* school improvements, thereby leading to more flexible and innovative reform – especially for teacher evaluation.

Understanding this paradox has additional value. This is because the various (mis)understandings of teaching in America makes it possible to understand why reforms, such as "Race to the Top" (and those before it), have failed. That is, our analysis of this paradox suggests that, essentially, the incomplete understanding of the diversity of American schools and the difficulty of successful teaching and learning, has allowed the media and policymakers to implement reforms that are costly, uninformed, and unsuccessful.

Now we are ready to move on to Chapter 2, which provides an understanding of: 1) what we currently know about teaching, 2) how it impacts student achievement, 3) the magnitude of those effects, 4) how that knowledge was obtained, and 5) what needs to be done to improve our knowledge base on effective teaching.

Notes

1 This report was from a committee appointed by the American Educational Research Association (AERA) and written by prominent educators in the field.
2 Rosenshine and Furst were well recognized as leading educational researchers.
3 Citizens may be concerned about schools for various reasons, such as they are underfunded or they are not safe. Still, independent of their specific concern these responses suggest that citizens are interested in their schools.
4 The Bureau of Labor Statistics provides detailed state-level information related to teacher compensation including: median teacher salary, all workers median salary data, per pupil expenditure, high school graduation rate, expected growth

of the profession, and cost of living. For labor statistics on kindergarten and elementary school teachers see: https://www.bls.gov/ooh/education-training-a nd-library/kindergarten-and-elementary-school-teachers.htm#tab-1 and for secondary school teachers see: https://www.bls.gov/ooh/education-training-and-libra ry/high-school-teachers.htm.

5 We do not intend to suggest that correctional officers are *over*paid, as we know that they work in dangerous and difficult situations (but many teachers do as well). We use this point only to show that other occupations, including those that do not require a college education, compensate employees better than is the case for teachers.

6 Although there are clear reasons as to why prison security and related expenses of caring for prisoners are expensive, nevertheless, it is instructive to see how expenses vary between teachers (and their students) and guards (and their prisoners).

7 Later in the chapter (p. 26, 27) we will show that negative media reporting can be attributed, at least in part, to government reports and the assessments of foundations about educational issues such as teacher quality.

8 We discuss Good (2014) because he directly responded critically to the *Time Magazine* article and vigorously supported teachers. Others have defended teachers generally and have been highly critical of poorly conceptualized reform efforts, including Berliner and Biddle (1995), Cuban (1990), Kuhn (2014), Nichols and Berliner (2007), and Ravitch (2011).

9 Good was not alone in his anger at the *Time Magazine*'s depiction of teachers as "bad apples." Alyssa Hadley Dunn (2014) noted that a petition in protest against the cover was circulated by the American Federation of Teachers (AFT), obtaining 50,000 signatures in a single day.

10 Gunda Tire, the national project manager for PISA in Estonia, was recently interviewed about the success of Estonia students on the PISA exam, and in this interview she gave credit for the marked educational success to various factors including a strong commitment to preschool education (Oakes, 2017).

11 For interactive, historical, state-level and gap-specific (Black-white, Hispanic-white, socioeconomic) National Assessment of Educational Progress (NAEP) data, we recommend that readers visit Stanford's Educational Opportunity Monitoring Project tool at: http://cepa.stanford.edu/educational-opportunity-m onitoring-project/achievement-gaps/race/.

12 Natriello's (1996) article appeared in a special issue edited by Good (1996) entitled "Educational researchers' comment on the Education Summit and other policy proclamations from 1983–1996." Authors in these special issues were commenting upon the mistakes that policymakers had made in the National Education Summit (1996).

13 The work at the Stanford Poverty Center—and in particular the work of Sean Reardon (2016) and colleagues (Owens, Reardon, & Jencks, 2016)—have illustrated that progress does occur. And we can find these effects if we look for the progress of students rather than looking only at their absolute level of performance.

14 McCaslin and Good (2008) and their colleagues reported their studies of school reform in Arizona in ten articles that were published in a special issue of *Teachers College Record*. In their comprehensive analysis based upon principal interviews, student surveys, and classroom observation, they concluded that students were engaged in assigned tasks and that teachers created productive and warm learning environments that involved teachers and students in a community of mutual support that the authors described as a sense of "we-ness."

15 Lower salaries are partially compensated for by better benefits packages (e.g., health coverage, and retirement benefits): However, the value of these benefits

will vary and in no place are these benefits sufficient to make up for low salaries (Allegretto & Mishel (2018).

16 Allegretto and Mishel (2018) performed a regression analysis in which weekly wages was the dependent variable and they examined the co-efficient on a dummy variable for public school k-12 teachers. The controls included education, age, marital status, region, race, ethnicity, and gender.

17 Teacher shortages are difficult to describe because the degree of shortage depends on location, and the type of teaching job. Some teacher positions have many openings (math and science) and other areas (such as social studies) have far fewer vacancies. Another issue in discussing teacher shortages is that in some locations there are certified teachers available but these teachers do not want to teach.

18 Ingersoll (2016) notes that retirement only explains approximately one-fifth of all teacher exits. Thus, it seems that a substantial number of teachers are leaving the field for non-retirement reasons.

19 As tempting as it is to blame policymakers and the media for the current demise of teaching, we caution readers to realize that because two events are correlated they do not necessarily have a causal- or cause-effect relationship. This logical error of inferring causality from correlational data is referred to as *cum hoc ergo propter*. Thus, the type of evidence available does not allow for any causal claims to be made between teacher pay and policymakers' beliefs (and negative media coverage). However, it is plausible that the cumulative effect of all these negatives—the plethora of negative reports about teaching and the facts that teacher salaries are decreasing, that fewer people want to be teachers, and that a majority of parents do not want their children to be teachers—strongly supports the possibility that media reports over a period of time may have impacted policymakers' willingness to pay teachers good salaries. Declining salaries and declining conditions of work arguably have further exasperated the problem.

20 These reports are about individuals and not teachers a group. Although teachers are portrayed favorably in books and movies, we note that these favorable depictions focus on an individual teacher and, perhaps, they are remembered fondly because they are *different than other teachers*. And, of course, some documentary films have depicted teachers and school pejoratively. For example, in the documentary film, *Waiting for Superman*, they talked about the "lemon dance" where principals pass on bad teachers to other principals and they described schools as "drop-out factories."

21 In the US most students are included in international tests. However, as Good and Braden (2000) pointed out, in some countries many students have been removed from academic tracks and placed in occupational vocational programs, and are therefore not include in the testing score averages. Bracey (1997) noted that many American teenagers hold part-time jobs. something that is not the case in many other countries. Further, he noted many of our 12th-grade students were being compared with 13th- or 14th-grade students. Berliner and Biddle (1995) noted that, unlike in Japan where all 8th-grade students are required to take algebra, in contrast, American 8th-grade students could be found in four different types of math classes. Indeed, American students who had actually taken algebra before the TIMSS test did better than Japanese students.

22 In 1994, the "Goals 2000: Educate American Act" was enacted, announcing that by 2000—just six years away—all children in America would start schools ready to learn and *all* children would have access to an appropriate preschool program.

References

Aaronson, D., Barrow, L., & Sander, W. (2007). Teachers and student achievement in the Chicago public high schools. *Journal of Labor Economics*, 25(1), 95–135.

ACT. (2016). *The condition of future educators 2015*. Retrieved from http://www. act.org/content/dam/act/unsecured/documents/Future-Educators-2015.pdf.

Allegretto, S., & Mishel, L. (2018). The teacher pay penalty has hit a new high: Trends in the teacher wage and compensation gaps through 2017. Economic Policy Institute. Retrieved from https://www.epi.org/publication/teacher-pay-gap-2018/.

Alvaredo, F., Atkinson, A. B., Piketty, T., & Saez, E. (2013). The top 1 percent in international and historical perspective. *Journal of Economic Perspectives*, 27(3), 320.

American Association of Colleges for Teacher Education. (2018). Colleges of education: A national portrait. Retrieved from https://secure.aacte.org/apps/rl/res_get. php?fid=4178&ref=rl.

Aristorenas, M. (2018, September 27). Solving the teacher shortage crisis: How some countries are working on it. National Center on Education and the Economy [NCEE]. Retrieved from http://ncee.org/2018/09/solving-the-teacher-shortage-crisis/.

Balfanz, R., & Byrnes, V. (2012). *Chronic absenteeism: Summarizing what we know from national available data*. Baltimore, MD: John Hopkins University Center for Social Organization of Schools.

Barr, A., Bechdolt, B., Gage, N., Orleans, J., Pace, C., Remmers, H., & Ryans, D. (1953). Second report of the committee on criteria of teacher effectiveness. *The Journal of Educational Research*, 46(9), 641–658.

Baumeister, R. F., Bratslavsky, E., Finkenauer, C., & Vohs, K. D. (2001). Bad is stronger than good. *Review of General Psychology*, 5(4), 323–370.

Berliner, D. C., & Biddle, B. J. (1995). *The manufactured crisis: Myths, fraud, and the attack on America's public schools*. Reading, MA: Addison-Wesley Publishing Company.

Berliner, D. C., & Glass, G. V. (Eds.). (2014). *50 myths and lies that threaten America's public schools: The real crisis in education*. New York, NY: Teachers College Press.

Berliner, D. C., & Tikunoff, W. J. (1976). The California beginning teacher evaluation study: Overview of the ethnographic study. *Journal of Teacher Education*, 27(1), 24–30.

Bracey, G. (1997). *The truth about America's schools: The Bracey reports, 1991–1997*. Bloomington, IN: Phi Delta Kappa Educational Foundation.

Brophy, J., & Good, T. L. (1986). Teacher behavior and student achievement. In M. Wittrock (Ed.), *Handbook of research on teaching* (3rd ed., pp. 328–375). New York, NY: Macmillan.

California Department of Corrections and Rehabilitation. (2018). Career opportunities: Pay and benefits. Retrieved from https://www.cdcr.ca.gov/career_opportuni ties/por/docs/payandbenefits.pdf.

California —Legislative Analyst's Office. (2016). Cal facts 2016. Retrieved from http s://lao.ca.gov/reports/2016/3511/CalFacts2016.pdf.

Carter, P. L., & Welner, K. G. (Eds.). (2013). *Closing the opportunity gap: What America must do to give every child an even chance*. London, UK: Oxford Press.

Cheng, A., Henderson, M., Peterson, P., & West, M. (2019, Winter). Public support climbs for teacher pay, school expenditures, charter schools, and universal vouchers. *Education Next*, *19*(1). Retrieved from https://www.educationnext.org/p ublic-support-climbs-teacher-pay-school-expenditures-charter-schools-universa l-vouchers-2018-ednext-poll/.

Coe, K., & Kuttner, P. J. (2018). Education coverage in television news: A typology and analysis of 35 years of topics. *AERA Open*, *4*(1), doi:2332858417751694.

Cohen, J. L. (2010). Teachers in the news: a critical analysis of one US newspaper's discourse on education, 2006–2007. *Discourse: Studies in the Cultural Politics of Education*, *31*(1), 105–119.

Cohen, J., Ruzek, E., & Sandilos, L. (2018). Does teaching quality cross subjects? Exploring consistency in elementary teacher practice across subjects. *AERA Open*, *4*(3), doi:2332858418794492.

Colorado Department of Higher Education. (2016, December 1). Individuals completing educator preparation programs declines for sixth straight year. Retrieved from https://highered.colorado.gov/Publications/Press/Releases/2016/ 20161201-Educator-Preparation-Report.pdf.

Cuban, L. (1990). Reforming again, again, and again. *Educational Researcher*, *19*(1), 3–13.

Dugan, K. (2018, September 17). Average Wall Street compensation hit $422K in 2017: report. *New York Post*. Retrieved from https://nypost.com/2018/09/17/the-a verage-wall-street-worker-made-more-than-600k-last-year/.

Eagen, K., Stolzenberg, E. B., Zimmerman, H. B., Aragon, M. C., Sayson, H. W., & Rios-Aguilar, C. (2017). The American freshman: National norms fall 2016. Retrieved from https://www.heri.ucla.edu/monographs/TheAmericanFreshman2016.pdf.

Fisher, C. W., Berliner, D. C., Filby, N. N., Marliave, R., Cahen, L. S., & Dishaw, M. M. (1981). Teaching behaviors, academic learning time, and student achieve-ment: An overview. *The Journal of Classroom Interaction*, *17*(1), 2–15.

Flannery, M. (2016, March 15). Survey: Number of future teachers reaches all-time low. *NEA Today*. Retrieved from http://neatoday.org/2016/03/15/future-teachers-at-all-tim e-low/.

Fottrell, Q. (2018, October 7). Public-school teacher jobs haven't recovered since the Great Recession: Earlier this year, teachers in Arizona, Kentucky, Oklahoma, and West Virginia protested for better wages and school funding. MarketWatch. Retrieved from https://www.marketwatch.com/story/there-are-still-fewer-public-school-teachers-than-there-were-before-the-great-recession-2018-10-05/print.

García, E., & Weiss, E. (2018, September 25). Student absenteeism: Who misses school and how missing school matters for performance. Economic Policy Insti-tute. Retrieved from https://www.epi.org/files/pdf/152438.pdf.

Gerstel-Pepin, C. (2002). Media (mis)representations of education in the 2000 pre-sidential election. *Educational Policy*, *16*(1), 37–55.

Goldhaber, D. (2016). In schools, teacher quality matters most. *Education Next*, *16*(2). Retrieved from https://www.educationnext.org/in-schools-teacher-quality-ma tters-most-coleman/.

Goldhaber, D., & Brewer, D. (1999). Teacher licensing and student achievement. In C. Finn & M. Kanstoroom (Eds.), *Better teachers, better schools* (pp. 83–102). Washington, D.C.: Thomas B. Fordham Institute.

Good, T. L. (2014). Teachers matter [Letter to *Time* Magazine]. Retrieved from https:// cloakinginequity.com/2014/10/31/teachers-matter-the-letter-defending-educators-tim e-wouldnt-print-timeapologize-timefail/.

Good, T. L. (1996). Educational researchers comment on the Education Summit and other policy proclamations from 1983–1996. *Educational Researcher, 25*(8), 4–6.

Good, T. L., Biddle, B., & Brophy, J. (1975). *Teachers make a difference*. New York, NY: Holt, Rinehart, and Winston.

Good, T. L., & Braden, J. (2000). *The great school debate: Choice, vouchers, and charters*. Mahwah, NJ: Lawrence Erlbaum Associates.

Good, T. L., & Grouws, D. (1979). The Missouri mathematics effectiveness project: an experimental study in fourth-grade classrooms. *Journal of Educational Psychology, 71*(3), 355–362.

Good, T. L., Grouws, D., & Ebmeier, H. (1981). *Active mathematics teaching*. New York, NY: Longman.

Good, T. L., & Lavigne, A. L. (2018). *Looking in classrooms* (11th ed.). New York, NY: Routledge.

Gould, E. (2018, October 5). Back-to-school jobs report shows a continued shortfall in public education jobs. Economic Policy Institute. Retrieved from https://www. epi.org/press/back-to-school-jobs-report-shows-a-continue-shortfall-in-public-e ducation-jobs/.

Hadley Dunn, A. (2014, October 27). Time after time: Why teachers are so frustrated with *Time's* "Rotten Apples" cover story. HuffPost. Retrieved from https://www. huffingtonpost.com/entry/time-rotten-apples_b_6049966.

Hansen, M., Levesque, E. M., & Valant, J. (2018, November 7). What do the 2018 midterm elections mean for education in America. Brown Center Chalkboard: Brookings Institution. Retrieved from https://www.brookings.edu/blog/brown-cen ter-chalkboard/2018/11/07/what-do-the-2018-midterm-elections-mean-for-educatio n-in-america/.

Hanushek, E. A. (2011). Valuing teachers: How much is a teacher worth. *Education Next, 11*(3), 41–45.

Hanushek, E. A. (2016). What matters for student achievement: Updating Coleman on the influence of families and schools. *Education Next, 16*(2), 18–26.

Hanushek, E. A., Kain, J. F., & Rivkin, S. G. (1998). Teachers, schools, and academic achievement. National Bureau of Economic Research (Working Paper #6691).

Hess, F. (2018, April 30). The facts behind the teacher strikes. *Forbes*. Retrieved from https://www.forbes.com/sites/frederickhess/2018/04/30/the-facts-behind-the-teacher-strikes/.

Hess, F., & Martin, R. (2018). How did major newspapers cover the 2018 teacher strikes? *Education Next*. Retrieved from https://www.educationnext.org/how-did-major-newspapers-cover-2018-teacher-strikes/.

Hill, H. C., Umland, K. L., Litke, E., & Kapitula, L. (2012). Teacher quality and quality teaching: Examining the relationship of a teacher assessment to practice. *American Journal of Education, 118*, 489–519.

Ingersoll, R. M. (2016, April 6). Ed Talk—Is there really a teacher shortage? [video file]. Retrieved from https://www.youtube.com/watch?v=KiZ2-4yJdrI.

Ingersoll, R. M., Merrill, E., Stuckey, D., & Collins, G. (2018). Seven trends: The transformation of the teaching force—updated October 2018. Retrieved from https://repository.upenn.edu/cgi/viewcontent.cgi?article=1109&context=cpre_resea rchreports.

Janus v. American Federation of State, County, and Municipal Employees, Council 31, No. 16-1466, 585 U.S. (2018).

Karp, S., & Sanchez, A. (2018, Summer). The wave of teacher strikes: A turning point for our schools. *Rethinking Schools, 32*(4). Retrieved from https://www.rethinkingschools.org/articles/the-2018-wave-of-teacher-strikes.

Keogh, J., & Garrick, B. (2011). Creating catch 22: Zooming in and zooming out on the discursive constructions of teachers in a news article. *International Journal of Qualitative Studies in Education, 24*(4), 419–434.

Konstantopoulos, S. (2014). Teacher effects, value-added models, and accountability. *Teachers College Record, 116*(1), 1–21.

Kuhn, J. (2014). *Fear and learning in America: Bad data, good teachers, and the attack on public education (the teaching for social justice series).* New York: Teachers College Press.

Lockhart, P. (2018, October 18). The lawsuit against Harvard that could change affirmative action in college admissions, explained. Vox. Retrieved from https://www.vox.com/2018/10/18/17984108/harvard-asian-americans-affirmative-action-racial-discrimination.

McCaslin, M., & Good, T. L. (2008). Special issue: School reform matters. *Teachers College Record, 110*(11), 2317–2496.

Malkus, N., Mulvaney Hoyer, K., & Sparks, D. (2015). *Teaching vacancies and difficult-to-staff teaching positions in public schools.* Washington, DC: U.S. Department of Education, National Center for Education Statistics. Retrieved from https://nces.ed.gov/pubs2015/2015065.pdf.

Mosle, S. (2018, September 6). Raising student performance the right way: Can good teaching be taught? *New York Times Magazine* [Special Issue Education]. Retrieved from https://www.nytimes.com/interactive/2018/09/06/magazine/student-performance-atlanta-teaching.html.

National Center for Education Statistics. (2017). Estimated average annual salary of teachers in public elementary and secondary schools, by state: Selected years, 1969–70 through 2016–17. Retrieved from https://nces.ed.gov/programs/digest/d17/tables/dt17_211.60.asp.

National Center for Education Statistics. (2018). Revenues and expenditures for public elementary and secondary education: School year 2014–15 (fiscal year 2015). Retrieved from https://nces.

National Education Association. (2017). 2016–2017 average starting teacher salaries by state. Retrieved from http://www.nea.org/home/2016-2017-average-starting-teacher-salary.html.

National Education Summit. (1996, March). Policy statement. Retrieved from http://www.summit96.ibm.com.

Natriello, G. (1996). Diverting attention from conditions in American schools. *Educational Researcher, 25*(8), 7–9.

Nichols, S. L., & Berliner, D. C. (2007). *Collateral damage: How high-stakes testing corrupts America's schools.* Cambridge, MA: Harvard Education Press.

Noack, R. (2018, October 10). Why are teachers in Europe paid so much better than those in the United States. *Washington Post.* Retrieved from https://www.washingtonpost.com/world/2018/10/10/why-are-teachers-europe-paid-so-much-better-than-united-states/?utm_term=.87b395dc136c.

Oakes, A. (2017, July 27). How Estonia became a world leader in science. Retrieved from https://all4ed.org/how-estonia-became-a-world-leader-in-science/.ed.gov/pubs2018/2018301.pdf.

OECD. (2018). Education at a Glance 2018: OECD Indicators. Retrieved from http s://doi.org/10.1787/eag-2018-en.

O'Neil, M. (2012, November). *Overarching patterns in media coverage of education issues: A core story of education report.* Washington DC: FrameWorks Institute. Retrieved from https://www.frameworksinstitute.org/assets/files/ed-core-story/ ecs_mca_overarching_final.pdf.

Owens, A., Reardon, S. F., & Jencks, C. (2016). Income segregation between schools and districts. *American Education Research Journal, 53*(4), 1159–1197.

Page, S., Nzanga, M., & Simon, C. (2018, September 12). Even when teachers strike, Americans give them high grades, poll shows: Unions fare worse. Retrieved from http s://www.usatoday.com/story/news/2018/09/12/teachers-union-strike-pay/1227089002/.

Pallas, A. M., Natriello, G., & McDill, E. L. (1989). The changing nature of the disadvantaged population: Current dimensions and future trends. *Educational Researcher, 18*(5), 16–22.

Passy, J. (2018, February 14). Fewer Americans are majoring in education, but will students pay the price?MarketWatch. Retrieved from https://www.marketwatch. com/story/fewer-americans-are-majoring-in-education-but-will-students-pay-the-p rice-2018-02-14.

Pew Research Center. (2013). Public esteem for military still high. Retrieved from http://www.pewforum.org/2013/07/11/public-esteem-for-military-still-high/.

Pew Research Center. (2017). After seismic political shift, modest changes in public's policy agenda: More view the environment, foreign trade as top policy priorities. Retrieved from http://www.people-press.org/2017/01/24/after-seismic-politica l-shift-modest-changes-in-publics-policy-agenda/.

Phi Delta Kappan. (2018). The 50th PDK poll of the public's attitudes toward the public schools. Retrieved from http://pdkpoll.org/assets/downloads/pdkpoll50_ 2018.pdf.

Phi Delta Kappan. (2015). The 47th PDK/Gallup poll of the public's attitudes toward the public schools. *Phi Delta Kappan, 97*(2), 52–57.

Phi Delta Kappan. (2017). The 49th PDK poll of the public's attitudes toward the public schools. Retrieved from https://journals.sagepub.com/doi/pdf/10.1177/ 0031721717728274.

Phi Delta Kappan. (2016). Why school? The 48th annual PDK poll of the public's attitudes toward the public schools. *Phi Delta Kappan, 98*(1), NP1–NP32. Retrieved from https://doi.org/10.1177/0031721716666049.

Ravitch, D. (2011). *The death and life of the great American school system: How testing and choice are undermining education.* New York, NY: Basic Books.

Reardon, S. F. (2016). School segregation and racial academic achievement gaps. *Russell Sage Foundation Journal of the Social Sciences, 2*(5), 34–57.

Riser-Kositsky, M., Will, M., & Burnette II, D. (2018, November 21). Over 170 teachers ran for state office. Here's what we know about them. *Education Week.* Retrieved from https://www.edweek.org/ew/section/multimedia/teachers-running- for-state-office.html.

Rosenshine, B., & Furst, N. (1971). Research in teacher performance criteria. In B. O. Smith (Ed.), *Research in teacher education: Symposium* (pp. 37–72). Engle- wood Cliffs, NJ: Prentice-Hall.

Rubie-Davies, C. (2014). *Becoming a high expectation teacher: Raising the bar.* London, UK: Routledge.

Schnell, L. (2018, November 3). "We're just fed up": Teachers running for office in record numbers, motivated by low pay and education cuts. *USA Today*. Retrieved from https://www.usatoday.com/story/news/politics/elections/2018/11/02/vote-teacher-education-ballot-election/1849995002/.

Stanford Center on Poverty and Inequality. (2014). State of the union. Retrieved from https://inequality.stanford.edu/sites/default/files/Pathways_SOTU_2018.pdf.

Strauss, V. (2018, October 22). Education professor: My students asked who I would vote for. Here's what I told them. *The Washington Post*. Retrieved from https://www.washingtonpost.com/education/2018/10/22/education-professor-my-students-asked-who-i-would-vote-heres-what-i-told-them/?utm_term=.1e0d734ab1bf.

Tamir, E., & Davidson, R. (2011). Staying above the fray: Framing a conflict in the coverage of education policy debates. *American Journal of Education*, 117(2), 233–265.

Thomas, S. (2011). Teachers in public engagement: An argument for rethinking teacher professionalism to challenge deficit discourses in the public sphere. *Discourse: Studies in the Cultural Politics of Education*, 32(3), 371–382.

Thompson, C. (2018, October 5). It's about standing up for what's right: How hundreds of teachers running for office are putting a jolt in the midterms. *TIME Magazine*. Retrieved from http://time.com/5413924/teachers-running-for-office-midterms/.

Time Magazine. (2014, November 3). The war on teacher tenure.

Ulmer, J. (2016). Re-framing teacher evaluation discourse in the media: An analysis and narrative-base proposal. *Discourse: Studies in the Cultural Politics of Education*, 37(1), 43–55.

U.S. Department of Education. (2015). A matter of equity: Preschool in America. Retrieved from https://www2.ed.gov/documents/early-learning/matter-equity-preschool-america.pdf.

U.S. Department of Education. (2017). Teacher shortage areas. Retrieved from https://www2.ed.gov/about/offices/list/ope/pol/tsa.html.

West-Rosenthal, B. L. (2017, September 7). 8 Celebrities reveal the teachers who have changed their lives. Weareteachers.com. Retrieved from https://www.weareteachers.com/celebrities-favorite-teachers/.

Will, M. (2018a, October 15). This road just got a lot harder: Teachers' unions hit with new round of lawsuits. *Education Week*. Retrieved from https://www.edweek.org/ew/articles/2018/10/15/this-road-just-got-a-lot-harder.html.

Will, M. (2018b, October 25). Post "Janus,' Nation's largest teachers" union sees signs of membership decline. *Education Week*. Retrieved from https://blogs.edweek.org/edweek/teacherbeat/2018/10/national_education_association_membership_loss.html.

Wong, A. (2018, November 8). The questionable year of the teacher politician. *The Atlantic*. Retrieved from https://www.theatlantic.com/education/archive/2018/11/midterms-year-of-the-teacher/575197/.

2

TEACHER EFFECTS ON STUDENT ACHIEVEMENT

A Review of the Literature

Introduction

In Chapter 1 we asserted that teachers impact student learning. Furthermore, we documented that teachers are valued by society, but, despite this, teachers are poorly paid. We suggested that conflicting opinions about teachers (value and effectiveness) arose, at least in part, for two reasons. First, a poor understanding of the complexity in which teaching unfolds together with a failure to recognize that teaching is difficult. Second, most policymakers and citizens, and even some educators, have an inadequate comprehension of what research has and has not demonstrated about effective teaching. This chapter addresses that knowledge base—what is known about effective teaching. We describe what teachers can accomplish but we also stress that there are limits on what teachers alone can do to overcome the effects of poverty.

This chapter explains how knowledge about effective teaching was obtained. First, we discuss the very earliest *research on teacher effectiveness*, from the 1960s through the 1990s. Then, we briefly review research conducted in the past two decades. In reviewing this body of literature we prioritize teacher-effectiveness research because it is both extensive and frequently replicated. We identify the specific ways teachers' actions influence students' achievements (the primary basis for teachers' effects on students' achievements comes from "process-product" and explicit teaching research areas). Then, we turn our attention to the relationship between *teachers' expectations* and students' achievements. Here, we identify and discuss how teachers communicate high- and low-performance expectations to individual students (or to entire classrooms) and identify how teachers' expectations and actions impact achievement.

And, finally, we examine research that describes the *magnitude of teachers' influence* on students' achievements—this literature flows primarily from the production function work of economists that seeks to attribute input/factors of production (e.g., labor, capital)/factors of production. We will learn that the effects of teachers are sufficiently great, both on students' achievements and their future economic productivity that they motivated policymakers to engage in reform efforts to enhance teaching and learning. Policymakers paid uneven attention to these three bodies of literature: 1) teacher effectiveness, 2) teacher expectations, and 3) magnitude of teacher effects. We will assert that they clearly heard and responded to the literature that emphasized the economic consequences of effective teachers but largely ignored the research literature on teacher effects and teacher-expectation effects.

It is useful to stress that our review of effective teacher research includes experimental evidence that relates teaching to student actions in causal ways. We explore the possibilities that this knowledge base (including research on teacher effects, the magnitude of these effects, and teacher expectations) holds for practice and policy. We acknowledge that although much remains to be learned about the relationship between teacher actions and student outcomes, current findings and concepts hold useful implications for teaching. Thus, when Race to the Top (RTTT) was conceptualized, as we will see, much was already known about teacher actions that impact student achievement.

What Do We Know About Teacher Effects and Their Impact on Students?

Chapter 1 reported that at one time the field of research on teaching had little information about *if* and *how* teachers enhanced student achievement. Dunkin and Biddle (1974) commented on the paucity of research this way:

> One of the striking things about product-oriented research on teaching to date is how often investigators have *failed* to observe a predicted relationship. More than half of all findings examine for both pupil achievement and pupil attitudes have reported insignificant relationships
>
> (Dunkin & Biddle, 1974, p. 417)

As recently as 1975, little consideration was given to the teachers' role in improving student achievement. Although teachers might be valued because they were kind, supportive, and good role models they were not seen as critical determinants of students' academic success. At that time, most social scientists believed that inherited IQ and social-class background (family status) were the important factors in whether students made good or poor academic progress. Although some social scientists believed that it was completely possible that students from low-income homes could make marked academic progress, most did not. Indeed, in Britain and in Europe generally in the 1950s, it was widely believed that talented students could be identified very early in their school career and students were placed into appropriate academic tracks. Some students learned advanced subject matter and were prepared for college and university. In contrast, students in less-challenging tracks received less-demanding academic work that was deemed sufficient for preparing these students for the jobs that they would take.

Teachers Do Not Make a Difference

The belief that teachers mattered but little was amplified by the Coleman Report (Coleman et al., 1966). Prior to this report, in the early 1960s, public and Congressional expectations for the progress of students from low-income homes increased considerably. The reason for this was that some social scientists felt that the infusion of money, especially into preschool programs, could change the academic trajectory for many students. Essentially, even if the effects of schooling could not overcome heredity, the effects of family income and social status could be compensated for by allowing less-advantaged students to have access to language stimulation, opportunity to read, and general intellectual stimulation (things that more advantaged students received at home). These beliefs led to the provision of vast amounts of public monies for preschool education programs.[1]

Unfortunately, the Coleman Report provided extensive research that seemingly dashed expectations that students from low-income families could make important educational gains (if provided with early enrichment). The Coleman Report involved an extensive survey of 4,000 public schools selected from across the country, and included 645,000 students. Data were collected on several standardized tests and information was also gathered about school characteristics and the neighborhoods in which they were located. Further, information was obtained about the characteristics and backgrounds of teachers' and students' aspirations and attitudes toward school. Coleman and his colleagues conducted the most comprehensive study of schooling ever performed.

The study yielded three major findings about the relationship between schools and achievement. First, students from low-income homes and minority groups performed at considerably lower levels than students from affluent homes and White students, with the performance gap between minority and majority students increasing over time. Second, the average quality of available school services varied considerably (both within and between regions and also within each region). Schools in the South provided lower average quality than anywhere else in the country. Third, school characteristics appeared to exert little, if any, influence upon student achievement. Indexes of school quality, such as per pupil expenditure and size of the school library appeared to have little relationship to achievement once the background characteristics of the pupils were controlled. The third conclusion was broadly interpreted to mean that schools and teachers did not influence student achievement. Although this conclusion was widely disseminated, it was wrong. Here is how Coleman reported the significance of this finding:

> Taking all of these results together, one implication stands out above all: That schools bring little influence to bear on a child's achievement that is independent of his background and general social context; and that this very lack of an independent effect means that the inequalities imposed on children by their home, neighborhood, and peer environment are carried along to become the inequalities with which they confront adult life at the end of school.
>
> (Coleman, et al., 1966, p. 325)

Teachers Do Make a Difference

The fundamental reason that the Coleman Report failed to find relationships between *inputs* (e.g., per pupil expenditure, teaching practices) and *outputs* (e.g., student achievements, graduation rates) was because processes within the school were *not observed*. Simply put, Coleman's analysis completely ignored teacher variation within schools. Good, Biddle, and Brophy (1975) explained this critically important deficiency this way:

> If teachers make a difference, and if pupils are to be exposed to both good and poor teaching as they progress through a given school, then small wonder if it turns out that there are only minor differences among schools in the average levels of achievement they produce! This does not mean that the determinants of pupil achievement are unknowable, however. If they vary with the individual teacher and are observable only within the classroom where pupils and teachers interact, then the data of the Coleman Report missed them completely!
>
> (Good, Biddle, & Brophy, 1975, p. 23)

This analysis has stood the test of time, as researchers now agree that the Coleman Report was flawed, and its erroneous conclusions are commonly acknowledged (see Hanushek, 2016). Despite its mistaken conclusion that schooling did not impact student achievement, the Coleman Report made important contributions to knowledge about schooling. Notably, the report provided a clear understanding of the vast achievement differences that existed among American schools and students, not only then, but also, as we have noted, that continue to exist today. Despite the methodological weaknesses in Coleman's original study, social scientists, especially economists, continue to note its historic impact on the field. Hanushek (2016) concludes that the Coleman Report dramatically altered how both the public and policymakers

41

value schools. Historically, schools were defined as good (or poor) on the basis of the resources that the school possessed. The Coleman Report shifted the language that surrounded schooling, so that when looking at the 'goodness' or quality of schools the focus is changed from inputs to outputs.

Teachers Can Influence Achievement

Good, Biddle, and Brophy (1975), after reviewing extant research, argued that it allowed for the plausible argument that teachers *do* impact student achievement. In making this case, they drew upon a wide range of studies: preschool programs (e.g., Beller, 1973; Gordon & Jester, 1973); elementary school studies (e.g., Vernon, 1969; Walburg, 1974); differences in teacher methods (e.g., Chall, 1967; Sears et al., 1972); affective variables (e.g., Aspy, 1973); and large-scale studies (e.g., Brophy, 1973; Brophy & Evertson, 1973); as well as: secondary school studies (e.g., Flanders, 1970); and higher education (e.g., Trent & Cohen, 1973). Using the extant literature they made a plausible, but not compelling, case that teachers influence student achievement. They called for more research to validate and to establish how these effects occur. Despite this demonstration that teachers likely impact student achievement, they and the field had little idea as to *how/why* teachers made a difference. Yet, their argument was sufficiently strong to encourage further study of instructional processes.

Early Attempts to Establish Teacher Actions that Influence Student Achievement

In actuality some correlational work existed before the Coleman Report on the relationship between teacher behavior and student achievement. In Chapter 1, we quoted Rosenshine and Furst (1971) and commented that they had begun their report by essentially offering an apology for the quality of their conclusions. Given the passage of time, it is now clear that they had little to apologize for, as some of their findings have stood the test of time very well. And if their work was flawed, it was because of the nature of the studies they had to review. The literature they reviewed contained but fragments of instruction for observers to examine. Further, what they did observe was often what teachers had been asked to do by researchers. Teaching, as it naturally unfolds in classrooms, was not observed. Despite this limitation of too little observation, their review identified several teacher actions that frequently related to student achievement including clarity, variability, enthusiasm, task-oriented and/or businesslike behavior, student opportunity to learn, use of student ideas, constructive criticism, use of structuring comments, types of questions, probing, and the level of difficulty of instruction. As we will see later, some of these teacher actions remain today as examples of how teachers can positively influence student achievement.

Evidence that Teachers Make a Difference

Although hundreds of studies had examined the possibility of teacher effects on student achievement, it was not possible to draw any compelling conclusions from this literature. Dunkin and Biddle (1974), in their seminal work entitled "The Study of Teaching," explained the weaknesses that had limited the productivity of this research. They identified four common characteristic weaknesses in these studies. First, they did not consider context such as grade level, subject matter being studied, time of year, and so forth. Second, little theory was used to inform these studies. Third, these studies had not defined the criteria of effectiveness that they studied. Fourth, they did not use observational data to link teacher characteristics and student outcomes.[2]

Many researchers moved into classrooms to investigate the possibility that teachers, even in the same school, varied in their actions and effects on students. Within a tradition called "process-product" (PP), researchers studied the relationship between teachers' classroom actions and student achievement (Berliner, 1976; Brophy & Evertson, 1974; McDonald, 1976; Stallings, 1976). Research in the PP tradition was an improvement on previous research because it drew upon earlier research findings and integrated that research (e.g., Rosenshine & Furst, 1971) and built upon the weaknesses and strengths that others had identified (e.g., Dunkin & Biddle, 1974). In particular, PP studies paid much more attention to context, included rich observational measures, and carefully defined their criteria for determining effective teaching.

PP research is extensive, has a long history, and it continues today in one form or another (e.g., value-added modeling). Research in this tradition especially flourished in the 1970s and 1980s, and an extensive review of this literature can be found elsewhere (Brophy & Good, 1986). This literature included both correlational studies and experimental studies that related teacher action to student achievement.

A Correlational Study

Here, we review one particular study from this tradition to illustrate how PP research was conducted. Good and Grouws (1977) conducted an observational study including over 100 third- and fourth-grade teachers. First, they identified a school district that was willing to let them examine past achievement data and to observe in classrooms. Importantly, teachers in the district were using the same textbook series and the student population in the district had been stable for over a decade. Second, effective teachers—

those who consistently had high (or low) effects on student achievement—were identified using data from the Iowa Test of Basic Skills (which generated residual gains scores for students across three consecutive years). And, third, they observed in classrooms to determine how more-effective and less-effective teachers actually taught.

Importantly, even within the relatively stable conditions of this teaching context, the median year-to-year correlation across residual gains scores on all Iowa subtests was only .20. Simply put, teacher effects on student achievement varied from year to year. Despite these fluctuations, it was possible to identify nine teachers who were relatively stable and *effective*, and, nine teachers who were stable and *ineffective* over three consecutive years. Stability was defined as teachers remaining in the top or bottom third of the distribution over consecutive years. Observations were made in 41 classrooms in order to protect the identity of all teachers (and knowledge of their effectiveness[3]). Data were collected with the Brophy Good Dyadic System[4] (Brophy & Good, 1970), which used how time was utilized during mathematics instruction (e.g., the ratio of time spent in development versus practice activities). High-inference measures were also used from the work of Emmer (1973) and Kounin (1970).

Details of the findings can be obtained in Good and Grouws (1977). They reported many relationships between various teacher actions and student achievement. However, the authors also performed a discriminate analysis that provided clusters of teaching that separated more-effective and less-effective teachers. The authors found that six dimensions distinguished more-effective from less-effective teachers. More-effective teachers a) had more student-initiated behavior, b) taught students in whole-class settings, c) were much clearer about classroom assignments and process, d) achieved classroom climates that were comparatively non-evaluative and relaxed, but were e) task-focused (had higher achievement expectations, were fast paced, and had more homework), and f) classrooms that were relatively free of major misbehavior.

These results were informative but, like much research, they led to other questions, including the basic issue: were there other factors not included in the research that might have caused the observed relationships between teacher actions and student achievement? Perhaps more-effective teachers knew more mathematics and thus were able to provide examples with greater clarity. Perhaps, teachers were able to engage students fully because they spent more time planning lessons, and thus could anticipate possible difficulties and hence avoid them. Simply put, these correlational data could not imply causality in themselves, as other factors may have been involved. And, of course, some possible questions did not receive the attention that they merited.[5]

An Experimental Study

As noted, Good and Grouws (1977) were able to document that teachers who were effective and stable over-time obtained more student achievement than did teachers who were less effective and stable over-time. This reported relationship between teacher actions and student achievement was clear. And, it is important to reiterate that these data were correlational and other factors (not studied) might have caused the relationship. To rule out other possible explanations, and to see if causal links could be drawn between teacher actions and student achievement, Good and Grouws (1979) conducted an experiment. The treatment group received a training program to improve teaching[6] (Good & Grouws, 1977). The training consisted of a workshop and a 45-page manual that was given to teachers describing the mathematics program and recommendation for teaching. This full manual including definitions of recommended teaching steps and variables coded can be found elsewhere (see Good, Grouws, & Ebmeier, 1981). The treatment (what teachers were asked to do when teaching mathematics) was based upon the results found in the earlier correlational study (Good & Grouws, 1977). However, in the treatment, attention was also given to the concept of lesson development (which focused on making the mathematical content being studied meaningful). This addition was based upon experimental research in mathematics education that showed the amount of time that teachers spent on *development* (focus on the meaning of the ideas presented) and the amount of time spent on *practice* (doing mathematics) were both important. These findings suggested that, in general, teachers tended to spend too much time on *practice* and too little time on *development*.

Two measures of student outcomes were assessed:[7] a standardized measure of student achievement and a test designed to measure the content actually taught. On both outcome measures students in experimental classrooms (those teachers who attended the training workshop and who received a program manual) exceeded the performance of students in control classrooms. The results were large and had both statistical and practical significance. This study provided prima facie evidence that information obtained in a correlational study (that described how more-effective teachers taught) could be taught to other teachers in ways that could lead them to teach differently and more successfully. Study results showed that teachers did implement the treatment program as intended (but more so in some classrooms than in others), and that these differences in teacher actions directly affected student achievement. Simply put, teachers made a difference in student learning in ways that could be attributed directly to the teachers themselves (not the curriculum or other variables). This study gained considerable attention, and, indeed, was later designated as a classic study in mathematics by the National Council of Mathematics Teaching (see Carpenter, Dossey, & Koehler, 2004).

Importantly, a follow-up study by Ebmeier and Good (1979) reanalyzed data from this experiment and qualified somewhat the findings reported in Good and Grouws (1979). Although the study reaffirmed that the treatment program had a generally good impact on student learning, it was found that certain combinations of teachers and students made more gains than other combinations. (For more information about how the clusters of teachers and students were formed, see Ebmeier & Good, 1979). Interestingly, these findings obtained a much smaller audience than Good and Grouws (1979),[8] which suggests that many readers are interested in what works *generally* rather than what works in some contexts. This does not mean that findings cannot be applied from one setting to another but it means that they have to be adjusted to the particulars of the teaching situation, including the particular students and the specific goals of instruction.

For example, the model used by Good and Grouws (1979) in fourth-grade classrooms was adopted by Sigurdson and Olson (1992) for use in eighth-grade classrooms when teaching lessons on ratios, rates, fractions, and geometry. In doing so, they combined lesson formats tested earlier with curriculum features associated with teaching mathematics for meaningful understanding. Subsequently, Sigurdson, Olson, and Mason (1994) extended and replicated these findings using a problem-solving dimension. So two points follow Sigurdson and colleagues work: First, research findings obtained in one setting can be applied elsewhere; second, these extensions may require some creative adaptation based upon students' mathematical knowledge, age, and the mathematical content taught.[9]

Continuing Research

Research like that of Good and Grouws, which was conducted in the PP tradition, stimulated a lot of further research on active teaching and explicit teaching. This research has continued to date and consistently shown similar relations between explicit teaching and student achievement. Work in this tradition has assumed different names (e.g., direct instruction, cognitive strategy instruction, active teaching, and, more recently, explicit teaching) and involves somewhat different emphases (e.g., greater or less emphasis on the teacher or student's processing information or demonstrating it). Still, in contrast to other instructional approaches (e.g., project-based or discovery learning, small-group work) these traditions have a similar emphasis that suggests that high-quality and active or explicit teaching can enhance student learning (Cohen, 2018; Cohen & Grossman, 2016; Connor et al., 2011; Hamre & Pianta, 2005; Hamre et al., 2013; Hughes, Morris, Therrien, & Benson 2017; McLeskey & Brownell, 2015; McLeskey, et al., 2018; Pianta, Belsky, Vandergrift, Houts, & Morrison, 2008; Swanson & Hoskyn, 1998). Matthews and Cohen (forthcoming) have provided an authoritative and succinct discussion of the distinctions between cognitive strategy, direct instruction, and explicit teaching approaches.

Teacher Actions Often Associated with Student Achievement

The work by Good and Grouws (1977, 1979) shows how correlational and experimental work identified and confirmed teacher actions associated with student achievement. These results, along with those of many other studies, collected over time—which examined various grade levels, explored different subject matter, and involved different types of school contexts—have yielded a profile of what we have learned from research on teaching effectiveness. Good teaching involves much *more* than these dimensions, but, without the knowledge and ability to enact them, other teaching tasks will not be realized. (For further elaboration, see Good & Lavigne, 2018 and Lavigne & Good, 2015). And, as others have noted, research needs to be applied and results can and do vary with context (Norwich, Koutsouris, & Bessudnov, 2018).[10]

Table 2.1 presents the 15 findings that have stood the test of time. Teacher actions identified therein have consistently related to student achievement at different grade levels and in different subjects. They can be viewed as examples of what teachers do to construct classrooms that value achievement, to respect individual differences in learners, and to create classrooms where most of the time is free from misbehavior. Clearly, other types of teaching are often appropriate, including discovery learning, project-based learning, individual learning via internet assignments, and so forth. However, success in these areas—also at least partly—is dependent upon the abilities of teachers to be able to have the knowledge and skill to carry out the actions identified in Table 2.1.

It is also the case that knowledge of teaching continues to suggest that learning specific subject matter often includes teacher actions that go beyond the teaching dimensions depicted in Table 2.1. It is beyond the scope of this chapter to discuss subject-matter knowledge, however information can be obtained from Good and Lavigne (2018) as well as other sources.[11]

The variables briefly mentioned in Table 2.1 will be discussed further in Chapter 5 when we look at the role of research findings for supplementing existing observation instruments. These teacher actions are presented here to illustrate research-based examples that linked teaching and student learning. Thus, when RTTT was implemented there was a body of research information that could be utilized. And this research suggested that more-successful teachers were those who built strong and supportive classrooms and who instructed in ways that emphasized both understanding and application.

Table 2.1 General Dimensions of Teaching that are Commonly Associated with Student Achievement

- **Appropriate Expectations:** Do all students receive an appropriately demanding curriculum? Are teacher expectations positive and forward-looking for students who vary in achievement level, ethnicity, gender, and socioeconomic status?

- **Supportive Classrooms:** Recognizing students as social beings as well as students, do teachers encourage students and support them at all times, especially when they struggle? Do teachers and students work in a climate of "we-ness" that supports individual differences?

- **Effective Use of Time:** Do teachers start classes promptly, plan transitions well, and help students focus on key ideas? Do they smoothly and effectively move from one activity to another within a lesson?

- **Opportunity to Learn:** Do teachers present content at various cognitive levels and give students a full range of learning opportunities?

- **Intellectual Push:** Do teachers encourage students to think, to learn from their mistakes, and strive to do better?

- **Coherent Curriculum in Sequence:** Given that content and expectations have been established for student performance, is the curriculum logically sequenced?

- **Active Teaching:** Do teachers actively present concepts and supervise students' initial work, and then encourage them to build and to extend meaningfully on teachers' initial presentations?

- **Balance Procedural and Conceptual Knowledge:** Do teachers encourage students to understand knowledge *and* apply it?

- **Proactive Management:** Do students know what to do, how to do it, and, when confused, how to access help? Do teachers prevent problems proactively rather than primarily reacting to misbehavior when it occurs?

- **Teacher Clarity:** Do teachers help students focus on the major lesson objectives? Do students understand what they are trying to learn or demonstrate? And why?

- **Teacher Enthusiasm and Warmth:** Do teachers express that they care about the content being studied as well as the students who study it?

- **Instruction Curriculum Pace:** Do teachers go through the curriculum reasonably briskly? Are teachers attentive to students' concerns and reteach content if necessary?

- **Teaching to Mastery:** Do teachers focus on students learning all material and minimize tangential material? This does not imply everything that is in the curriculum is fully understood but it does imply that students must understand fully those key concepts that are needed for later learning.

- **Review and Feedback:** Are students presented with frequent review? Do teachers give frequent feedback to students so that they know if they are making adequate progress and how to correct difficulties when they occur? Do teachers offer students opportunities to apply feedback to improve their work in future lessons or activities? Are students sometimes allowed to conduct their own reviews individually or in groups?

- **Adequate Subject-Matter Knowledge:** Do teachers display adequate subject-matter knowledge? Are students allowed to use knowledge but also to understand it?

Source: Adapted from Lavigne and Good (2014) and Good and Brophy (2008).

Research Emphasis Evolves over Time

Just as American education has moved from reform to reform, it has also moved from one to another important pedagogical approach. A method of practice (e.g., individualized instruction) becomes highly recommended only to eventually, and often abruptly, be discarded for another 'new' approach (e.g., discovery learning). Educators, including researchers, have a long history of overvaluing a single variable to the point of making it a panacea or silver bullet.[12] Given this, educators have moved back and forth in terms of recommended pedagogy (e.g., from phonics to whole language and then back to phonics). As Good (2014) and Good and Lavigne (2018) have concluded, there are no simple solutions and any learning involves multiple variables and complex interactions between them. Additionally, most learning outcomes can be achieved in multiple ways by using various different methods, although some approaches may be more effective in some contexts than others.

Thousands of studies were conducted prior to the time that PP studies became highly salient—and thousands have been conducted since then. Following PP research, with its central perspective on which teacher actions or behaviors influence student achievement, the field moved to a more central focus on teacher beliefs, then student-led instruction, then teachers' subject-matter knowledge, and so forth. These research paradigms have yielded useful concepts and findings but have not replaced, nor substantially improved, the knowledge provided by PP studies, in terms of how teachers influence student learning on standardized tests. Thus, in the last two decades, the knowledge base for explaining how teacher actions influence students' achievement has not changed in any fundamental way (although, the subsequent research studies frequently replicated earlier research and, thereby, strengthened the field's confidence in these relationships).

However, in the past decade, there has been a renewed interest in studying what teachers do ... their behaviors and actions (see Loewenberg Ball, & Forzani, 2009). Also, much attention has been placed on high-leverage (explicit) teaching practices (McLeskey et al., 2018). In particular, the many studies commonly called valued-added are highly similar to the PP studies we reviewed earlier. These studies use more sophisticated statistical techniques for controlling (attempting to equate) conditions that are involved[13] in trying to adjust for variables that might impact achievement. However, these studies, to date, have not found anything to contradict earlier PP studies, and have essentially replicated them (see, for example, Ferguson & Danielson, 2014).

Teacher Expectations

Research on teacher expectations is also directly relevant to the improvement of classroom teaching and student learning. Like teacher-effectiveness research, research on teacher expectations has a long history (Rosenthal,

1967; Rubie-Davies, 2018). Although discussion of the history of this research paradigm has to necessarily be brief, we provide a quick review to justify our conclusion that this literature is relevant to our analysis of productive classroom teaching. For an extended discussion of this history, see Good and Lavigne, 2018; Good, Sterzinger, and Lavigne, 2018; and a special issue of *Educational Research and Evaluation* edited by Timmermans, Rubie-Davies, and Rjosk, 2018, and Rubie Davies, 2014 and 2018.

Laboratory Studies and Early Conceptions of Beliefs as Self-Fulfilling Prophecies

Beliefs may become self-fulfilling. Consider George Bernard Shaw's 1913 play *Pygmalion* or the 1948 essay by Merton ("The Self-Fulfilling Prophecy"). We know, from Shaw's fictional play, that a flower girl (Eliza) was transformed into a duchess through the positive expectations and instructional opportunities that Professor Henry Higgins provided. Merton (1948) provided an illustration of how a negative self-fulfilling prophecy might become true. He described how a solvent bank was completely undermined because of the false rumor that it was not solvent. Customers acting upon this false belief showed up in mass demanding their money, with the result that the bank was quickly depleted of its funds and ruined. Although beyond the scope of our chapter, it is useful to note that several laboratory studies have illustrated that, in experimental conditions, when given false information about the subjects they were working with, experimenters often fulfilled these false expectations. For example, in one experiment, rats described as 'maze-bright' or 'maze-dull' received different patterns of interaction with the experimenter in ways that led 'maze-dull' rats to have much more difficulty in mastering a maze task than did rats that had been described as 'maze-bright.' For reviews of this literature, see Rosenthal (1966, 1967) and Barber and Silver (1968). And for more recent discussions, see Good et al. (2018) and Timmermans et al. (2018).

This laboratory work is complex, but it provides clear evidence that expectation effects can influence both how experimenters treat subjects and how subjects actually perform. Elsewhere, there is an extensive literature to suggest that our own beliefs may influence our own responses. A classic example of this occurs in medicine where it is most usually termed a *placebo effect*. Simply put, the belief that a drug (or a treatment) may lead to improvement sometimes has been associated with an actual improvement, even though there was no medical reason for this. Thus, before drugs can be marketed they need to be tested against a placebo to be sure that the drug, and not just the belief of relief, causes the reduction in pain.

Merton (1948) has argued persuasively that not only individuals hold beliefs but so does society. As we know all too well, the pejorative views of others (those who differ from us in some way, including racial, ethnic, or sexual identity) may lead us to expect less from them (or to fear them unnecessarily) to the extent that these beliefs actually influence behavior and outcomes. Further, as we noted in Chapter 1, it is possible (and we argue that it is likely) that exaggerated beliefs about schools being *in crisis* (as Berliner and Biddle (1995),[14] refuted long ago) and incompetent teachers may lead to conditions that inadvertently make it more likely that they will fail (e.g., unwarranted reform efforts, low pay, and below-par working conditions). Simply put, false beliefs can become self-fulfilling. Expectations may be explicit or implicit.[15]

Pygmalion *in the Classroom*

Robert Rosenthal was a primary contributor to laboratory studies that induced expectations and explored their consequences in experimental settings. Building on this, in 1968 Robert Rosenthal and Lenore Jacobson published a book entitled, *Pygmalion in the Classroom* (Rosenthal & Jacobson, 1968), which was highly controversial and drew not only considerable public interest, but also attracted serious professional criticism (e.g., Snow 1969; Thorndike 1968). In the experiment, teachers were told that some of their students would bloom intellectually in the coming year. The information given to teachers was false (for the sake of the experiment). In actuality, students reported to be bloomers were chosen at random. Thus, there was no reason to believe that these students would make unusual gains during the year, except for the expectations that teachers held (that is, if they believed the information that some students would bloom). Although Rosenthal and Jacobson reported that students described as "bloomers" did better than expected in grades 1 and 2, critics disagreed. Among the criticisms levelled at the study was the fact that the tests used in grades 1 and 2 had not been properly normed for those grades. No observational data were collected (to see if teachers treated "bloomers" more favorably), and some teachers did not even remember which students were described as "bloomers."

In part, because the well-conducted laboratory studies that preceded *Pygmalion in the Classroom* (e.g., Rosenthal, 1966) were sufficiently striking, some critics (including Snow and Thorndike) thought that the idea appeared interesting and promising enough to merit additional research, even though the 1968 study was flawed in major ways (see Good et al., 2018). This possibility attracted many researchers to make classroom studies that examined how teachers interacted with students believed to be more capable or less capable. However, the literature that followed *Pygmalion* was not based upon false information. For example, Brophy and Good (1970, 1974) studied teachers' natural expectations (i.e., teachers' own ranking of students) as opposed to artificially creating expectations by giving teachers false information. This literature eventually produced hundreds of studies that explored *if* and *how* teachers interacted differently with students they believed to be more capable or less capable.

Teachers Interact Differently with Individual Students Believed to be More Capable or Less Capable

In time, this literature produced a clear understanding that some teachers treated students differently based upon their expectations but that other teachers did not. Further, this literature identified a rich summary of how teachers communicated high or low expectations to individual students. And over time this literature was supplemented with many studies that explored whether students were aware of differential teacher expectations and the consequences of those expectations. Again, it was found that in some classrooms—those in which teachers interacted notably differently with students believed to be more capable or less capable—students were aware of teachers' differential expectations in ways that influenced their performance (see Weinstein, 2009).

In Table 2.2, we describe a few of the numerous ways in which teachers interact differently with students believed to be more talented or less talented. These dimensions are drawn from a broad source of literature that have provided summary statements about differential behavior toward students believed to be more capable and less capable including Brophy (1983), Good

Table 2.2 Teachers' Interactions with Students who are Perceived to be More Capable or Less Capable

Teachers' Actions with Students Believed to Be Less Capable	*Teachers' Actions with Students Believed to Be More Capable*
• Less time to answer a question (before giving an answer/ calling on another) • Less or inappropriate reinforcement • Less praise: more often criticism for failure • Fewer chances to respond • Less challenging questions: asking only easier or nonanalytic questions • Less teacher proximity: seating is further away from the teacher • Less public interaction (more private interaction) • Less friendly interactions: less smiling and fewer other nonverbal indicators of support • Less and briefer informative feedback to questions from low achievers • Less acceptance of suggestions	• Greater opportunity to perform publicly on meaningful tasks • Greater opportunity to think • More honest, contingent feedback (feedback emphasizes students' behaviors in the task) • More assignments that deal with comprehension, understanding • Greater respect for the learner as an individual with unique interests and needs • Greater opportunity for self-evaluation • Greater autonomy (more choice in assignments, fewer interruptions) • Greater acceptance and use of ideas • Greater nonverbal attention, including smiles and head nods • Generally more attention paid to these students

and Weinstein (1986), Harris and Rosenthal (1985), Rosenthal (1973), Rubie-Davies (2014, 2018), and Weinstein and McKown (1998).

Teachers also Hold Expectations for the Whole Class

Teacher-expectation research focused initially on how teachers treated individual students differently on the basis of their beliefs about student potential. Subsequently, Rubie-Davies (2007) explored the possibility that teachers may hold different expectations for the entire class (that is, teachers may believe that their class is composed of many competent learners or only a few). Rubie-Davies (2007, 2014) found that some teachers held higher expectations for classes of students than did other teachers. Further, she found that high-expectation teachers interacted with the class as a whole differently than did low-expectation teachers. The major ways that high- and low-expectation teachers differed are summarized in Table 2.3.

An Experimental Study

Rubie-Davies (2014) conducted an experimental study based upon information obtained from past research on how teachers communicated differently with classes believed to have more potential or less potential. Her study attempted to change teachers' expectations, their classroom actions, and student achievement. Teachers had the opportunity to learn how high-expectation teachers taught and they also had the opportunity to plan (with other teachers and with the project staff) how to incorporate these expectation practices into their own lessons. The results indicated that, in the experimental group (the teachers who received treatment information), the students gained 28% in mathematics

Table 2.3 Rubie-Davies' Findings Regarding how Beliefs and Practices of High-Expectation Teachers Differ from those of Low-Expectation Teachers

High-Expectation Teachers	Low-Expectation Teachers
Hold malleable beliefs about intelligence	Hold fixed beliefs about intelligence
Think that all students need generally similar learning tasks; no ability grouping	Think that students' learning tasks and grouping should be based on ability
Believe that learning focus is on understanding and comprehension	Believe that learning focus is on correctness
Take time to review and update student goals/progress	Do not review or update students' goals/progress
Believe that motivation incentives are primarily intrinsic	Believe that motivation incentives are primarily extrinsic
Provide frequent choice to students[16]	Provide no or limited choice to students

achievement more than students in the control group. The gains and achievement were observed in all schools, at all socioeconomic levels, and across ethnic and gender groups of students. The teaching of expectation research resulted in significant improvements for students generally.[17]

None of the dimensions presented in Tables 2.2 or 2.3 are necessarily a sign of low expectations, but the presence of several of these teacher actions suggests that expectations are likely too low for students. Clearly, teachers can communicate high and low expectations in many ways (e.g., written notes on students' assignments, comments in the hallway, and so forth). The information presented in Tables 2.2 and 2.3 indicates ways to think about the extent to which all students are encouraged to learn significant material, and when appropriate, to be given some choice and autonomy.

Teachers Treat Students in Ability Group Instruction Differently

We have seen that individual students, or whole classes of students, believed to be more capable or less capable are sometimes treated differently by their teachers. For decades, educators have argued for ability grouping or tracking on the grounds that this allows teachers to focus on specific instructional goals that are not possible when students are taught in classes or groups of heterogeneous ability levels. This literature is lengthy and complex. Part of the difficulty in interpreting effects is because separating the effects of grouping per se from the curriculum content is exceedingly difficult to do. That is, students placed in different ability groups often receive very different curriculum content. This is true in both conceptual focus and content. Students placed in higher ability groups often receive greater opportunity to learn advanced content than students placed in less-capable groups. Further, the instructional orientation often differs with students in higher ability groups receiving more focus on the meaning of the content being studied, whereas those in less-knowledgeable groups receive a more factual and drill-oriented curriculum. The literature is replete with many reviews of the advantages and disadvantages of using ability groups for instruction (Francis, et al., 2017; Gamoran, 1992; Oakes & Lipton, 1990; and Slavin, 1987).

Clearly there are times when students can be grouped for instruction appropriately, as some students may need focused work on vocabulary development or basic arithmetic skills. But, too often, when students are defined by their deficits, too much instructional emphasis is placed on what they lack and not enough attention is paid to their need for meaning and challenging work. When students are grouped for instruction, teachers need to be sure that students are not recipients of low expectations and a watered-down curriculum; they need to ensure that all students receive an appropriately challenging curriculum. Good and Lavigne (2018) recommend that students generally be taught in heterogeneous groups and provide suggestions for using ability grouping in ways that minimize the communication of low expectations (which unnecessarily reduce the opportunities for students to learn). Six of these suggestions are presented in Table 2.4.

Although these guidelines may seem simplistic, in reality they are very often difficult to implement. Students perceived as less able (especially if they are seen as racially, culturally, or linguistically different from majority students) are less likely to receive intellectual encouragement and emotional support than other students.

Teacher Effects: Their Magnitude and Stability

The teacher-effectiveness experiment (Good & Grouws, 1979) and the teacher-expectation experiment (Rubie-Davies, 2014) both provided conclusive information that teachers impacted student achievement. Up to this point, we have mainly discussed which teacher actions influence student achievement, but we have said little about the size of teacher effects. We now discuss the magnitude or size of teacher effects. What does it mean to have an effective teacher? Does it have consequences for students now? In the future?

Table 2.4 Key Considerations for Grouping

1. The number and composition of the groups should depend on the variation in achievement and instructional needs among students. If you use within-class grouping to achieve homogeneity among students assigned to the same group, then make sure that such homogeneity is achieved—don't just arbitrarily divide the class into three equal-sized groups.

2. Grouping should lead to more effective meeting of instructional needs, not merely to differentiated pacing through the curriculum. Teaching will still have to be individualized within groups, and students who continue to have trouble will need additional instruction.

3. Group assignments should be flexible. Assignments should be reviewed regularly with an eye toward disbanding groups that have outlived their usefulness.

4. Group scheduling and instructional practices should be flexible (a particular group might best meet for 40 minutes on one day and 20 minutes the next day).

5. Because of the potential dangers of labeling effects and because grouping affects peer contacts, teachers should limit the degree to which group membership determines students' other school experiences. Members of the same reading group should not be seated together or otherwise dealt with as a group outside of reading instruction, and, if ability grouping is used for mathematics or other subjects, group assignments should be based on achievement in these subjects rather than in reading.

6. Groups should be organized and taught in ways that provide low achievers with extra instruction. For example, you can assign more students to high-achievement groups and fewer students to low-achievement groups, thus arranging for more intensive instruction of low achievers within the group setting. Or, you can spend more time teaching to low-achievement groups while high-achievement groups spend more time working cooperatively or independently.

Below, we review evidence to show that if teacher effects are sufficiently large, we should be concerned about them. Then, we turn to related issues that deal with the stability of teacher effects. Are teachers generally effective or do they vary from year to year? And we consider other related issues, for example does effectiveness vary in terms of a particular context?

Teacher Effects Are Large

Teacher effects have been studied extensively by production-function researchers (often conducted by economists). Educational production-function research, like the teacher-effectiveness and teacher-expectation paradigms, also has a long and continuing history (e.g., Bowles, 1970; Li, Miranti, & Vidyattama, 2017; Monk, 1989; Pigott, Williams, Polanin, & Wu-Bohanan, 2012; Polachek, Kniesner, & Harwood, 1978). In these studies, the process of teaching is ignored and the inputs (money spent on education, amount of teacher experience, and so forth) are related to outcomes (primarily student achievement). Although these types of studies do not provide process information about *what teachers do* to influence student achievement, they are given much consideration by policymakers because they bring money and economics into the equation. Simply put, do teachers add value that is economically important to students? To society? The answer is *yes*—the differences are sufficiently large to prompt possible policy action.

Nye, Konstantopoulos, and Hedges (2004) summarize 18 studies that showed that teachers account for 7–21% of the variance in student-achievement gains. Their review estimated how much variance teachers accounted for in student achievement and it remains an accurate summary of the magnitude of teacher effects (see Konstantopolous, forthcoming). So what does this magnitude of teacher effect mean for student achievement? Nye and colleagues noted that these findings equate to a one standard deviation increase in teacher effectiveness to improving student achievement by about one-third of a standard deviation.

Nye et al. (2004) illustrate how teacher effects are determined. In their experiment, they included four years of teacher and student-achievement information collected in a study that also examined the effects of class size on student achievement. Their study was carefully controlled as they assigned students randomly to classrooms (something that typically cannot be done in production-function research). Further, they verified that students in treatment and control groups were comparable. (They did this because sometimes randomization does not yield equal control and experimental groups.) This careful study allowed the authors not only to report the size of teacher effects in both control and experimental conditions but also to compare naturally-occurring teacher effects with the effects found in classes with smaller class sizes.

What did they find? First, they demonstrated (as had earlier research) that teacher effects are considerably larger than school effects. In other words, the differences between teachers are larger than the differences between schools (as noted earlier, Good et al., 1975; and as found in other countries as well, Luyten & Snijders, 1996). They also found that there are substantial differences between teachers in their ability to obtain achievement gains from their students. How large are these differences? They note:

> these findings would suggest that the difference in achievement gains between having a 25th percentile teacher (a not-so-effective teacher) and a 75th percentile teacher (an effective teacher) is over one third of a standard deviation (.035) in reading and almost half a standard deviation (.048) in mathematics
>
> (Nye et al., 2004, p. 253)

Differences of this magnitude are important and a major reason that policymakers created RTTT high-stakes testing reform (we discuss RTTT in Chapter 3). Further, they noted that teacher effects are much larger in schools serving students from low-SES (socioeconomic status) homes than they are in schools serving high-SES students. Nye et al. (2004) emphasized that it matters more which teacher a child is assigned to in low-SES schools than in high-SES schools. And, as noted above, given that teacher effects are larger than school effects, it matters more which teacher a student has than the school that the student attends. Konstantopoulos (forthcoming) notes that these conclusions continue to be valid today.

When Nye and colleagues conducted their work in 2004 much emphasis was placed on the importance of reducing class size,[18] because class size was considered an important determinant of achievement, however the authors showed in this study that teacher effectiveness has a larger effect than does reducing class size from 25 to 15. And when compared to the *costs* of reducing class size, the importance of teacher effects are again apparent. Also, increasing teacher effectiveness would appeal to most policymakers as an easier and less costly way to improve student achievement.

Arguments about the importance of teacher effects and their magnitude quickly led to policymaker (and researcher) questions, such as what difference would it make if a student had an effective teacher for several consecutive years? Chetty, Friedman, and Rockoff (2011) found that value-added measures of teacher quality had large impact on students. For example when students were taught by high-value-added teachers, they graduated at higher rates from high school and they were more likely to attend college, to be productively employed, and to earn higher wages. What does this mean in terms of dollars? Chetty and colleagues estimated that replacing a teacher whose value-added is in the bottom 5% of the distribution with an *average* teacher would increase students' lifetime income by more than $250,000. What then would the teachers' impact (value) have for the entire class of students? In a single year, a teacher at the 60th percentile would raise students' aggregate earnings by a total of $106,000 (lifetime earnings for a class of students). This value increases to $212,000 for an even better teacher at the 69th percentile, and to $400,000 for a teacher at the 84th percentile (Hanushek, 2011).

Hanushek (2011), after noting the positive effects of effective teachers on students, considered the negative consequences of having an ineffective teacher. He put it this way, "Alternatively, replacing the bottom 5–8% of teachers with average teachers could move the US near the top of international math and science rankings with a present value of $100 trillion" (Hanushek, 2011, p. 466). These economic data of course are very attractive to policymakers as they suggest that, potentially, student productivity in school and in later life would dramatically improve with effective teachers. The results of such improvements would have important consequences.

Replacing Less-Effective Teachers

Economists have described an overly idealistic and a likely unobtainable economic situation in which superintendents and principals should recruit teachers in a more selective manner, thereby gaining teachers who are more effective. This is much like when a football coach is pressured to recruit new athletes that are better than players from previous years. Would this improve the quality of the team? Yes, it is true that a football team with a losing record for many years could improve dramatically if they had a top-five recruiting class two years in a row. But this is not in the cards as many potential recruits prefer (and select) teams with winning records, better facilities, and so forth. Also, the number of five- and four-star athletes is very limited.

As well as the economists being insensitive to a number of variables (e.g., teacher supply, lack of stability), there are other considerations: new (better) athletes could get injured in preseason, an amazing teacher could experience the loss of a parent, etc. Additionally, and unfortunately, little is done to change the conditions that will attract and keep teachers in the schools where they matter the most – low-SES schools. Clearly, RTTT policymakers were listening to economists informing policy (with an eye toward improving economic productivity by removing incompetent teachers through high-stakes evaluation). Unfortunately, policymakers did not listen to educational researchers who had also studied classroom practice and explicated the conditions in which teachers work, identifying the inadequate resources that educators had for overcoming the effects of poverty on students' learning.

Stability of Teacher Effects

However, this possibility of radically improving student achievement, is sharply undercut if teacher effects on student achievement vary from year to year. This possibility was not considered as policymakers concluded that the effects of good teaching had important economic consequences. The equation policymakers used was A − B = C, or (a) retain good teachers − (b) remove ineffective ones = (c) productive schools, economy, and society. This simple equation, and its implication for policy, was irresistibly attractive to reformers. However, as a simple policy goal, this was also illusionary for many reasons. One basic reason is the lack of teacher stability, but there are other problematic assumptions that we address in Chapters 4 and 5. However, to prefigure these assumptions, we note that they included that, once an ineffective teacher was identified, it would be easy to improve their teaching, and, that if that was not possible, other teachers could easily be obtained to replace them.

Unrealistic Economic Forecasts

The increased gain in economic productivity promised in the strategy—retain effective teachers and remove (or retrain) less-effective ones—assumes that effective teachers are stable in their effects on student achievement and do not vary from year to year. Unfortunately, the opposite is the case: teacher effects do vary, and often considerably so, from year to year.

That teacher effects vary was shown in research that we examined earlier (see Good & Grouws, 1977). We reiterate that effects of teachers vary because instructional practice varies, as do the life circumstances of teachers and the students they teach. We know that seemingly "small" changes in student composition can have huge effects on the classroom environment. Researchers have observed variations such as: across lessons (Patrick, Mantzicopoulos, & French, 2018); across different groups of students who experience the same lesson (Rosenshine, 1970); across a single year (Emmer, Evertson, & Brophy, 1979; Rosenshine, 1970); and across multiple years with different groups of students (Brophy, 1979). Given the multiple ways teachers' instructional practices, and the effectiveness of those practices, vary, the stability of teacher effects is low (Konstantopoulos, 2014, forthcoming) within a period of two weeks (Berliner, 1976).

Problematic Policy Implications

When RTTT, high-stakes teacher evaluation, and attempts to improve teacher effectiveness were initiated, there was clear evidence that there was considerable variation in teachers' abilities to increase student achievement in a given year (Hanushek & Rivkin, 2012). Thus, in any given year, some teachers are more effective than others. However, teacher stability over consecutive years is low and this limits policy actions. For example, does it make sense to replace a teacher who is ineffective one year but who may be highly effective the next year?

Some Teachers are Stable

Nonetheless, as we saw earlier (in the review of process-product research), some researchers have found that a subset of teachers are stable in their effects on students over time. More recently, there has appeared some evidence that teachers who are most effective tend to be more stable over time than those who are least effective (Konstantopoulos, forthcoming). Further, as we have seen, considerable research has been conducted to identify those actions of teachers who are effective and stable.

When RTTT began, at least five things were highly salient:

1   Teacher effects in a given year can be very large.
2   Having effective teachers over consecutive years can further increase student achievement.
3   Unfortunately, the difficulty and reality of teaching (and life circumstances) are sufficiently important that teacher effects can and do vary.
4   There is a limited, but useful amount, of information describing teacher actions that increase student achievement (i.e., the knowledge gained from teacher-effectiveness and teacher-expectations research).
5   It had been asserted that increasing teacher effectiveness (as noted earlier in this chapter) could have enormous economic consequences on students and the economy. Given what was known about the instability of teacher effectiveness (in the literature), this "salubrious" effect was unlikely.

Policymakers acted on the belief that improvements in teacher effectiveness would reap large economic benefits, but policymakers appeared to be unaware of the points enumerated above—the things that the literature had established (e.g., only some teachers were effective over consecutive years). However, these five things *were* knowable, as they were clearly evident in the literature. It appears that policymakers and researchers engaged in high-stakes teacher evaluation had not read or understood the relevant research. If they had, they would have realized that there were many errors in their reasoning (e.g., a selective review of the literature ... see Lavigne and Good 2017 for explication) as well as factual mistakes (e.g., teachers are not stable in their effects on students over consecutive years ... see Good and Lavigne, 2015). In future chapters (see Chapters 4 and 5), we will show that not only were policymakers partially/largely ignorant of the research on teaching, but also that they failed to utilize what they did know.

Conclusion

In Chapter 1, we started our book with a paradox. That is, good teaching should equal adequate compensation—but, it doesn't. In explaining this paradox, we noted that policymakers and citizens did not fully understand the complexities of teaching. Accordingly, simple and misguided reforms were mandated, because schools were characterized by policymakers as being *in crisis* and it was believed that too many of our teachers were inadequate. These reforms were inaccurate, excessive, and failed to to take account of the conditions of schooling and teaching. Nonetheless, because the criticisms stuck (together with their suggested quick solutions), the reforms were enacted in ways that expended great resources but failed to bring about change.

Here in Chapter 2 we have demonstrated how the research literature has developed into three separate research tradition: 1) *teacher effectiveness*, 2) *teacher-expectation effects*, and 3) *the magnitude of teacher effects*. Within a focus on student achievement (as measured by standardized achievement tests) we have considered correlational evidence about the types of teacher actions and classroom environments that correlate with student achievement. We have also presented experimental literature to show that these teacher actions are *causally* related to student achievement. This research information is directly related to the most central RTTT concern: How do teachers increase student achievement on standardized tests?[19, 20]

The knowledge base from earlier reforms and the availability of literature on teacher effects was overlooked by policymakers. They certainly heard that if students had effective teachers (or could be spared from ineffective ones) their achievement, and life-long earnings would improve substantially. However, many other messages from the literature were ignored when RTTT was mandated (e.g., teacher effectiveness varies). Given this lack of understanding, policymakers design and implementation of RTTT was seriously flawed, as we will see in Chapter 3.

Notes

1 Lyndon Johnson was notable for gathering a panel of experts to develop a comprehensive early childhood program that would address the needs of disadvantaged children. From this panel emerged "Head Start," a program designed to serve the emotional, social, health, nutritional, and psychological needs of low-income children and pregnant women through comprehensive child care. Since its beginning, Head Start has served over 35 million children and pregnant women (Head Start, 2017).

2 For example, teacher warmth, or some other teacher characteristics, might be correlated to student achievement or to student attitudes but studies failed to measure if/how teacher warmth (or other teacher characteristics) influenced their interactions with students.

3 Observations were made without observers knowing whether teachers were classified as effective or not.

4 This observation system measured a teacher's interactions with individual students and recorded the frequency with which students were called upon, the type of questions they were asked, how teachers responded to student answers, and so forth.

5 Although PP researchers reported that relatively few teachers were stable in their effects on student achievement from year to year, this finding failed to generate curiosity or research about *why* teachers varied from year to year. As we will see later, value-added research that was utilized in RTTT reform, would have been much more valuable if that question had been addressed.

6 As we describe later in the chapter (p. 60), sometimes improvements can occur because people are aware that they are a part of a study and this attention may lead them to make greater efforts (known as placebo or Hawthorne effects). To reduce these possible effects, control teachers (who did not receive information about strategies for improving mathematics instruction) were told that they were involved in a study of effective mathematics teaching. And that pre- and post-tests of students' mathematical performance would be collected. Further, these teachers were observed as frequently as the experimental teachers; thus, control teachers were likely motivated to teach mathematics as effectively as they could.

7 By using two outcome measures, information could be obtained both on how the mathematical performance of students in the study compared to that of students elsewhere (the standardized test) and also the extent to which students mastered the material that teachers actually taught (i.e., what was emphasized in the textbook).

8 According to Google Scholar, as of November 2018, Ebmeier and Good (1979) have been cited 75 times, whereas Good and Grouws (1979) have been cited 587 times, thus the main effect study was cited approximately eight times more frequently than was the more contextual study.

9 The importance of adapting instructional practice to meet students' needs has long been asserted (Good & Brophy, 1973) and is still asserted today (Good & Lavigne, 2018). Findings do not translate themselves. They have to be used by teachers, as decision-makers, with the knowledge of their students and instructional goals.

10 Norwich et al. (2018) provide an important example illustrating how subtle issues in context and implementation can have important effects on findings.

11 For reviews of subject-matter knowledge in science see Windschitl and Calabrese-Barton (2016); for social studies see Barton and Avery (2016), and Hicks, van Hover, Doolittle, and VanFossen (2012); for literacy see Tracey and Morrow (2017); for guided or structured inquiry see Bevins and Price (2016), and Furtak, Seidel, Iverson, & Briggs (2012); for mathematics see Franke et al. (2015).

12 The field has had many "silver bullets" that were often seen at that time as transformative—but all of which proved illusionary. Among these silver bullets were smaller class sizes, small-group instruction, technology-infused instruction, whole-language/phonics instruction, discovery learning, project-based learning, and so forth. Each of these highly recommended approaches certainly had some advantages, but all of them had distinct weaknesses as well. In many of these approaches the role of the teacher was greatly unappreciated and all of them assumed that teaching could be improved by one single variable.

13 For example, value-added attempts to make comparisons across teachers as equal as possible. Still, it is very clear that these models only do so imperfectly and some variables cannot be corrected … for example, several special-education students in a classroom versus no special-education students.

14 Berliner and Biddle (1995) provided an exhaustive review, refuting policymakers' claims that American schools were *in crisis*.

15 We make this point to illustrate that expectations are not explicitly held about an individual student but they may be held about a general category of students. For

example, teachers may hold implicit beliefs that female students have high levels of math anxiety or lack potential to do it well, and thereby may inadvertently expect less and demand less (thus inadvertently lowering the female students' mathematical performance).

16 Student choice is another variable that ranges from desirable to undesirable. In the work of Rubie-Davies, choice refers to students choosing among acceptable and appropriate educational tasks. At times, schools have been lambasted because they provide but limited choice (see Silverman, 1970), and, at other times, for allowing students to have too much choice (see Heidelberg, 1971). Attitudes toward choice vary from one extreme to the other.

17 Significant gains were not found in reading. As we have noted several times in this chapter, teacher actions that are successful in one context are not always successful in another context or with other students. (See also Norwich et al., 2018.)

18 See Glass and Smith (1978) and Glass, Cahen, Smith, and Filby (1982). But, over time, support for reducing class size lessened as more data became available.

19 As we have argued elsewhere, standardized tests are overused in evaluating both teachers and students. They have many flaws, including the fact that they emphasize absolute achievement and do not consider the important relative gains (small wins) that students exhibit. Elsewhere we have argued that standardized achievement tests need to be supplemented with many other measures that have important outcomes for teaching and learning (see, for example, Lavigne & Good, 2014, 2015; Good & Lavigne, 2018).

20 We do not want to convey the impression that research on active and explicit teaching is the only literature available. We have noted from time to time that other important literature is available for informing teaching practice and development. We have emphasized aspects of explicit teaching because they are most central to the narrow question: How do teachers influence student achievement on standardized tests? Elsewhere Good and Lavigne (2018) have examined other literature relevant to teaching, including motivation, classroom management, use of technology, cultural diversity, and assessment.

References

Aspy, D. (1973). A discussion of the relationship between selected student behavior and the teacher's use of interchangeable responses. Paper presented at the annual meeting of the American Educational Research Association, New Orleans.

Barber, T. X., & Silver, M. J. (1968). Fact, fiction, and the experimenter bias effect. *Psychological Bulletin Monograph Supplement, 70*, 1–29.

Barton, K. C., & Avery, P. G. (2016). Research on social studies education: Diverse students, settings, and methods. In D. Gitomer & C. Bell (Eds.), *Handbook of research on teaching*, (pp. 985–1038). Washington, D.C.: American Educational Research Association.

Beller, E. (1973). Research on organized programs of early education. In R. Travers (Ed.), *Second handbook of research on teaching* (pp. 530–600). Chicago, IL: Rand McNally.

Berliner, D. C. (1976). A status report on the study of teacher effectiveness. *Journal of Research in Science Teaching, 13*, 369–382.

Berliner, D. C., & Biddle, B. J. (1995). *The manufactured crisis: Myths, fraud, and the attack on America's public schools*. Reading, MA: Addison-Wesley Publishing Company.

Bevins, S., & Price, G. (2016). Reconceptualising inquiry in science education. *International Journal of Science Education*, 38(1), 17–29.

Bowles, S. (1970). Towards an educational production function. In *Education, income, and human capital* (pp. 11–70). NBER.

Brophy, J. E. (1973). Stability of teacher effectiveness. *American Educational Research Journal*, 10, 245–252.

Brophy, J. E. (1979). Teacher behavior and its effects. *Journal of Educational Psychology*, 71(6), 733–750.

Brophy, J. E. (1983). Research on self-fulfilling prophecy and teacher expectations. *Journal of Educational Psychology*, 75(5), 631–666.

Brophy, J. E., & Evertson, C. M. (1973). The Texas teacher effectiveness project: Presentation of non-linear relationships and summary discussion. Research Report, the Research and Development Center for Teacher Education, University of Texas at Austin.

Brophy, J. E., & Evertson, C. M. (1974). Process-product correlations in the Texas teacher effectiveness study: Final report (res. Rep. 74–74). Austin, Texas: Research and Development Center for Teacher Education. (ERIC No. ED 091 394).

Brophy, J. E., & Good, T. L. (1970). Brophy-Good system (teacher-child interaction). In A. Simon & E. Boyer, *Mirrors for behavior: An anthology of observation instruments continued, 1970 supplement* (Vol A). Philadelphia, PA: Research for Better Schools, Inc.

Brophy, J. E., & Good, T. L. (1974). *Teacher-student relationships: Causes and consequences*. New York, NY: Holt, Rinehart and Winston.

Brophy, J. E., & Good, T. L. (1986). Teacher behavior and student achievement. In M. Wittrock (Ed.), *Handbook of research on teaching* (3rd ed., pp. 328–375). New York, NY: Macmillan.

Carpenter, T. P., Dossey, J. A., & Koehler, J. L. (2004). *Classics in mathematics education research*. National Council of Teachers of English.

Chall, J. (1967). *Learning to read: The great debate*. New York, NY: McGraw Hill.

Chetty, R., Friedman, J. N., & Rockoff, J. E. (2011). The long-term impacts of teachers: Teacher value-added and student outcomes in adulthood (No. w17699). National Bureau of Economic Research.

Cohen, J. (2018). Practices that cross disciplines?: Revisiting explicit instruction in elementary mathematics and English language arts. *Teaching and Teacher Education*, 69, 324–335.

Cohen, J., & Grossman, P. (2016). Respecting complexity in measure of teaching: Keeping schools and students in focus. *Teaching and Teacher Education*, 55, 308–317.

Coleman, J. S., Campbell, E., Hobson, C., McPartland, J., Mood, A., Weinfeld, F., & York, R. (1966). The coleman report. Equality of educational opportunity. Washington D.C.: Superintendent of Documents, U.S. Government Printing Office.

Connor, C. M., Morrison, F. J., Schatschneider, C., Toste, J. R., Lundblom, E., Crowe, E. C., & Fishman, B. (2011). Effective classroom instruction: Implications of child characteristics by reading instruction interactions on first graders' word reading achievement. *Journal of Research on Educational Effectiveness*, 4(3), 173–207.

Dunkin, M. J., & Biddle, B. J. (1974). *The study of teaching*. New York, NY: Holt, Rinehart & Winston.

Ebmeier, H., & Good, T. L. (1979). The effects of instructing teachers about good teaching on the mathematics achievement of fourth grade students. *American Educational Research Journal*, 16(1), 1–16.

Emmer, E. T. (1973). Classroom observation scales. Austin, TX: Research and Development Center for Teacher Education.

Emmer, E. T., Evertson, C. M., & Brophy, J. E. (1979). Stability of teacher effects in junior high classrooms. *American Educational Research Journal*, 16(1), 71–75.

Ferguson, R., & Danielson, C. (2014). How framework for teaching and tripod 7cs evidence distinguish key components of effective teaching. In T. Kane, K. Kerr, & R. Pianta. (Eds.), *Designing teacher evaluation systems* (pp. 98–143). San Francisco, CA: Jossey-Bass.

Flanders, N. (1970). *Analyzing Teacher Behavior*. Reading Mass.: Addison-Wesley.

Francis, B., Archer, L., Hodgen, J., Pepper, D., Taylor, B., & Travers, M. C. (2017). Exploring the relative lack of impact of research on "ability grouping" in England: A discourse analytic account. *Cambridge Journal of Education*, 47(1), 1–17.

Franke, M. L., Turrou, A. C., Webb, N. M., Ing, M., Wong, J., Shin, N., & Fernandez, C. (2015). Student engagement with others' mathematical ideas: The role of teacher invitation and support moves. *The Elementary School Journal*, 116(1), 126–148.

Furtak, E. M., Seidel, T., Iverson, H., & Briggs, D. C. (2012). Experimental and quasi-experimental studies of inquiry-based science teaching: A meta-analysis. *Review of Educational Research*, 82(3), 300–329.

Gamoran, A. (1992). Synthesis of research: Is ability grouping equitable?. *Educational Leadership*, 50, 11–17.

Glass, G. V., Cahen, L., Smith, M. L., & Filby, N. (1982). *School class size*. Beverly Hills, CA: Sage.

Glass, G. V., & Smith, M. L. (1978). *Meta-analysis of research on the relationship of class size and achievement*. San Francisco, CA: Far West Laboratory for Educational Research and Development.

Good, T. L. (2014). What do we know about how teachers influence student performance on standardized tests: And why do we know so little about other student outcomes. In A. L. Lavigne, T. L. Good, & R. M. Marx (Eds.), High-stakes teacher evaluation: High cost-big losses [Special issue]. *Teachers College Record*, 116(1).

Good, T. L., & Brophy, J. (1973). *Looking in classrooms* (1st ed.). New York, NY: Harper and Row.

Good, T. L., & Brophy, J. (2008). *Looking in classrooms* (10th ed.). Boston, MA: Pearson.

Good, T. L., Biddle, B., & Brophy, J. (1975). *Teachers make a difference*. New York, NY: Holt, Rinehart, and Winston.

Good, T. L., & Grouws, D. A. (1977). Teaching effects: A process-product study in fourth-grade mathematics classrooms. *Journal of Teacher Education*, 28(3), 49–54.

Good, T. L., & Grouws, D. A. (1979). The Missouri mathematics effectiveness project: An experimental study in fourth-grade classrooms. *Journal of Educational Psychology*, 71(3), 355.

Good, T. L., Grouws, D. A., & Ebmeier, H. (1981). *Active mathematics teaching*. New York, NY: Longman.

Good, T. L., & Lavigne, A. L. (2015). Issues of teacher performance stability are not new: Limitations and possibilities. *Education Policy Analysis Archives*, 23, 2.

Good, T. L., & Lavigne, A. L. (2018). *Looking in classrooms* (11th ed.). New York, NY: Routledge.

Good, T. L., Sterzinger, N., & Lavigne, A. L. (2018). Expectation effects: Pygmalion and the initial 20 years of research. *Educational Research and Evaluation, 24*(3) 1–25.

GoodT. L., & Weinstein, R. (1986). Teacher's expectation: A framework for exploring classrooms. In K. Zumwalt (Ed.), *Improving teaching* (pp. 63–86). Alexandria, VA: Association for Supervision and Curriculum Development.

Gordon, I., & Jester, E. (1973). Techniques of observing teaching in early childhood. In R. Travers (Ed.), *Second Handbook of Research on Teaching* (pp. 184–217). Chicago, IL: Rand McNally.

Hamre, B. K., & Pianta, R. C. (2005). Can instructional and emotional support in the first-grade classroom make a difference for children at risk of school failure?. *Child development, 76*(5), 949–967.

Hamre, B. K., Pianta, R. C., Downer, J. T., DeCoster, J., Mashburn, A. J., Jones, S. M., … Brackett, M. A. (2013). Teaching through interactions: Testing a developmental framework of teacher effectiveness in over 4,000 classrooms. *The Elementary School Journal, 113*(4), 461–487.

Hanushek, E. A. (2011). Valuing teachers: How much is a teacher worth. *Education Next, 11*(3), 41–45.

Hanushek, E. A. (2016). What matters for student achievement: Updating Coleman on the influence of families and schools. *Education Next, 16*(2), 18–26.

Hanushek, E. A., & Rivkin, S. G. (2012). The distribution of teacher quality and implications for policy. *Annual Review of the Economy, 4*(1), 131–157.

Harris, M., & Rosenthal, R. (1985). Mediation of interpersonal expectations effects: Thirty-one meta-analyses. *Psychological Bulletin, 97*, 363–386.

Head Start. (2017). Head Start program facts: Fiscal year 2017. Retrieved from http s://eclkc.ohs.acf.hhs.gov/sites/default/files/pdf/hs-program-fact-sheet-2017_0.pdf.

Heidelberg, R. (1971). The cafeteria concept: curricular malnutrition?. *The Phi Delta Kappan, 53*(3), 174–175.

Hicks, D., van Hover, S., Doolittle, P., & VanFossen, P. (2012). Learning social studies: An evidence-based approach. *APA Educational Psychology Handbook, 3*, 283–307.

Hughes, C. A., Morris, J. R., Therrien, W. J., & Benson, S. K. (2017). Explicit instruction: Historical and contemporary contexts. *Learning Disabilities Research & Practice, 32*(3), 140–148.

Konstantopoulos, S. (2014). Teacher effects, value-added models, and accountability. In A. L. Lavigne, T. L. Good, & R. M. Marx (Eds.), High-stakes teacher evaluation: High cost – big losses [Special Issue]. *Teachers College Record, 116*(1).

Konstantopoulos, S. (forthcoming). Teacher effects: Their stability and magnitude. In T. L. Good & M. M. Mccaslin (Eds.), Educational psychology section; D. Fisher (Ed.), *Routledge encyclopedia of education* (online). New York, NY: Taylor & Francis.

Kounin, J. S. (1970). *Discipline and group management in classrooms*. New York, NY: Holt, Rinehart, and Winston.

Lavigne, A. L., & Good, T. L., (2014). *Teacher and student evaluation: Moving beyond the failure of school reform*. New York, NY: Routledge.

Lavigne, A. L., & Good, T. L. (2015). *Improving teaching through observation and feedback: Beyond state and federal mandates*. New York, NY: Routledge.

Lavigne, A. L., & Good, T. L. (2017). Citing, being cited, not citing, and not being cited: Citations as intellectual footprints. In J. Plucker & M. Makel (Eds.),

Toward a more perfect psychology: Improving trust, accuracy, and transparency in research (pp. 97–116). Washington, D.C.: American Psychological Association.

Lavigne, A. L. , Good, T. L., & Marx, R. M. (Eds.), High-stakes teacher evaluation: High cost-big losses [Special issue]. *Teachers College Record, 116*(1).

Li, J., Miranti, R., & Vidyattama, Y. (2017). What matters in education: a decomposition of educational outcomes with multiple measures. *Educational Research and Evaluation, 23*(1–2), 3–25.

Loewenberg Ball, D., & Forzani, F. M. (2009). The work of teaching and the challenge for teacher education. *Journal of Teacher Education, 60*(5), 497–511.

Luyten, H., & Snijders, T. A. B. (1996). School effects and teacher effects in Dutch elementary education. *Educational Research and Evaluation: An International Journal on Theory and Practice, 2*(1), 1–24.

McDill, E., Meyers, E., & Rigsby, L. (1967). Institutional effects on the academic behavior of high school students. *Sociology of Education, 40*, 181–199.

McDonald, F. I. (1976). *Beginning teacher evaluation study. Phase II summary*. Princeton, NJ: Educational Testing Service.

McLeskey, J., Barringer, M-D., Billingsley, B., Brownell, M., Jackson, D., Kennedy, M., ... Ziegler, D. (2017, January). *High-leverage practices in special education*. Arlington, VA: Council for Exceptional Children & CEEDAR Center.

McLeskey, J., & Brownell, M. (2015). High-leverage practices and teacher preparation in special education (CEEDAR Document No. PR-1). Retrieved from University of Florida, Collaboration for Effective Educator, Development, Accountability, and Reform Center website: http://ceedar. education. ufl. edu/tools/best-practice-review.

Matthews, H., & Cohen, J. (Forthcoming). Explicit instruction: A brief review of what we know and next directions for research. In T. L. Good & M. M. McCaslin (Eds.), Educational Psychology Section; D. Fisher (Ed.), *Routledge encyclopedia of education* (Online). New York, NY: Taylor & Francis.

Merton, R. K. (1948). The self-fulfilling prophecy. *Antioch Review, 8*, 193–210.

Monk, D. H. (1989). The education production function: Its evolving role in policy analysis. *Educational Evaluation and Policy Analysis, 11*(1), 31–45.

Norwich, B., Koutsouris, G., & Bessudnov, A. (2018). An innovative classroom reading intervention for Year 2 and 3 pupils who are struggling to learn to read: Evaluating the Integrated Group Reading Programme. University of Exeter. Retrieved from https://ore.exeter.ac.uk/repository/handle/10871/32881.

Nye, B., Konstantopoulos, S., & Hedges, L. V. (2004). How large are teacher effects?. *Educational Evaluation and Policy Analysis, 26*, 237–257.

Oakes, J., & Lipton, M. (1990). Tracking and ability grouping: A structural barrier to access and achievement. In J. I. Goodlad & P. Keating (Eds.), *Access to knowledge: An agenda for our nation's schools* (pp. 187–204). New York, NY: College Entrance Examination Board.

Patrick, H., Mantzicopoulos, P., & French, B. (2018). The utility and value of observation measures of instruction: differences for research and practice. In The problematic relationship of research to practice. Symposium presented at the Annual American Psychological Association (San Francisco).

Pianta, R. C., Belsky, J., Vandergrift, N., Houts, R., & Morrison, F. J. (2008). Classroom effects on children's achievement trajectories in elementary school. *American Educational Research Journal, 45*(2), 365–397.

Pigott, T. D., Williams, R. T., Polanin, J. R., & Wu-Bohanon, M. J. (2012, Spring). Predicting Student Achievement with the Education Production-Function and Per-Pupil Expenditure: Synthesizing Regression Models from 1968–1994. Society for Research on Educational Effectiveness.

Polachek, S. W., Kniesner, T. J., & Harwood, H. J. (1978). Educational production functions. *Journal of Educational Statistics*, 3(3), 209–231.

Rosenthal, R. (1966). *Experimenter effects in behavioral research*. East Norwalk, CT: Appleton-Century-Crofts.

Rosenthal, R. (1967). Unintended communication of interpersonal expectations. *American Behavioral Scientist*, 10(8), 24–26.

Rosenthal, R. (1973). The mediation of Pygmalion effects: A four-factor "theory". *Journal of Education*, 9, 1–12.

Rosenthal, R., & Jacobson, L. (1968). *Pygmalion in the classroom*. New York, NY: Holt, Rinehart, and Winston.

Rosenshine, B. (1970). The stability of teacher effects upon student achievement. *Review of educational research*, 40(5), 647–662.

Rosenshine, B., & Furst, N. (1971). Research in teacher performance criteria. In B. O. Smith (Ed.), *Research in teacher education: Symposium* (pp. 37–72). Englewood Cliffs, NJ: Prentice-Hall.

Rubie-Davies, C. M. (2007). Classroom interactions: Exploring the practices of high-and low-expectation teachers. *British Journal of Educational Psychology*, 77(2), 289–306.

Rubie-Davies, C. M. (2014). *Becoming a high expectation teacher: Raising the bar*. London, UK: Routledge.

Rubie-Davies, C. M. (2018). *Teacher expectations in education*. London, UK: Routledge.

Sears, P. S., Bloch, M., Hubner, J., Gamble, J., Adenubi, M., & Crist, J. (1972). Effective reinforcement for achievement behavior in disadvantaged children: the first year. Technical report no.30, Stanford Center for Research in Development in Teaching, Stanford University. Retrieved from https://files.eric.ed.gov/fulltext/ED067442.pdf.

Sigurdson, S. E., & Olson, A. T. (1992). Teaching mathematics with meaning. *Journal of Mathematical Behavior*, 11(1), 37–57.

Sigurdson, S. E., Olson, A. T., & Mason, R. (1994). Problem solving and mathematics learning. *The Journal of Mathematical Behavior*, 13(4), 361–388.

Silverman, D. (1970). *The theory of organizations*. Exeter, NH: Heinemann.

Swanson, H. L., & Hoskyn, M. (1998). Experimental intervention research on students with learning disabilities: A meta-analysis of treatment outcomes. *Review of Educational Research*, 68(3), 277–321.

Slavin, R. E. (1987). Ability grouping and student achievement in elementary schools: A best-evidence synthesis. *Review of Educational Research*, 57(3), 293–336.

Snow, R. E. (1969). Unfinished Pygmalion review of Pygmalion in the Classroom. *Contemporary Psychology*, 14, 197–200.

Stallings, J. A. (1976). How instructional processes relate to child outcomes in a national study of follow through. *Journal of Teacher Education*, 27(1), 43–47.

Thorndike, R. L. (1968). Review of Pygmalion in the Classroom. *American Educational Research Journal*, 5, 708–711.

Timmermans, A. C., Rubie-Davies, C. M., & Rjosk, C. (Eds.). (2018). Pygmalion's 50th anniversary: the state of the art in teacher expectation research [Special issue]. *Educational Research and Evaluation*, 24(3–5), 91–98.

Tracey, D. H., & Morrow, L. M. (2017). *Lenses on reading: An introduction to theories and models.* New York, NY: Guilford Publications.

Trent, J., & Cohen, A. (1973). Research on teaching in higher education. In R. Travers (Ed.), *Second handbook of research on teaching* (pp. 997–1071). Chicago, IL: Rand McNally.

Vernon, P. (1969). *Intelligence and cultural environment.* London, UK: Methuen.

Walburg, H. (1974). Optimization reconsidered. In H. Walburg (Ed.), *Evaluating educational performance: A source book of methods, instruments, and examples.* Berkeley, CA: McCutchan.

Weinstein, R. S. (2009). *Reaching higher.* Cambridge, MA: Harvard University Press.

Weinstein, R. S., & McKown, C. (1998). Expectancy effects in (context): Listening to the voices of students and teachers. In J. Brophy (Ed.), *Advances in research on teaching: Expectations in the classroom* (pp. 215–242). Greenwich, CT: JAI Press.

Windschitl, M., & Calabrese Barton, A. (2016). Rigor and equity by design: Locating a set of core teaching practices for the science education community. In D. Gitomer & C. Bell (Eds.), *Handbook of research on teaching* (pp. 1099–1158). Washington D.C.: American Educational Research Association.

3

A BRIEF HISTORY OF EDUCATION REFORM AND RACE TO THE TOP

Introduction

In Chapter 1, we set the table by presenting the paradox that teachers are highly valued, but receive low pay. We discussed the conditions that give rise to this, which allowed us to understand why simple reforms emerge. Chapter 2 indicated what reform can and cannot do and identified what research evidence exists to inform reform and improve instruction. In this chapter, we review education reform leading up to RTTT to demonstrate that the challenges that haunt RTTT are by no means new. Like other reforms, RTTT policy was not well informed by research. We discuss the aspects of RTTT and how states won RTTT dollars.

Our review of education reform from over four decades[1] demonstrates that research is rarely translated into policy, and this continues today. We review the major education reforms from the last 40 years to provide a historical context for understanding modern-day educational reform. We describe what innovations were tried in each reform, the existing evidence to support each reform, and how each reform impacted education, including the reform that followed. For this review, we examine four reforms: *A Nation at Risk* (1983), *No Child Left Behind* (2002), *Race to the Top (RTTT)* (2009), and the Every Student Succeeds Act (2015) (U.S. Department of Education, 2015a). In doing so, we note that policymakers are generally uninformed, problems are not well developed, solutions are not well researched, the reforms are misguided or lack adequate pilot data, and education reform efforts are ineffective. This wastes time, resources, and, even worse, it may harm teaching and learning. Yet, the cycle continues.

After providing a brief history of U.S. education reform, we take a close look at our most recent reform, the one at the heart of this book—Race to the Top (RTTT). How did policymakers arrive at RTTT? What did RTTT entail? We describe RTTT's assumptions, mandates, and intended independent and dependent variables. We will see that RTTT demanded increased accountability on teacher effectiveness, a shift that some have described as a war on teachers (Cowen, Brunner, Strunk, & Drake, 2017). We then address the following questions:

- Who applied to RTTT?
- How were applications rated and scored?
- Who won RTTT dollars (and why)?

In Chapter 4, we will analyze the effects of RTTT on teacher supervision and evaluation as we know it today.

Thirty-Five Years of Education Reform

Teachers and principals, aside from their immediate duties, also have to negotiate the never-ending cycle of failed education reforms, while coping with the "unrelenting criticism of failing public schools" (Cuban, 2001). It is no easy task. According to a recent survey of 500 K-12 teachers by the Education Week Research Center, nearly 84% of teachers reported that, as soon as they get a handle on the new reform, it changes. Perhaps the most discouraging finding from the report, and one we will return to later in the chapter, is that 68% of teachers reported that "new" education reforms or changes aren't really new, they have all been tried before (Loewus, 2017)— this must be incredibly frustrating for veteran teachers who have experienced previous reforms. This must be especially frustrating for teachers who know that the policymakers, who have introduced the new reform, are unaware that their new reform is actually old and previously unsuccessful. Cuban (2013) notes that in the complex world of schools what results is:

[classrooms] marked by continuity and many small changes— seldom ones that fundamentally turn around the dynamic of that complex world. In that world, the basic teacher–student relationship, one that is shaped by both persistent continuity and incremental changes, one that is constantly negotiated and renegotiated, determines the degree to which good and successful teaching occur ... structures that policymakers believe will reshape what teachers do—such as district and school governance; new curricular standards; organizing schools into K-8, 7–12; or other configurations; or going from big to small schools—have had few effects on classroom practices, and consequently, students' academic outcomes. In short, new structures and changes in existing ones may be necessary to get teachers to consider changes in routines, but those new and renovated structures are insufficient to change significantly what happens daily in classrooms and then produce student learning.

(p. 186)

Yet, new reforms continue to emerge with the promise of 'fixing' American schools for good. Perhaps the narrative below will illuminate why the education reform pendulum swings as it does.

Reform movements that have emerged since the 1980s have been described as standards-based, curriculum-based, test-based, and accountability-driven (Cuban, 2001). And the reform efforts that characterized RTTT are no different. In a brief review of the last forty years of education reform, it will become apparent that all of these reforms began with great expectations that they would yield swift and powerful change. Yet, little change in the desired outcomes was observed, and so a new reform, often drastically different from the last, emerges, and is costly both in terms of time and money.

A Nation at Risk

In April of 1983, *A Nation at Risk* was released, a scathing report on the quality of education in the United States. Twelve million copies of the report were sold, implying significant public interest (Fiske, 1986). The report, written by the National Commission on Excellence in Education (NCEE), argued that society had lost sight of the purpose of education, so much so that our students were not only mediocre, but that the nation was vulnerable to complete collapse. The NCEE framed the failure of public schools this way:

> If an unfriendly foreign power had attempted to impose on America the mediocre educational performance that exists today, we might well have viewed it as an act of war. As it stands, we have allowed this to happen to ourselves. We have even squandered the gains in student achievement made in the wake of the Sputnik challenge. Moreover, we have dismantled essential support systems which helped make those gains possible. We have, in effect, been committing an act of unthinking, unilateral educational disarmament.
> (National Commission on Excellence in Education, 1983, p. 2)[2]

One issue identified in the report was the rapid decline in student achievement, as evidenced by a decline in high school science achievement from 1966 to 1973 and 1977, as well as an increase in remedial math courses offered at four-year institutions. The report also highlighted that 23 million American adults were illiterate and only one-fifth of 17-year old students could write a persuasive essay. Who or what was to blame? The report pointed to high teacher turnover rates—driven by low salaries and weak preparation, poorly-managed instructional time, low-quality teachers, as well as low expectations for student learning. Recommendations were packaged into what the Committee called the New Basics—curriculum recommendations for English, mathematics, science, social studies, and computer science. The recommendations also underscored the need that

72

students start to learn a foreign language in elementary school. A report from the President's Commission on Foreign Language and International Studies (1980) indicated that "America's incompetence in foreign languages is nothing short of scandalous, and it is becoming worse" (p. 12). Schools, colleges, and universities were encouraged to design more rigorous standards.

Other recommendations included the reorganization of time—specifically, that schools should be spending more time on the New Basics as well as extending the school day to 7 hours and the school year to 220 days. In the spirit of finding more time for core subjects, many recommendations were made that involved cutting activities, for example experiences in music and art, physical education, and recess. Now, years later, society has reacted sharply to school decisions to ignore issues of health and physical education. The awareness of the benefits of recess (time to renew) and of physical education, in an era of growing youth obesity, has led to social media and professional associations recommending that recess and physical education both need to be an important part of today's school curriculum. Thus, despite the considerable waste of time and energy in ridding American schools of nonessential subjects (Hobbs, 2017), those aspects of schooling are now seen as essential.

The final recommendation pinpointed teaching. Teacher accountability for student learning focused primarily on the role of teacher-preparation programs to ensure high educational standards and to prepare competent and effective teachers. The report explicitly illustrated that American schools were failing society but were also responsible for fixing the "problem" of dismal achievement outcomes. The narrative that U.S. schools are failing because U.S. students are not competitive with international peers (on standardized achievement tests) continues to drive debate and education reform today.

Effects

Despite these initial challenges, some aspects of *A Nation at Risk* are still felt 30 years later. For example, since the 1980s there has been closer monitoring of how well high school graduates are equipped for the marketplace and higher education. Most states, districts, and schools have adopted more rigorous and measurable standards, and, as of 2009, this has manifested in the hotly debated Common Core State Standards (Graham, 2013). Other changes included adjustments in the preparation of future teachers such as: additional testing and curriculum requirements, the introduction of field experiences earlier in the preparation pipeline, and additional continuing education requirements after graduation (Jones, 2009). The National Board for Professional Teaching Standards, established in 1987, reflects *A Nation at Risk*'s focus on quality teaching, as well as the push by accreditation agencies (such as the Council for the Accreditation of Educator Preparation) for higher standards for entry requirements (such as Grade Point Average

(GPA)) to promote teacher-preparation programs, with the hope of recruiting more students from the top of their class to enter the profession.

Despite *A Nation at Risk*'s recommendations, and its lasting effects, today only a limited number of U.S. students graduating from the top third of their high school class enter teaching. For example, Auguste, Kihn, and Miller (2010) report that countries such as Finland, Korea, and Singapore recruit 100% of their teachers from the top third of the academic cohort, whereas, the US is only able to recruit 23% from the top third. Further, there is growing evidence that education reform has not been able to encourage teachers with higher scores to enter the teaching profession (Kraft, Brunner, Doughtry, & Schwegman, 2018).

Likewise, many of the issues addressed in *A Nation at Risk* remain. For example, there has been relatively little improvement in teachers' salaries and retention (Graham, 2013). And, despite *A Nation at Risk*'s call for a 7-hour school day, the increase in time spent on learning has been relatively small—in 2011–2012, the average number of hours in the school day was 6.7 (U.S. Department of Education, 2016). And recommendations to extend the school year to upward of 220 days has had no effect. This number has remained steady at 180 days since the release of *A Nation at Risk* (U.S. Department of Education, 2016).

To what extent changes initially prompted by *A Nation at Risk* have actually improved the teacher workforce and educational outcomes for students is unclear. For example, imposing additional testing requirements on teachers for licensure was a misguided attempt to improve the teacher workforce. Evidence suggests that these licensure tests have little or no relationship to teacher effectiveness and that the predictive validity of these tests on the student performance acquired by teachers varies by teacher and student race/ethnicity match (Goldhaber & Hansen, 2010). As earlier noted by the Education Commission of the States (ECS) and more broadly argued by Lavigne and Good (2014), reforms oftentimes propose an oversimplified "fix," yet expect drastic changes to result. But change is relatively slow and classroom life is complex. This is especially true if the "problem" is not well developed. Notably, at least one report emerged in the 1990s to reassess the data presented in *A Nation at Risk*, and it found steady and improving trends in student-achievement outcomes (Huelskamp, 1993). Guthrie and Springer (2004) note that *A Nation at Risk* overlooked the positive trends of disadvantaged students' SAT scores, which had increased over time. In their analysis of the problematic presentation of student achievement in *A Nation at Risk*, they note:

> It may have been more accurate for *A Nation at Risk* to assert that achievement by American students has historically matched or exceeded that of previous generations, whereas societal expectations have risen at a disproportionately faster rate. Had the NCEE

done so, it would have recognized that education reform is more complex and challenging than it seemed.

(Guthrie and Springer, 2004, p. 18)

With misguided problems and solutions, and expectations for drastic change, it quickly became apparent that reform expectations embedded in *A Nation at Risk* were unattainable.

No Child Left Behind

Nearly 20 years later, on January 8, 2002, the *No Child Left Behind Act* (NCLB) became law. As illustrated in its title, greater focus was placed on the achievement of particular student groups. Under NCLB, states were now required to annually test students in Grades 3–8 in reading and mathematics and report disaggregated scores by race, special education, and English-language learners. NCLB required that, by 2014, all students in all subcategories demonstrate proficiency in all tested subject areas. The goal was ambitious—and impossible to achieve. Schools that were unable to achieve adequately yearly progress (AYP) for any of the subgroups would receive sanctions, such as: ability for students to transfer to another school, corrective action, supplemental education services, reconstitution (including the replacement of school staff), and restructuring (including state takeover, private management, or reconstitution as a charter school) (Lipman, 2007). Essentially NCLB assumed that focusing on student outcomes with the threat of sanctions and being labeled as failing, would force changes from students, teachers, and principals that would yield higher performance outcomes. Although the pressure was universally felt across the system, it also placed a greater focus on teachers as the lever for school improvement, mandating that teachers be "highly qualified" (Jones, 2009). Furthermore, in order to protect their jobs and their schools from being labeled as "failing," teachers had to meet the student-achievement expectations set by NCLB. Dee and Jacob (2010) argued that it was the most far-reaching education policy initiative in the United States of the last four decades (p. 149). We agree.

Effects

Were states able to implement NCLB? In the 2003–2004 school year, 24 states had adopted accountability systems that threatened reconstitution for low-performing schools (Olson, 2004). An initial analysis two years into NCLB by the Education Commission of the States gave states a "B" overall, but indicated that many states were still struggling to implement the key requirements and had yet to comply with the most challenging ones, such as sending home report cards that reflect child's test scores, the school, together with those of other schools locally and statewide, and ensuring that all teachers were highly qualified (Toppo, 2004).

In the context of these implementation efforts, did NCLB work? Many would argue that the focus on failing schools actually attacked both urban schools and schools that served students of color and students from less affluent homes (Meier, 2007). In a careful analysis of high-stakes pressure and student achievement in 25 states, Nichols, Glass, and Berliner (2006) found no relationship between earlier accountability pressure and later cohort mathematics achievement at 4th or 8th grade, as measured by the National Assessment of Educational Progress. Dee and Jacob (2010) found that NCLB yielded gains in mathematics for younger students, particularly those from disadvantaged backgrounds, but yielded no gains in reading. The authors suggested that any observed gains may have been a function of increases in per-pupil expenditures, particularly on instruction. Their findings also suggest that NCLB led to increases in teacher pay and the share of teachers with graduate degrees. As Nichols and Berliner (2007) noted, instructional time was shifted towards greater allocation to mathematics and reading—the tested subject areas (Dee & Jacob, 2010).

Damage left in the wake of NCLB included: narrowed and watered-down curriculum, teaching to the test, strategically pushing students with low test performance out of the classroom and schools (known as student pushout), cheating, misrepresentation of scores, and the undermining of teacher practice (Nichols & Berliner, 2007). Because of how schools, states, and districts were held accountable for student test scores, pressure to increase the number of students who met proficiency led to score inflation and hindered the growth opportunities of student groups historically marginalized by U.S. schooling. Furthermore, attention was placed on students in the "bubble" of proficiency levels, hindering the growth opportunities of the most proficient students. Finally, Murnane and Papay (2010) noted that AYP rules yielded teacher migration patterns that drove experienced teachers out of the highest-need schools—the same schools serving the students that NCLB intended to serve best. Teachers who remained in those schools felt conflict between what they were supposed to do under NCLB to improve test scores and what they felt they should do to best serve their students.

Left Behind

Taken together, despite the extensive cost and effort of NCLB, most students have reaped no gains. Considering this and the unintended consequences of NCLB, the general conclusion is, and we agree, that NCLB left most, if not all, of our children behind. In 2009, the NEA agreed with this conclusion, calling NCLB "President Bush's failed education experiment," one that judged "schools and children based solely on standardized test scores at the expense of preparing them with 21st century skills."

Cuban (2008) notes that, "policymakers turn religiously to school-based solutions for national problems. If society has an itch, schools get scratched" (p. 100). Yet, these reforms rarely make a difference in schools, as already noted in the two reforms described above (pp. 73 and 75), and reforms continue to return again, again, and again—as we present two additional reforms below. Why is this? One explanation that Cuban (2008) presents is the rational explanation for recurring reforms:

> Reforms return because policymakers fail to diagnose problems and promote correct solutions. Reforms return because policymakers use poor historical analogies and pick the wrong lessons from the past (Katz, 1987). Reforms return because policymakers fail, in the words of Charles Silberman 2 decades ago, "to think seriously about educational purposes" or question the "mindlessness" of schooling (Silberman, 1971, pp. 10–11). Reforms return because policymakers cave in to the politics of a problem rather than the problem itself. Reforms return because decision-makers seldom seek reliable, correctly conducted evaluations of program effectiveness before putting a program into practice (Slavin, 1989).
>
> (Cuban, 2008, p. 93)

Lavigne and Good (2014) noted, in their review of five recent education reforms, a number of commonalities. They noted that each crisis is characterized by a concern for low achievement on standardized tests, typically relative to other countries. These crises are often misdiagnosed because the problem and the independent variable are not well researched or well developed. The "solution" to the "problem" calls for something new that has not been piloted (or sometimes old efforts return in a new form). We see that the new reform has not resolved the problem and the cycle begins again. Classroom practice, though, remains remarkably unchanged (Cuban, 2013).

RTTT

As noted, all education reforms, historically, establish their need in response to a problem (whether it be real, fabricated, or misguided). RTTT was a response to the increased demands for more education, even for the middle class—a status that was attainable in the past to individuals who did not finish high school, but was identified as no longer the case (U.S. Department of Education, 2015a). The recession of 2009 further exacerbated the existing gap between more-affluent and less-affluent communities as well as White communities and those of color. The housing crisis was, in part, to blame, as the recession was particularly financially damaging to minorities, who were more likely to have held subprime mortgages. While homeownership dropped for communities of color following the recession, homeownership among Whites increased. Likewise, education had made very limited progress on closing these gaps (U.S. Department of Education, 2015a)—a gap central to NCLB, but one that NCLB failed to close. And as noted in Chapter 1, teachers were blamed for the failure to close the achievement gap. The renewed awareness that teachers matter, coupled with the belief that many "bad apples" remain in the classroom (see Chapter 1), led some to recommend the use of high-stakes teacher evaluation to weed out inadequate teachers. These pressures, based largely on perceptions, led to RTTT.

Despite attention to research that indicates that teachers matter, unfortunately, policymakers selectively ignored other aspects of research on teacher effects (the research we presented in Chapter 2)—we would give policymakers a D+ for their knowledge of this research. Yes, they did learn from the teacher-effects literature that some teachers matter more than others and from the teacher-magnitude literature that these teacher effects are impactful. Unfortunately, they overestimated these results from the teacher-effect literature (by not understanding that teacher effects are not stable from year to year) and from the teacher-magnitude literature (that most students do not have effective teachers two years in a row). Further, observational measures commonly recommended used only limited insights from the teacher-effect literature, and made no use of knowledge from the teacher-expectation literature. One consistent finding they ignored was the magnitude of teacher effects. Although we note that teachers are the most important in-school factor, they still only account for 7–21% of the variance in student achievement. Thus, teachers can only do so much, and, therefore, reforms that are intended to change teachers' practices can *also* only achieve so much. Policymakers also ignored that teacher effects on student learning are not stable over time. Thus, efforts to capture a teacher's true effectiveness, particularly for evaluation, is limited. The research findings presented in Chapter 2 have rich implications for policy, yet the gap between research and policy is great.

So, like previous reforms, it was out with the old, in with the new. Rather than shaming or scaring schools into improving outcomes for all learners, RTTT approached this challenge by focusing on innovation. The competitive program, launched in 2009 by President Barack Obama, allocated more than $4 billion to RTTT-winning entities (U.S. Department of Education, 2015a). In the application process, states were required to develop (and implement) comprehensive reforms to improve their entire educational systems, specifically around four areas:

1   High, challenging, and college and career readiness standards and expectations for student learning.
2   Effective instruction and leadership.
3   Data systems and technology to improve instruction.
4   Turnaround of lowest-performing schools.

(U.S. Department of Education, 2015a)

With principal and teacher effectiveness as one central component of RTTT, states were required to construct better ways to develop and identify effective teachers, primarily through teacher evaluation. Here, teachers were being held accountable both in what they were doing in the classroom and also, in significant part, by the student-learning growth outcomes they were able to achieve (U.S. Department of Education, 2015a). There was substantial evidence of the harmful effects and ineffectiveness of high-stakes testing at the time RTTT emerged. In a report by the Learning Policy Institute, Darling-Hammond et al. (2016) note that results from NCLB revealed that:

> the reliance on student test scores as a measuring stick for gauging school effectiveness did not always translate into schools that were teaching students the relevant skills needed to apply knowledge to real-world situations. Instead, in many cases, improved scores signaled the greater use of test-taking strategies, rather than more durable learning; sometimes, gains were also achieved by eliminating low-scoring students from the testing pool.
>
> (Darling-Hammond et al., 2016, p. 4)

Despite this, under RTTT high-stakes testing continued, now in the form of high-stakes teacher evaluation.

RTTT distributed awards in three phases. Two Phase I winners were announced on March 29, 2010. Ten Phase 2 winners were announced on August 24, 2010, which included nine states and the District of Columbia. And, finally, Phase 3 winners were announced on December 23, 2011, adding seven states to the tally, resulting in a total of 19 RTTT winners—eighteen states and the District of Columbia. We describe the winners and how they were rated later in the chapter.

Variations of RTTT also emerged that funded innovation at the district level (RTTT – District) as well as for younger students (RTTT – Early Learning Challenge). All initiatives that fell under "RTTT" will be described in greater detail later in the chapter, and its effectiveness and effects in Chapter 4.

Every Student Succeeds Act

Today's education context is shaped by the *Every Student Succeeds Act*. The *Every Student Succeeds Act* (ESSA) was signed into law on December 10, 2015 (U.S. Department of Education, 2015b). It reauthorized the *Elementary and Secondary Education Act* (ESEA) and put an end to NCLB-era accountability. It also eliminated the AYP system. Further, states can cap the amount of time students spend taking annual tests, and allow districts greater flexibility in choosing the annual standardized test. Note that, under ESSA, states are still required to annually test students in Grades 3–8 (and one grade in high school) in English Language Arts and mathematics. Yet, ESSA signifies a more holistic approach to school reform, as it encourages multiple measures of school and student success, beyond standardized test scores and graduation rates (Darling-Hammond et al., 2016, p. 1). Under the ESSA, states are still required to identify the bottom 5% (or lowest-performing) public schools and develop comprehensive school improvement plans for these schools. Yet, states are given greater responsibility for the evidence driving their school improvement efforts, including monitoring and evaluating them (Kane, 2017). The law also provides that states have the responsibility of designing systems that address inequities (Darling-Hammond et al., 2016).

The ESSA is driven by two goals: 1) college- and career-readiness, and 2) equity as it pertains to students in poverty, students of color, English learners, and students with disabilities. Other components include:

- The sharing of public information on statewide assessments of students' progress.
- Local innovation (e.g., evidence-based and place-based interventions developed by local leaders and educators).
- Accountability and improvement efforts for the lowest-performing schools.

The ESSA also recognizes the importance of paraeducators (also known as teacher aides, paraprofessionals, or teaching assistants)—their voice as well as professional development needs. The law provides opportunities to extend early learning through Preschool Development Grants (U.S. Department of Education, 2015a).

Finally, and relevant to RTTT's "Great Teachers and Leaders" (as described in greater detail below, p. 82), the ESSA does away with mandating teacher evaluations or defining teacher effectiveness (Sawchuk, 2016). The implementation of ESSA means that the Highly Qualified Teacher provision from NCLB is no longer recognized. Under ESSA, states must collect, and make publicly available, the number of ineffective teachers across schools serving different populations of students. Furthermore, states are no longer required to include student achievement as a significant component in a teacher's evaluation. The law allows states to redesign their teacher evaluation systems and submit them to the U.S. Department of Education. Other changes to teacher evaluation include:

- The Secretary of Education is not to determine any aspect of states' teacher evaluation systems or mechanism/model for defining and determining teacher effectiveness.
- State-developed goals that utilize a broad range of factors to gauge school performance.

- The requirement to utilize multiple-measure teacher-evaluation systems that employ: 1) high-quality evaluation tools and training, 2) training for school leaders and evaluators on differentiating performance, providing useful feedback, and aligning evaluation results with professional development opportunities and personnel decisions, and 3) a quality assurance system to continually evaluate the evaluation system and its related supports.
- Measuring and ensuring that low-income and minority students are not disproportionately served by ineffective, out-of-field, or inexperienced teachers.

Some states have used this opportunity to allow districts to determine how they assess teachers, particularly to what extent student growth measures are used (Loewus, 2017) and how they will define ineffective teachers (Berg-Jacobson, 2016). Kane (2017) argues that, under this new role and new flexibility, states should conduct pilots for any initiative that will impact 100 classrooms or more. We extend our discussion of this in Chapter 5 and describe to what extent states have used lessons from RTTT to make changes to their teacher-evaluation models under this new reform.

A Closer Look at RTTT

Now we shift to take a closer look at RTTT. We will discuss the initiative and related changes across the United States, broadly, and we will also take extensive space to discuss changes to teacher supervision and evaluation. This is particularly important, as RTTT marked a distinct and significant shift away from teacher-evaluation practices of the past, both in how teachers were rated as well as holding teachers accountable for student-learning gains (especially in ways different than the past for a number of RTTT-winning states).

It is important to recognize that RTTT had a number of iterations. Klein (2014) provides a road map that briefly describes all of the versions. The first is *RTTT Classic*. This is the most well-known aspect of RTTT and was the initial competition announced by President Obama. It is also linked to the greatest amount of funding and perhaps the most profound changes (or planned changes). Thus, this is the version we dedicate the most space to in this text. This original form of RTTT was first created as part of the *American Recovery and Reinvestment Act* (ARRA) of 2009, which was signed into law on February 17, 2009. As part of the ARRA, $4.35 billion in funds was allocated to RTTT. Phase 1 and 2 applications were rated, based on six criteria: state success factors, standards and assessments, data systems to support instruction, great teachers and leaders, turning around the lowest-achieving schools, and general selection criteria (U.S. Department of Education, 2009). A list of sub-elements is provided in Table 3.1.

Figure 3.1 describes the weight assigned to each element when rating RTTT applications.

In Phases 1 and 2, states were awarded funds based on innovative statewide reforms that included more rigorous teacher-evaluation models based on

Table 3.1 Selection Criteria for Phase 1 and Phase 2 RTTT Applications

---

A. *State Success Factors (125 points)*
  (A)(1) Articulating state's education reform agenda and LEAs' participation in it (65 points)
  (A)(2) Building strong statewide capacity to implement, scale up, and sustain proposed plans (30 points)
  (A)(3) Demonstrating significant progress in raising achievement and closing gaps (30 points)

B. Standards and Assessments (70 points)
  (B)(1) Developing and adopting common standards (40 points)
  (B)(2) Developing and implementing common, high-quality assessments (10 points)
  (B)(3) Supporting the transition to enhanced standards and high-quality assessments (20 points)

C. Data Systems to Support Instruction (47 points)
  (C)(1) Fully implementing a statewide longitudinal data system (24 points)
  (C)(2) Accessing and using state data (5 points)
  (C)(3) Using data to improve instruction (18 points)

D. Great Teachers and Leaders (138 points)
  (D)(1) Providing high-quality pathways for aspiring teachers and principals (21 points)
  (D)(2) Improving teacher and principal effectiveness based on performance (58 points)
  (D)(3) Ensuring equitable distribution of effective teachers and principals (25 points)
  (D)(4) Improving the effectiveness of teacher- and principal-preparation programs (14 points)
  (D)(5) Providing effective support to teachers and principals (20 points)

E. Turning Around the Lowest-Achieving Schools (50 points)
  (E)(1) Intervening in the lowest-achieving schools and LEAs (10 points)
  (E)(2) Turning around the lowest-achieving schools (40 points)

F. General Selection Criteria (55 points)
  (F)(1) Making education funding a priority (10 points)
  (F)(2) Ensuring successful conditions for high-performing charters and other innovative schools (40 points)
  (F)(3) Demonstrating other significant reform conditions (5 points)

Source: U.S. Department of Education (2009). RTTT Executive Summary. Retrieved from http s://www2.ed.gov/programs/racetothetop/executive-summary.pdf

student outcomes, better state data systems, and aggressive school turnaround efforts. Those who adopted rigorous, common standards were given an advantage – this initially referred to the hotly debated Common Core State Standards (eventually abandoned by some states). As noted in Figure 3.1, "Great Teachers and Leaders" represented the largest piece of the RTTT pie and is an essential focus for this text, but before we go into greater detail about "Great Teachers and Leaders," let us take a look at RTTT more broadly.

Forty states plus the District of Columbia submitted applications in Phase 1 and, of these, two were designated winners—Tennessee and Delaware. They were awarded $500 million and $120 million, respectively. This accounted for 10% and 5.7% of the two states' annual budgets for K-12 education,

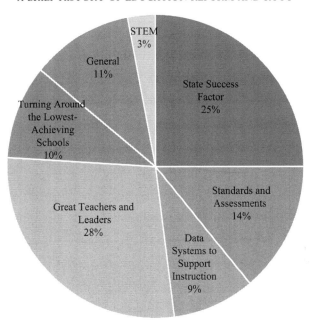

Figure 3.1 Allocation of RTTT Points
Adapted from: U.S. Department of Education (2009). RTTT Executive Summary.
Retrieved from https://www2.ed.gov/programs/racetothetop/executive-summary.pdf

respectively. Thirty-five states plus the District of Columbia submitted applications in Phase 2. Ten in total, nine states—Florida, Georgia, Hawaii, Maryland, Massachusetts, New York, North Carolina, Ohio, Rhode Island—plus the District of Columbia were awarded funds ranging from $75 million to $700 million (Howell, 2015). Awards were distributed in 2010 for Phase 1 and 2 winners. A list of winners and the amounts each one received is provided in Table 3.2.

RTTT Roadmap

RTTT, Common Tests

The administration used some of the RTTT funds and distributed them to two consortia of states charged with creating assessments that would align with the Common Core State Standards—the Partnership for the Assessment of Readiness for College and Careers (PARCC) and the Smarter Balanced Assessment Consortium. These awards were distributed in 2010. In total, $360 million was allocated to the two winners.

Table 3.2 RTTT Winners and Amounts Awarded

Winner	Amount (in $ millions)	Phase
Florida	700	2
New York	700	2
Tennessee	500	1
Georgia	400	2
North Carolina	400	2
Ohio	400	2
Maryland	250	2
Massachusetts	250	2
Delaware	120	1
D.C.	75	2
Hawaii	75	2
Rhode Island	75	2
Illinois	43	3
Pennsylvania	41	3
New Jersey	38	3
Arizona	25	3
Colorado	18	3
Kentucky	17	3
Louisiana	17	3

RTTT, Silver Edition

Although the funds allocated to RTTT from the ARRA had been utilized in Phases 1 and 2, Congress approved funds for a Phase 3 (Howell, 2015). Runners-up with high scores from Phase 1 and Phase 2 submissions were invited to split an additional $200 million. States were permitted to choose smaller elements of their original proposals to move forward on. Awards were distributed to seven Phase 3 winners (Arizona, Colorado, Illinois, Kentucky, Louisiana, New Jersey, and Pennsylvania) in 2011, in RTTT, Silver Edition, which was essentially an extension of the Classic. Awards ranged from $17 to $43 million.

RTTT, Goes to Preschool

Known as the "RTTT – Early Learning Challenge," RTTT allocated funds to encourage innovative early-learning programs. In 2011, nine winners (California, Delaware, Maryland, Massachusetts, Minnesota, North Carolina, Ohio, Rhode Island, and Washington) were awarded $500 million to improve early-learning programs, which included developing an early-learning rating system, developing appropriate standards and assessments for early-learning programs and student outcomes, and establishing standards for teachers.

RTTT, Goes to Preschool, Silver Edition

Five top runners-up from the initial RTTT—Goes to Preschool competition were awarded a total of $133 million to split and fund a small portion of its overall request. These funds were split among 5 winners: Colorado, Illinois, New Mexico, Oregon, and Wisconsin.

RTTT, Goes to Preschool, Silver Medal Edition Part II

In 2013, the U.S. Department of Education awarded $89 in the RTTT Early Learning Competition silver medal winners (Colorado, Illinois, New Mexico, Oregon, and Wisconsin) as well as California, which was funded initially.

RTTT Districts, Personalized Learning

In this iteration of RTTT, districts were awarded $400 million to develop personalized learning or customized instruction that was tailored to meet individual students' needs, interests, and abilities. Sixteen districts received funding and these awards were distributed in 2013.

RTTT Districts. Personalized Learning, Rural Edition

RTTT was criticized for showing bias towards urban districts (Hart, 2010). In response, rural applications were prioritized in the second round of awards, including five winners as well as one urban district—Houston. $120 million in awards was distributed in 2013.

RTTT, Goes to Preschool, Again

Six states that did not win an early-learning grant were awarded $281 million: Georgia, Kentucky, Michigan, New Jersey, Pennsylvania, and Vermont. A total of 20 states won RTTT Early Learning Challenge grants. For a review of this RTTT roadmap visit: https://www.edweek.org/ew/section/multimedia/rtt-road-map.html.

Arriving at RTTT Teacher Evaluation

In looking closer at the "classic" version of RTTT, how did we arrive at this particular education reform. What were its origins and assumptions pertaining to teacher evaluation? The 'problem' identified by RTTT is similar to other reforms—low student achievement. RTTT outlines a four-pronged solution approach (as noted earlier), with effective instruction and leadership linking teacher ineffectiveness to low student-achievement outcomes. Since there was a belief that few teachers were being identified as ineffective (see Chapter 1 and Chapter 5), RTTT encouraged multipoint scales (as opposed to binary) in a multiple-measure system that would require more measures of teacher effectiveness and more often. The hope was that this would help us to identify more accurately the ineffective teachers we supposedly had not been identifying. Since there was a renewed awareness that teachers mattered, student-achievement growth needed to be a significant component of these new models, and principals were required to be in classrooms observing and providing feedback more often. The assumption was that these changes would do two things: 1) teachers would improve by receiving more frequent feedback; and 2) there would be better personnel decision-making (specifically more "bad" teachers would be identified and replaced by effective ones, and effective teachers would be rewarded). RTTT described success as student-achievement growth and narrowed achievement gaps (see State Success Factors – (A)(3)). We review the extent to which RTTT met these assumptions in Chapter 4. [3]

RTTT A General Review of Policy to Practice

In Chapter 4, we provide a detailed analysis of RTTT and its ripple effect on teacher-evaluation practices across the nation, as well as its effectiveness. In setting up this smaller-grain analysis that follows in Chapter 4, here we present a broad overview of the changes that emerged from RTTT, primarily summarizing an analysis conducted by Howell (2015). Howell examined the policymaking process in RTTT and, in particular, the extent to which the policies described in RTTT were adopted by states. He compared the policy changes in the 19 RTTT states plus the District of Columbia to those of the losers or non-applicants in order to answer the question: Did RTTT impact the production of education policy across the US? Notably, Howell did not assess the effectiveness of the policies or how states and districts enacted RTTT, a task we tackle in Chapter 4. After collecting data on trends in policy enactments across the 50 states plus the District of Columbia from 2001 and 2014, Howell found that awards were not necessarily biased toward what states had already done, but that RTTT award status did appear to be related to what states had already done *and* had outlined in their applications. For example, states that were already piloting or utilizing growth measures on a large scale were at an advantage (e.g., Tennessee and Florida) as this element, state success, was second in weight in "Great Teachers and Leaders."

When examining the extent to which *all* states enacted policies related to RTTT, Howell (2015) found that, between 2001 and 2008, states enacted approximately 10% of RTTT reform policies compared to 68% enacted between 2009 and 2014. Thus, Howell's (2015) analysis points to the ripple effect of RTTT. Enactment was not only limited to winners. All three groups—winners, applicants, and those that never applied—increased in their RTTT policy-adoption with an uptick in enactment around the announcement of RTTT, with enactment increases much steeper for winners and applicants.

Notably, the uptick in enactment seemed to be significant in 2008—almost an entire year prior to the announcement of RTTT. The steep rate at which winners enacted policies is reflective of some winners taking proactive steps to put policies in place regardless of winning RTTT funding. For example, Howell notes that, Illinois, which did not win RTTT funcing until Phase 3 in 2011, implemented a new teacher-evaluation policy nearly a year before winning RTTT funding. Thus, some states took steps to strengthen their applications by fulfilling the commitments described in their applications. Dillon (2010) notes similar trends by other states. Last-minute legislative efforts by states to strengthen their RTTT applications included California and Wisconsin repealing laws that banned linking student-achievement data to teachers. Also, states made efforts to get districts to sign on prior to submitting their applications—Florida persuaded more than 60 of its 67 districts, Colorado 135 of 178 districts, and California 804 of 1,729 school districts and charter schools, all to sign on. In Ohio, 250 of the state's 613 districts had agreed to participate. Thus, district buy-in across the states varied significantly, as is also demonstrated in Table 3.3.

Despite significant legislative efforts as part of the application process, by 2014, there were important differences in the three groups, as one might expect—winning states had adopted 88% of the policies relative to 68% for losing states and 56% for states that had never applied. Since almost all states applied for RTTT funding, the impact of RTTT was significant, both across the country and for both winning and losing states. Winning and losing states were more likely to have enacted a RTTT policy than those states that had never applied. Winning states were 37 percentage points more likely to have enacted a RTTT with an estimated effect approximately twice as large as losing states. Notably, though, in nearly half the states that had no plans to apply for RTTT funding, RTTT policies were enacted (Howell, 2015).

Beyond Howell's own external analysis, an internal one was also conducted in 2015 by the U.S. Department of Education. The results were released in a report entitled, *Fundamental Change: Innovation in America's Schools under RTTT*, summarizing the findings from the first 12 RTTT winners. In just these 12 winners, by 2015, RTTT had impacted 10,668,155 students, 746,795 teachers, and 21,543 principals (U.S. Department of Education, 2015b). See Table 3.3.

Sweeping Changes Across the Nation

Basic changes that occurred in teacher evaluation were the use of multiple measures (to determine a teacher's effectiveness) and multiple-rating categories, pushing states away from binary rating systems (e.g., satisfactory, unsatisfactory) to rating systems that included three or four levels. Most

Table 3.3 Students, Teachers, and Principals Participating in RTTT States.

RTTT Winner	K-12 Students (% of all students)	Teachers (% of all teachers)	Principals (% of all principals)
Delaware	128,467 (99%)	8,896 (99%)	448 (98%)
District of Columbia	60,145 (91%)	5,230 (74%)	186 (81%)
Florida	2,514,365 (94%)	166,234 (92%)	2,844 (92%)
Georgia	692,526 (41%)	44,732 (40%)	2,404 (41%)
Hawaii	175,456 (95%)	11,967 (94%)	255 (88%)
Maryland	649,296 (78%)	46,217 (78%)	1,167 (81%)
Massachusetts	640,596 (69%)	48,840 (66%)	1,280 (68%)
New York	2,317,192 (87%)	177,132 (87%)	4,175 (86%)
North Carolina	1,453,468 (97%)	97,534 (97%)	2,482 (97%)
Ohio	931,474 (55%)	58,247 (57%)	2,034 (57%)
Rhode Island	137,370 (99%)	11,313 (99%)	499 (99%)
Tennessee	967,800 (100%)	70,453 (100%)	3,769 (100%)

Note: All data are as of June 2014.

Total Student and Educator Participation	10,668,155 K-12 Students	746,795 Teachers	21,543 Principals

Adapted from U.S. Department of Education (2015b), *Fundamental Change: Innovation in America's Schools under Race to the Top.*
https://www2.ed.gov/programs/racetothetop/rttfinalrptfull.pdf

states chose to utilize four levels and include student growth as one measure of a teacher's effectiveness (U.S. Department of Education, 2015b).

Other early changes included reduction in force. During the initial start of RTTT, the Education Commission on the States released a report on reduction-in-force policies across the 50 states in 2012. In regard to teacher evaluation, 11 states—Colorado, Florida, Georgia, Illinois, Indiana, Louisiana, Maine, Michigan, Oklahoma, Tennessee, and Texas—in 2012 required teacher evaluations to be considered a primary factor in making reductions in force (Thomsen, 2014a).

A report by the Education Commission of the States (2014), that examined policy trends in relationship to teacher evaluation across the 50 states, found that in 16 states—Alaska, Colorado, Connecticut, Delaware, Florida, Illinois, Indiana, Louisiana, Michigan, Nevada, New Jersey, Oklahoma, Rhode Island, Tennessee, Washington, and Wyoming—teacher-evaluation ratings were a factor in tenure decisions. Seven states—Arizona, Colorado, Idaho, Indiana, Louisiana, Nevada, and Tennessee—required that non-probationary teachers, if rated "ineffective," must be returned to probationary status. This policy threatens teachers' contract renewals and also translates to further observation during probationary years (Thomsen, 2014b).

In sum, although only 18 states plus the District of Columbia were awarded RTTT funding, 45 submitted applications. Thus, nearly all states have revised their teacher evaluation models in salient ways (Howell, 2015; National Council on Teacher Quality, 2017). For example, in 2009, only 15 states required student achievement to be a significant component in a teacher's evaluation (Weisberg, Sexton, Mulhern, & Keeling, 2009). But today nearly 40 do (NCTQ, 2017)—down from 43 only two years prior (National Council on Teacher Quality, 2015).

Conclusion

This chapter has provided a concise but thorough review of two previous reforms: *A Nation at Risk* (1983) and *No Child Left Behind* (2002). In both cases we indicated the context and problem they identified, the specific issues they addressed, and what they did and did not achieve. Although two decades apart, both reforms suffered from specific and similar flaws.

We have discussed the general conditions of past reform efforts and noted that reforms are based on identified problems with student achievement. These problems quickly become exaggerated and are generalized from possible limited problems to include most, if not all, students and their teachers. Typically schools and teachers, or both, are identified as *the* problem. The escalated problem moves quickly to a crisis situation that is widely discussed in public media (see Chapter 1); and this problem then becomes sufficiently salient to cause policymakers to act. Their actions are not based upon reasoned research nor do their recommendations start with modest proposals that invest in exploratory pilot projects. Rather what policymakers do is call for immediate and sweeping reform that leads to massive expenditures of time and money. These poorly conceived plans, unsurprisingly, lead to limited gains, if any, and no real progress. The collateral damage is that, once again, students, principals, teachers, and schools are depicted as being "in trouble."

Finally we discussed a new reform RTTT. Here we detailed its purpose, funding criteria, and winning and losing states. We stressed where RTTT differed from and where it was similar to past reforms. In Chapter 4 we extend the work done by Howell (2015) by examining how states, districts, and, specifically, principals implemented RTTT-inspired teacher-evaluation models and whether such changes were effective. In other words, did RTTT improve teaching and learning?

Notes

1 Educational reform has been attempted at several points in American education. Earlier reforms have included Individualized and Humanistic reform movements, and notably included the Sputnik-generated reform in the 1950s. Readers may be

interested in learning about these earlier reforms, especially Sputnik, which is a good example. The Soviet's launching of Sputnik sparked considerable anxiety in Americans that centered on both economic and military concerns (e.g., Were we losing the scientific battle?) and raised questions such as: What do we need to do to make our school curriculum (especially math and science) better so as to compete with engineers and physicists in the Soviet Union? To learn more about these earlier reforms see comprehensive reviews by Good and Braden, 2000, Payne, 2010, or Ravitch, 2010.

2   Some critics would question whether there were any gains to squander or not. Some have argued, for example, Good and Braden (2000), that the new math reforms did not lead to improved student learning. But it is possible to argue that funding associated with Sputnik concerns did lead to higher levels of scholarship, allowing a greater number of talented people to pursue careers in science and mathematics.

3   RTTT policymakers also made a number of other assumptions in their teacher-evaluation policy, noted throughout this book and elsewhere including: that what constituted good teaching was commonly known, that good teaching was independent of context (Good, 2018), that teaching was stable (Good & Lavigne, 2015), and that observing teachers on a few occasions would provide a reliable and accurate illustration of teacher effectiveness (Good, 2018).

References

Auguste, B., Kihn, P., & Miller, M. (2010). Closing the talent gap: Attracting and retaining top-third graduates to careers in teaching (McKinsey & Company Report). Retrieved from https://www.mckinsey.com/~/media/mckinsey/industries/social%20sector/our%20insights/closing%20the%20teaching%20talent%20gap/closing-the-teaching-talent-gap.ashx.

Berg-Jacobson, A. (2016). Teacher effectiveness in the Every Student Succeeds Act: A discussion guide. Center on Great Teachers & Leaders. American Institutes for Research. Retrieved from https://gtlcenter.org/sites/default/files/TeacherEffectiveness_ESSA.pdf.

Cowen, J., Brunner, E., Stunk, K., & Drake, S. (2017). A war on teachers? Labor market responses to statewide reform. Education Policy Innovation Collaborative (White Paper #1). Retrieved from http://education.msu.edu/epic/documents/White-Paper-1-A-War-on-Teachers.pdf.

Cuban, L. (2001, May 30). How systemic reform harms urban schools. *Education Week*, 20(38).

Cuban, L. (2008). *Frogs into princes: writings on school reform.* New York, NY: Teachers College Press.

Cuban, L. (2013). *Inside the black box of classroom practice: change without reform in American education.* Cambridge, MA: Harvard Education Press.

Darling-Hammond, L., Bae, S., Cook-Harvey, C. M., Lam, L., Mercer, C., Podolsky, A., & Stosich, E. L. (2016). Pathways to new accountability through the Every Student Succeeds Act. Learning Policy Institute. Retrieved from https://learningpolicyinstitute.org/product/pathways-new-accountability-through-every-student-succeeds-act.

Dee, T. S., & Jacob, B. A. (2010, Autumn). The impact of No Child Left Behind on students, teachers, and schools. *Brookings Papers on Economic Activity*, 149–207.

Dillon, S. (2010, January 18). Education grant effort faces late opposition. *New York Times*. Retrieved from https://www.nytimes.com/2010/01/19/education/19educ.html.

Education Commission of the States. (2014). Teacher tenure: Laws governing tenure status. Retrieved from https://files.eric.ed.gov/fulltext/ED561923.pdf.

Fiske, E. B. (1986, April 26). Effort to improve U.S. schools entering a new phase. *New York Times*, p. 32.

Goldhaber, D., & Hansen, M. (2010). Race, gender, and teacher testing: How informative a tool is teacher licensure testing?. *American Educational Research Journal*, 47(1), 218–251.

Good, T. L. (2018). Federal educational reform has failed again: Why? Paper presented as part of the symposium, The problematic relationship of research to practice, at the Annual Convention of the American Psychological Association. San Francisco, CA.

Good, T. L., & Braden, J. S. (2000). *The great school debate: Choice, vouchers, and charters*. Mahwah, NJ: Lawrence Erlbaum Associates.

Good, T. L., & Lavigne, A. L. (2015). Issues of teacher performance stability are not new: Limitations and possibilities [Peer commentary on the paper, "The stability of teacher performance and effectiveness: Implications of policies concerning teacher evaluation" by G. B. Morgan, K. J. Hodge, T. M. Trepinksi, & L. W. Anderson]. *Education Policy Analysis Archives*, 23(2), 1–16.

Graham, E. (2013, April 25). "A Nation at Risk" turns 30: Where did it take us?. NEA Today. Retrieved from: http://neatoday.org/2013/04/25/a-nation-at-risk-turns-30-where-did-it-take-us-2/.

Guthrie, J. W., & Springer, M. G. (2004). "A Nation at Risk" revisited: Did "wrong" reasoning result in "right" results? At what cost?. *Peabody Journal of Education*, 79(1), 7–35.

Hart, K. (2010). Critics see east coast, urban biases in Race to the Top awards. NEA Today. Retrieved from http://neatoday.org/2010/08/26/critics-see-east-coast-urban-biases-in-race-to-the-top-awards/.

Hobbs, T. D. (2017, June 13). A favorite subject returns to schools: Recess; after playtime was dropped amid focus on academic performance, educators now take playground breaks seriously. *Wall Street Journal* (Online) Retrieved from http://ezproxy.library.arizona.edu/login?url=https://search.proquest.com/docview/1908766961?accountid=8360.

Howell, W. G. (2015). Results of President Obama's Race to the Top. *Education Next*, 15(4). Retrieved from http://educationnext.org/results-president-obama-race-to-the-top-reform/.

Huelskamp, R. M. (1993). Perspectives on education in America. *Phi Delta Kappan*, 74(9), 718–721.

Jones, L. (2009). The implications of NCLB and a Nation at Risk for K-12 schools and higher education. *International Journal of Educational Leadership and Preparation*, 4(1), 1–4.

Kane, T. J. (2017). Making evidence locally: Rethinking education research under the Every Student Succeeds Act. *Education Next*, 17(2), 52–58.

Katz, M. (1987). *Reconstructing American education*. Cambridge, MA: Harvard University Press.

Klein, A. (2014, April 15). RTTT: A roadmap. *Education Week*, 33(28). Retrieved from https://www.edweek.org/ew/section/multimedia/rtt-road-map.html.

Kraft, M. A., Brunner, E. J., Dougherty, S. M., & Schwegman, D. (2018). Teacher accountability reforms and the supply of new teachers. Retrieved from https://scholar.harvard.edu/files/mkraft/files/teacher_accountability_reforms_march_2018.pdf.

Lavigne, A. L., & Good, T. L. (2014). *Teacher and student evaluation: Moving beyond the failure of school reform.* New York, NY: Routledge.

Lipman, P. (2007). "No Child Left Behind": Globalization, privatization, and the politics of inequality. In E. W. Ross & R. Gibson (Eds.), *Neoliberalism and education reform* (pp. 35–58). Cresskill, NJ: Hampton Press.

Loewus, L. (2017). Are states changing course on teacher evaluation? Test-score growth plays lesser role in six states. *Education Week, 37*(13), 1–7.

Meier, D. (2007, May 21). Evaluating No Child Left Behind. *Nation, 28*(2), 20–21.

Murnane, R. J., & Papay, J. P. (2010). Teachers' views on No Child Left Behind: Support for the principles, concerns about the practices. *Journal of Economic Perspectives, 24*(3), 151–166.

National Commission on Excellence in Education. (1983). *A nation at risk.* Retrieved from https://www2.ed.gov/pubs/NatAtRisk/risk.html.

National Council on Teacher Quality. (2015). State of the states: Evaluating teaching, leading, and learning. Retrieved from https://www.nctq.org/dmsView/StateofStates2015.

National Council on Teacher Quality. (2017). Running in place: How new teacher evaluations fail to live up to the promises. Retrieved from http://www.nctq.org/dmsView/Final_Evaluation_Paper.

Nichols, S. L., & Berliner, D. C. (2007). *Collateral damage: How high-stakes testing corrupts America's schools.* Cambridge, MA: Harvard Education Press.

Nichols, S. L., Glass, G. V., & Berliner, D. C. (2006). High-stakes testing and student achievement: does accountability pressure increase student learning?. *Education Policy Analysis Archives, 14*(1).

Olson, L. (2004, December 6). Taking root. *Education Week.* Retrieved from https://www.edweek.org/ew/articles/2004/12/08/15nclb-1.h24.html.

Payne, C. (2010). *So much reform so little change.* Cambridge, MA: Harvard Education Press.

President's Commission on Foreign Language and International Studies. (1980). Strength through wisdom: A critique of U.S. capability. *Modern Language Journal, 40,* 383–390.

Ravitch, D. (2010). *The death and life of the great American school system: How testing and choice are undermining education.* New York, NY: Basic Books.

Sawchuk, S. (2016, January 5). ESSA loosens reins on teacher evaluations, qualifications. *Education Week.* Retrieved from https://www.edweek.org/ew/articles/2016/01/06/essa-loosens-reins-on-teacher-evaluations-qualifications.html.

Silberman, C. (1971). *Crisis in the classroom.* New York, NY: Alfred Knopf.

Slavin, R. (1989). PET and the pendulum: Faddism in education and how to stop it. *Phi Delta Kappan, 90,* 750–758.

Thomsen, J. (2014a). A closer look: Teacher evaluations and reduction-in-force policies. Denver, CO: Education Commission of the States. Retrieved from https://www.ecs.org/clearinghouse/01/12/43/11243.pdf.

Thomsen, J. (2014b). A closer look: Teacher evaluations and tenure decisions. Denver, CO: Education Commission of the States. Retrieved from https://www.ecs.org/clearinghouse/01/12/44/11244.pdf.

Toppo, G. (2004, July 15). States adapting to No Child Left Behind. *USA Today,* p. 4D.

U.S. Department of Education. (2009). RTTT executive summary. Retrieved from https://www2.ed.gov/programs/racetothetop/executive-summary.pdf.

U.S. Department of Education. (2015a). Fundamental change: Innovation in America's schools under Race to the Top. Retrieved from https://www2.ed.gov/programs/racetothetop/rttfinalrptfull.pdf.

U.S. Department of Education. (2015b). Every Student Succeeds Act. Retrieved from https://www.ed.gov/essa.

U.S. Department of Education. (2016). Digest of education statistics 2015: 51st edition. Retrieved from https://nces.ed.gov/pubs2016/2016014.pdf.

Weisberg, D., Sexton, S., Mulhern, J., & Keeling, D. (2009). *The widget effect: Our national failure to acknowledge and act on difference in teacher effectiveness.* Brooklyn, NY: The New Teachers Project. Retrieved from http://widgeteffect.org/downloads/TheWidgetEffect.pdf.

4

RACE TO THE TOP

Its Effects on Principal Practice, Teaching, and Learning

Introduction

In Chapter 3, we described RTTT's assumptions, mandates, and intended outcomes. In this chapter we review evidence of how RTTT was implemented and its effects on principal practice, teaching, and learning. We analyze and interpret these effects and ask: Did RTTT work? As noted in Chapter 3, nearly all states have implemented new 'teacher-evaluation models (Walsh, Joseph, Lakis, & Lubell, 2017). Thus, we do not limit our review to research conducted only in RTTT states, but instead focus on research on new teacher-evaluation models that emerged in any state post-RTTT.

We start our review by focusing on those primarily responsible for implementing RTTT high-stakes teacher evaluations—principals—and their practices. Did RTTT change how principals engaged in teacher evaluation and supervision? How often were teachers formally or informally observed? What was the quality and quantity of feedback offered for teachers? How did school leaders use multiple sources of data to make personnel decisions? Then we examine the measures. What measures were used to evaluate teachers? How good were the measures (e.g., observational, student-achievement growth, and student surveys) used to evaluate teachers? We answer the following question: Is there any evidence that RTTT improved teaching and learning? In doing so, we summarize findings from two of the studies (perhaps the only two) that tied RTTT changes to student-achievement outcomes (Garet et al., 2017; Stecher et al., 2018). After we provide our conclusions from the evidence, we tap into research that examined principals' and teachers' perceptions of RTTT high-stakes teacher evaluation. Did principals and teachers believe RTTT was a success? What did teachers and principals observe as the benefits and drawbacks of the new teacher-evaluation models? Do their views offer anything to build on in future reforms? We end by providing our summative conclusions about RTTT's effectiveness by assessing the two assumptions that we presented in Chapter 3 and that informed RTTT—that teaching and learning would improve by reme-diating and removing ineffective teachers, and by requiring principals to spend more time in classrooms observing and providing teachers with feed-back. We show that RTTT did not improve teaching and learning.

Race to the Top: Principals and Principal Practice

Here we review principals' practices in the context of RTTT—how they were prepared to enact new teacher-evaluation models, how they engaged in obser-vation and feedback, how they used teacher-evaluation data, and the imple-mentation challenges they faced. We then address the question: Did RTTT change how principals engaged in teacher evaluation and supervision?

How Well Were Principals Prepared in Order to Enact New Teacher-Evaluation Models?

Research findings raise many concerns about the quality and adequacy of the training that principals received to successfully implement new teacher-evaluation systems. For example, Herlihy et al. (2014) analyzed states' plans to implement and assess teacher-evaluation systems. One positive finding was that all states required evaluators to complete training on the new teacher-evaluation system. However, since not all states required evaluators to pass the training, it was unclear what level of proficiency states expected of evaluators in order to be qua-lified to make high-stakes decisions. Fewer states had included best practices when it came to rater training and monitoring. Such practices would include, for example: randomly selecting teachers to be double-coded during observation, frequent recalibration and retraining to account for coder drift, and specific training on providing feedback to teachers.

Despite these limitations, did principals find the training useful? Lavigne and Chamberlain (2017) explored the perceptions of principals enacting a new tea-cher-evaluation model in an RTTT state, in this case Illinois. Like many other states (Donaldson & Woulfin, 2017; Herlihy et al., 2014), Illinois required prin-cipals to pass an online training unit. Illinois' training consisted of five modules (four of which had end-of-module assessments that each required a passing score). When participants in the study were asked if the training improved their understanding of the Illinois Growth through Learning Performance Evaluation requirements and standards of practice, their understanding of reliability and validity, and their ability to accurately rate a teacher during an observation, a majority agreed or strongly agreed (71–73%). However, only 46% of principals agreed or strongly agreed that the training was effective in preparing them to use student-growth data as a measure of teacher effectiveness.

The training was also time consuming—63% of principals spent over 41 hours on the training. The excessive amount of time spent on the training was because more than half (61%) failed one or more modules. Module 2 proved to be the most difficult. For Module 2, principals had to establish reliability on the Danielson Framework for Teaching by rating video-recorded instruction. Nearly 30% failed this module, relative to 3–5% failure rates on other modules. As classroom researchers who have worked with numerous observation instruments, we do not find this failure rate alarming. Observing and rating instructional practice and becoming reliable in doing so is incredibly difficult. However, principals encountered additional challenges with technology (e.g., video quality, glitches) and the assessment itself (e.g., clarity, alignment between training material and assessment). What was most concerning was that some principals received none or only poor feedback when they failed a module (Lavigne & Chamberlain, 2017), even though feedback is very important in high-quality observational training. Establishing reliability with a master coder requires rich discussions about differences in scoring, perceptions of instructional practice, and conversations that serve to establish consensus. Instead, in the absence of feedback, those taking the training turned to colleagues who advised them to lower or raise their standards. This doesn't help evaluators improve their understanding of why a teachers is coded a "3" as opposed to a "4" on pacing, for example.

In another study, principals received limited training in differentiating between teachers, particularly in the upper and lower thresholds of the rating system (e.g., an ineffective teacher who is not trying to improve vs. a struggling teacher who may lack skills, but could improve). Principals also received limited training on observing and interpreting instructional practice and providing feedback, which meant that they provided positive affirmations of teachers' practices rather than suggestions for improvement. This was oftentimes the case for principals who entered the profession with limited or no teaching experience (Kraft & Gilmour, 2017).

These findings suggest that principals were not well trained prior to implementing new teacher-evaluation models, and could have, indeed should have, been better prepared in order to: use student growth data in teacher evaluations, differentiate between teachers and ratings, observe and interpret instructional practice, and provide useful feedback to teachers. To ensure the reliability of evaluations, some principals did not have, but should have had, opportunities for recalibration and retraining to address coder drift.

How Often Were Teachers Formally or Informally Observed?

After principals received training on the new teacher-evaluation models, some states rolled out the observational components of the model first, with student-achievement growth or student-learning objectives implemented in subsequent years. Most RTTT-inspired models required principals to observe all teachers annually, and multiple times within a given year (Walsh et al., 2017) with most states requiring one to four observations annually (Lavigne & Good, 2015). In Florida, some teachers reported that administrators were in their classrooms once or twice throughout the year, whereas others indicated weekly (Pressley, Roehrig, & Turner, 2018). In Connecticut, for example, in the first pilot year of the new teacher-evaluation model, principals were required to observe every teacher six times (three informally, three formally). However, because of the time demands this requirement imposed, some principals did not complete the number of observations designated by policy (Donaldson & Woulfin, 2018). In Tennessee, experienced teachers were required to be observed four times, and teachers with three or fewer years of experience, six times. This doubled the number of observations principals were conducting in the state (Wright, 2012). In order to reduce the burden on principals, some states made modifications to this in subsequent years of implementation, such as reducing the number of observations required for teachers who received high evaluation scores.

How Often Should Teachers Be Observed?

RTTT required principals to conduct more observations, but are more observations better? Usually, yes. As we note in Chapter 5, there is significant variation in teachers' practices. Thus, a single observation may not be very representative of a teacher's practice. Furthermore, Berliner (2018a) notes how difficult it is for one observer to rate a teacher on one occasion using an instrument and how the stability of certain teacher practices may also matter. He describes findings from a project in which Richard Shavelson was helping him determine how many observers and observations he needed to reliably code teacher behavior:

> Shavelson found that only one observer visiting a classroom on one occasion can reliably code only a few behaviors. These easy to code behaviors are usually "high inference" variables, such as a rating of the teachers' enthusiasm, orderliness, preparedness, and other "trait-like" characteristics of teachers—behaviors that are likely to persist throughout the day, and also from day to day.
>
> (Berliner, 2018a, p. 13)

For these reasons multiple observations are recommended and multiple observers. For example, a single classroom visit can receive substantially different ratings depending on the observer. Ho and Kane (2013) found that reliability coefficients of a single observation ranged from .27 to .45 depending on whether or not an administrator, peer, or teacher observed the teacher. Others have reported similar reliabilities of .31 and .51 for a single observation on the widely used Classroom Assessment Scoring System and the Danielson Framework for Teaching, respectively (Garet et al., 2017). Because of this, many call for *at least three classroom visits* by *multiple individuals* to acquire modest reliability of .70 (Hill, Charalambous, & Kraft, 2012; Ho & Kane, 2013; Kane & Staiger, 2012). Herlihy et al. (2014)

note that only rarely did states have plans for multiple observers (only 3 of 17 states), and that the principal fulfilled the responsibility of conducting most (if not all of) the observations and evaluations of teachers (and still does) (Cherasaro, Brodersen, Reale, & Yanoski, 2016).

However, the number of visits may depend on the purpose. Van der Lans, van de Grift, van Veen, and Fokkens-Bruinsma (2016) have found that to provide reliable feedback to teachers requires that three different observers view a teacher's classroom instruction on three different occasions. Teachers deserve to receive both reliable feedback and summative evaluations of their teaching practices. Given that teachers fluctuate significantly in their practices, high-stakes teacher evaluation requires systematically effective or ineffective practice over multiple occasions. In this particular study, the authors found that ten observations are needed in order to reliably promote or dismiss a teacher (a reliability of .90 or higher)!

These findings suggest that even though RTTT required principals to conduct more observations than in the past, this likely did little to increase the reliability of observational measures since teachers were still being observed by a single observer (Kane & Staiger, 2012; Whitehurst, Chingos, & Lindquist, 2014). The prospects of achieving adequate reliability in real schools is further challenged by the fact that the reliabilities achieved in some of the above-mentioned studies were from observers who were rigorously trained on observation instruments and, oftentimes, when no stakes were attached to evaluations. Achieving the same level of reliability is likely impossible considering the training principals received and the complex nature of schools. More value (in reliability) could have been achieved by leveraging multiple observers as opposed to increasing the number of observations. However, RTTT teacher evaluations did not provide the support, time, and resources for teachers to be observed an appropriate number of times by multiple individuals. Conducting ten observations per teacher, as noted by Van der Lans et al. (2016), would be impossible, even in the best case scenario.

What was the Quality and Quantity of Feedback that Principals Offered to Teachers?

Perhaps teachers benefited from more frequent observations because they received feedback more often? Unfortunately, we were unable to identify any studies that gathered direct observations of the quantity and quality of feedback that principals offered to teachers. However, there are data on *teachers'* perceptions of the feedback they received under these new models. For example, Cherasaro et al. (2016) examined teachers' (*n* = 243) perceptions of the feedback they received in seven school districts across two states implementing new teacher-evaluation systems during the 2014–2015 school year. As expected, teachers most often received feedback from their principal (70%) or assistant principal (27%), receiving written and verbal feedback one to four times a year. Notably, almost

25% of teachers received verbal feedback and nearly 30% written feedback five or more times during the year. This finding suggests that some principals spent significant time providing feedback to all teachers and/or to specific teachers. Most teachers agreed or strongly agreed that their evaluator was credible (74%) and the feedback they received was accurate (70%). Just a little more than half (55%) felt that the feedback they received was useful. Most teachers agreed or strongly agreed that the feedback was timely (70%), frequent (67%), and included specific suggestions for improvement (66%).

Albeit this was only one study, these findings indicate that in RTTT-inspired teacher evaluations, teachers received accurate feedback and they viewed the feedback provider—most often their principal—as a credible source of feedback. Principals spent significant time on the feedback process and provided frequent and timely feedback. However, only 55% found the feedback to be useful and only 66% of teachers received specific suggestions for improvement. If instructional leadership continues to play an important aspect of the principal's role, these results suggest a need to better support and prepare principals in providing teachers with useful feedback that includes specific, concrete, and actionable suggestions for improvement.

How much Time Did Principals Spend Observing and Providing Teachers with Feedback and Why?

As noted in Chapter 3, RTTT increased the number of observations that principals conducted in a given year. If feedback followed after each observation, time spent on feedback should have increased, too. So how much time did principals spend observing and providing teachers with feedback? Many researchers look more generally at principals' instructional leadership practices (which include, but are not limited to, observing and providing teachers with feedback). For example, Grissom, Loeb, and Master (2013) collected data on elementary, middle, and high school principals' time allocations in 2011 and 2012. In 2011, high school principals spent 10.0% of their time on instructional leadership, middle school principals 13.7% of their time, and elementary school principals 14.1% of their time. In 2012, these values were 10.1%, 12.0%, and 16.5%, respectively.

Was this amount significantly more than before RTTT? Not necessarily. Data from 2011 and 2012 indicate that principals still spent a relatively small amount of their time on instructional leadership tasks—similar to what researchers found in 2008. As in 2008, in 2012 there was great variation—instructional tasks accounted for anywhere between .1% and 28.3% of a principal's time. And, again, some principals spent *no time* on walk-throughs, formal evaluations, coaching, professional development, or developing the educational program. These findings suggest that instructional leadership has played, and continues to play, a secondary role in the principalship.

However, it is possible that time allocated to instructional leadership remained the same, but the way principals spent their time did not. For example, Flores and Derrington (2017) noted that because of RTTT, principals spent more time in the office writing their evaluations and recording data from observations, reducing the time they could dedicate to conducting walk-throughs. The glaring irony of this finding is that high-stakes teacher evaluation was intended to *increase* principals' time in *classrooms*, and instead, may have inadvertently reduced it.

Principals' Observation and Feedback Practices: A Note

In summarizing principals' observation and feedback practices under RTTT, it is important to recognize that principals often adapted new teacher-evaluation models to fit their context. Sometimes these modifications served to enhance the existing model (e.g., creating tools for efficiency), and at other times it may have undermined it (e.g., failing to conduct in-person, post-observation conferences). Donaldson and Woulfin (2018) found that principals exercised discretion as it pertained to the observation process, observation rubric, and feedback conversations. Principals indicated making modifications, such as focusing on only a few indicators, developing new forms for observing and providing feedback, and making adjustments to the observation time line. Here are two excerpts from principals in Donaldson and Woulfin's study that indicate the types of modifications principals made:

> Because one of the problems I'm running into now is I'll do the observation, but then try to find time to meet with them for the post-observation. It's very difficult. So maybe a week or two goes by, and then that's no good. That defeats the purpose, because I do think that—and I know the plan's set up that way— you do your observation, then you meet within five days. You've got to meet right after.
> (Donaldson and Woulfin, 2018, p. 543)

> I think we got our three formals in for everybody. We didn't get three informal for everybody, but most people—well, more than half got all six. And I just had to call it quits. I think it was Memorial Day weekend, and I just said, "Whatever's done by Memorial Day is done, and we're just not doing anymore." And I think that's life.
> (Donaldson and Woulfin, 2018, p. 544)

How Did Principals Rate Teachers?

We know from the evidence provided above RTTT required principals to spend more time in the classroom and providing teachers feedback, but in practice, that did not always occur. Did, though, RTTT teacher-evaluation models change how principals rated teachers? Kraft and Gilmour (2017) analyzed teacher-evaluation ratings from 24 states (14 of which were RTTT winners)[1] that had fully implemented a new teacher evaluation model by the 2014–2015 school year. Their findings indicated that in most states, less than 1% of teachers were rated unsatisfactory.[2] Variations across states, in some cases, were notable. For example, in Hawaii only .7% of teachers were rated as developing/needing improvement or ineffective/unsatisfactory whereas in New Mexico, 28.7% were rated as needing improvement. Notably, New Mexico utilized a 5-point scale. The primary differentiation between teachers occurred in the top two categories on 4-point rating scales and in the top three categories on 5-point rating scales. In general, the use of more rating categories has not changed the distribution of how teachers are rated in terms of effectiveness, and has done little to help differentiate between teachers in the lower end of the scale. Few ineffective teachers were identified by RTTT high-stakes teacher evaluation.

State reports from the last eight years validate these trends, as noted by Kraft and Gilmour (2017) and they continue today. For example, in 2016–2017 in Illinois, 97% of teachers were rated as proficient or excellent (Illinois State Board of Education, 2017). In Michigan, in the 2017–2018 year, less than 1% of teachers were rated as ineffective, with 98% rated as effective. These percentages are similar to those of the past. In 2011–2012, 2012–2013, and 2013–2014, 1% of teachers were rated as ineffective, with anywhere from 97 to 98% rated as effective (Michigan State Board of Education, 2017). In New Jersey, .2% of teachers were rated as ineffective in 2013–2014 and 2014–2015, with 97.3%–98.4% rated as effective or highly effective; and .1% were rated as ineffective in 2015–2016, with 98.9% rated as effective or highly effective (New Jersey State Board of Education, 2017). With the exception of New Mexico,[3] few ineffective teachers were identified by RTTT high-stakes teacher evaluation, as was the case prior to RTTT (Weisberg, Sexton, Mulhern, & Keeling, 2009).

How Did Principals Use Multiple Sources of Teacher Effectiveness Data to Make Personnel Decisions?

Few teachers were rated ineffective, but perhaps principals became more skilled at hiring effective teachers and counseling out ineffective ones? With more sources of data on teacher effectiveness than ever before, did principals use the data better than before? Despite the use of multiple-measure teacher-evaluation systems, principals relied primarily on observational data when hiring, promoting, or dismissing teachers. For hiring candidates, the use of data by principals was low to moderate. When they did use data to inform hiring practices, principals reported using teacher-observation scores (71%) more often than student-achievement growth measures (62%), in part, because they had greater access to observational data either through the central office or by asking candidates to self-report (Cannata et al., 2017). Some of this was a function of timing—observational data were readily available, whereas student-achievement growth measures, such as value-added measures (VAMs) were not (Goldring et al., 2015). Even when principals and teachers did have access to VAMs electronically, only half were found to actually access and view the growth data (Garet et al., 2017). Another problem lies in the use of school as opposed to individual VAMs. For example, in one study, a principal questioned how principals could even use school-wide VAMs to make good hiring decisions (Cannata et al., 2017).

Principals' Personnel Decision-Making: A Note

We think it is important to note here that principals make deliberate decisions and actions to maximize the effectiveness of their teachers. And that they do this despite reform efforts. These intentional personnel strategies are likely attributed to the principal and not the evaluation system itself (Stecher et al., 2018).

For example, Grissom and Bartanen (2018) found that in a RTTT state that was enacting a single teacher-evaluation model, principals' strategic retention patterns varied. For example, suburban schools were better able to leverage strategic retention in important ways than their rural or urban counterparts because they had far more applicants for open positions. Thus, their ability to replace low-performing teachers who had exited the profession with higher-performing ones was greater. The cost of having an unfilled position for some principals was worse than keeping a low-performing teacher in the classroom. They found that teachers who received low observation scores were in fact more likely to leave schools with effective principals,[4] regardless of whether they had high or low VAMs.

Loeb, Kalogrides, and Béteille (2012) have also noted similar variations. In particular, schools that achieved greater gains in student achievement, hire, assign, develop, and retain teachers differently than do schools with lower gains in student achievement. The authors found that more-effective schools differed from less-effective schools in four ways. First, when filling vacancies, effective schools were able to attract and hire more-effective teachers from other schools. Second, they assigned novice teachers to students in an equitable fashion. Third, growth spurs growth—teachers in schools that were more effective at achieving student growth in the past, improved more rapidly in acquiring student-achievement gains. Finally, more-effective schools were better able to retain high-quality teachers, as has been documented by others (Grissom & Bartanen, 2018).

What Implementation Challenges did Principals Face?

In reviewing principals' practices following RTTT, we pointed to a few of the challenges principals faced when enacting new teacher-evaluation systems. Clearly, the success of any reform rests on accurate problem conceptualization and research-based solutions, however, success also rests on capacity. Here we explore implementation challenges, barriers, and whether or not resources and support were provided to account for the increased expectations and demands placed on principals. Did RTTT-inspired teacher-evaluation models provide adequate time, resources, and support for principals to enact the new models well? We will show that they didn't.

The biggest implementation challenge principals encountered was *lack of time*, as we predicted (Lavigne & Good, 2014). Principals were overwhelmed by the increased demands of the new teacher-evaluation models (Donaldson & Woulfin, 2018; Goldring et al., 2015; Kraft & Gilmour, 2016; Lavigne & Chamberlain, 2017; Range, Scherz, Holt, & Young, 2011). Lavigne and Chamberlain (2017) noted that principals spent almost eight hours per teacher evaluation. The consequences of these increased demands meant that some principals did not have adequate time to provide feedback. Instead, feedback was infrequent and brief, undermining teacher development (Kraft & Gilmour, 2016). Likewise, time demands impeded their ability to document deficiencies (Range et al., 2011) and limited the time they could dedicate to other duties (Lavigne & Chamberlain, 2017). Some teachers noted that principals cut observations short or were not available to address their concerns. Some districts had to shift plans to allow for shorter and more frequent observations, or use other school administrators to conduct observations (Stecher et al., 2018). Some principals scaled back on the number of observations they conducted or double-dipped with their observations (Donaldson & Woulfin, 2018).

What barriers did principals face pertaining to making personnel decisions, or specifically rating teachers ineffective? In examining principals' perceptions of teacher effectiveness as well as actual summative ratings, principals perceived over three times as many teachers as being below proficient than they actually rated as needing improvement in their summative evaluations (Kraft & Gilmour, 2017). Kraft and Gilmour (2016) found that principals reported that they were reluctant to rate teachers ineffective because it required significant documentation and support for teachers' professional growth,[5] it undermined teachers' potential and motivation, specifically for new teachers, replacing teachers is costly (financially and otherwise), and principals experience personal discomfort—having difficult conversations with teachers is not pleasant, particularly in the context of high-stakes teacher evaluations. Furthermore, principals' perspectives on removing teachers may wax and wane based on teacher supply. Some principals might prefer to retain a mediocre or low-performing teacher if it means avoiding a teacher vacancy in the upcoming year because of teacher shortages (Grissom & Braeten, 2018; Berliner, 2018a).

We provided a research summary of principals' preparation to and actual enactment of new teacher-evaluation models. To remind readers, here is a summary of our main findings:

- Principals were not well trained to implement new teacher-evaluation models (Herlihy et al., 2014; Kraft & Gilmour, 2017; Lavigne & Chamberlain, 2017).
- Even the increased number of observations was not enough to reliably measure teacher effectiveness, with the commonly used single observer—the principal (Hill et al., 2012; Ho & Kane, 2013; Kane & Staiger, 2012; Van der Lans et al., 2016).
- Only 55% of teachers found principals' feedback to be useful and only 66% received specific suggestions for improving instructional practice (Cherasaro et al., 2016).
- Increased requirements for documentation from new teacher-evaluation models meant that principals actually spent less time in classrooms and providing feedback (Flores & Derrington, 2017).
- No more ineffective teachers were identified by RTTT (Kraft & Gilmour, 2017).
- Despite multiple measures of teacher effectiveness, principals still relied on observational data to make personnel decisions (Cannata et al., 2017; Goldring et al., 2015).
- Principals experienced a number of challenges in implementing new teacher-evaluation models, with the most significant challenge being lack of time (Donaldson & Woulfin, 2018; Goldring et al., 2015; Kraft & Gilmour, 2016; Lavigne & Chamberlain, 2017; Range et al., 2011; Stecher et al., 2018).

An Analysis of RTTT Effects

We return to the question: Did RTTT change how principals engaged in teacher evaluation and supervision? RTTT teacher evaluation required principals to engage in more observation and provide more frequent feedback to teachers, but, because of the increased demands placed on principals, these expectations were impossible to fulfill. Instead, principals' time for observation and feedback was constrained by the need to complete the necessary paperwork. Principal practice changed but not in ways that would have fostered improvements in teaching and learning. RTTT required multiple-measure teacher evaluations with the intent to better differentiate between teachers and to aid principals in strategic personnel decision-making. Instead, principals relied on observational measures—those mostly commonly used before RTTT—to make personnel decision and the distribution of teacher-evaluation ratings remained unchanged. Notably, principals engaged in strategic personnel decision-making, but this was not attributed to new teacher-evaluation models. In sum, RTTT did not change principal use of teacher-evaluation data or teacher-evaluation ratings.

Race to the Top: Assessment of Commonly Used Teacher-Evaluation Measures

Now we move from the principal and the practices to the tools they had to measure teacher effectiveness. Given that a majority of a teacher's evaluation under RTTT was composed of two main sources of data—observational data and student-achievement growth data—we focus our efforts on assessing these two commonly used indicators of teacher effectiveness.

What Observation Instruments were used to Evaluate Teachers?

The most commonly adopted tool for observing teachers was (and still is) the Danielson Framework for Teaching (FFT), or a modification of the FFT (Donaldson & Woulfin, 2018; Kane, Taylor, Tyler, & Wooten, 2011; Lash, Tran, & Huang, 2016; Sartain, Stoelinga, & Brown, 2011). As teacher-evaluation reform was at its peak in 2011, the FFT was an approved model in New Jersey, Florida, and Washington, the default tool in Illinois, the only recommended framework in New York City schools, and adopted statewide in Arkansas, Delaware, Idaho, and South Dakota. It was also adopted in large districts, such as Los Angeles Unified School District, Pittsburgh Public Schools, Hillsborough County Public Schools, and 14 other districts in Florida (PRNewswire-USNewswire, 2011). And it was one of the instruments used in the Measures of Effective Teaching project. The FFT is organized into four domains:

1   *Domain 1: Planning and preparation.* This domain includes components involved in instructional design. How does a teacher organize and structure content and lessons, and what evidence does the teacher use to make those decisions?
2   *Domain 2: Classroom environment.* This domain entails the extent to which a teacher provides a safe and warm environment that cultivates learning and students' risk-taking.
3   *Domain 3: Instruction.* This domain includes how a teacher engages students in the content/lesson. Are students engaged? Are students cognitively challenged?
4   *Domain 4: Professional responsibilities.* This domain assesses teachers' engagement outside of the classroom—in the community, with parents, with colleagues, and with professional organizations and learning opportunities.

For each domain, there are a number of components and elements, equating to a total of 22 components and 76 elements rated on a 4-point scale: unsatisfactory, basic, proficient, distinguished. Usually, teachers received a single, average score.

How Good Were the Observation Instruments Used to Evaluate Teachers?

Unlike student-achievement measures, observational measures offer perhaps greater promise, because they are a direct indicator of a teacher's competency and indicate what teachers *do* in the classroom (Berliner, 2018a). We know that many of teachers' interactions happen with individual students as opposed to the whole class. However, many of the tools used to observe teachers (such as the FFT or similar modifications) seek to capture the average experience of a student in the classroom, or how a majority of students experience the classroom. Unfortunately this tells principals and teachers very little about students who may be receiving the most opportunities to learn as opposed to those receive the least (Lavigne & Good, 2014, 2015). As noted in Chapter 2, this has real implications for student-learning outcomes, as does the low reliability of these instruments, as noted earlier (and later in this chapter).

Observations are Biased

It is possible that some teachers are more likely to receive a higher or lower rating because of the students they serve. For example, Whitehurst, Chingos, and Lindquist (2014) found that teachers serving students with higher achievement levels receive higher observation scores than those teachers serving students with lower achievement scores. The difference is significant—37% of teachers who taught the highest-achieving students achieved an observation score in the top 20% compared to only 9% for teachers who taught the lowest-achieving students. These patterns suggest that teachers would be penalized for taking on certain teaching and, as a result, teachers may avoid teaching the lowest-performing students unless scores are adjusted to account for student demographics (see Whitehurst et al., 2014 for an example).[6]

How Were Student-Achievement Growth Outcomes Accounted for in Teacher-Evaluation Models?

In 2015, 43 states required that measures of student achievement be a significant factor in a teacher's evaluation (National Council on Teacher Quality, 2015). As noted in Chapter 3, states that adopted student-learning measures typically assigned this indicator a weight of 30–50% of a teacher's evaluation. In 2014, 40 states plus D.C. were in the process of developing or piloting some type of growth or value-added model. See Appendix A (pp. 129) for information about the differences between student-growth percentiles and value-added models.

How Good Were the Student-Achievement Growth Measures Used to Evaluate Teachers?

Given the role that value-added modeling played in fostering RTTT-inspired teacher evaluation, we examine the benefits and limitation of VAMs.

Value-added Benefits

Proponents of VAMs (Chetty, Friedman, & Rockoff, 2014a, 2014b; Hanushek & Rivkin, 2010) suggest that they are the best statistical tool for isolating the effects of an individual teacher, and, thus, hold promise for identifying teacher effectiveness and making personnel decisions. For example, Hanushek (2009) suggested that student test scores could be used to remove the bottom 5–10% of teachers and replace them with average or excellent teachers. VAMs were further publicized when Hanushek and Rivkin (2010) estimated a difference of three-month learning gains for a teacher at the 84th percentile relative to an average teacher. Then, three years later, Chetty et al. (2014a) indicated that replacing a teacher in the bottom 5% with an average teacher would yield an increase in college attendance by 2.2% and earnings by 1.3% (by age 28). In sum, proponents of VAMs argue their value in citing evidence that VAMs relate positively to teachers' instructional practices (Hill, Kapitula, & Umland, 2011), and are a valid predictor of student achievement in the short- (Chetty et al., 2014a; Kane & Staiger, 2008) and long-term (Chetty et al., 2014b).

Value-added Limitations

Others have questioned the use of VAMs (e.g., American Statistical Association, 2014; Darling-Hammond, Amrein-Beardsley, Haertel, & Rothstein, 2012), pointing to the numerous variables that can influence a teacher's VAM score and are not appropriately accounted for in current models, such as:

- non-random assignment of students to teachers (Braun, 2005; Paufler & Amrein-Beardsley, 2014; Rothstein, 2010);
- classroom composition (Hill et al., 2011);
- school characteristics (McCaffrey, Lockwood, Koretz, Louis, & Hamilton, 2004);
- principal leadership (Corcoran, 2010); and
- effectiveness of colleagues (Corcoran, 2010).

Another concern, and perhaps not surprising given what we know about how teaching practices vary, is that VAMs are not stable either. Findings suggest that VAMs vary:

- from year to year (Braun, 2005; Collins & Amrein-Beardsley, 2014; Corcoran, 2010);
- from content area and class to another content area or class (Darling-Hammond et al., 2012); and
- across different tests of the same content area (Darling-Hammond et al., 2012; Papay, 2011), as long known (see Chapter 2).

This, of course, adds to the complexity of using VAMs, especially for making personnel decisions. One outcome is the low reliability of VAMs. Garet et al. (2017) noted reliabilities of .44–.46 in English Language Arts and .67–.68 in mathematics. Another consideration is high error rates, which will lead to the misclassification of teachers. Schochet and Chiang (2010) indicate that error rates, even when using the recommended three years of data, are 25%. When data for one year only are available, error rates are 35%. The real implications of this for students is significant. Schochet and Chiang note that these errors rate mean:

> that in a typical performance measurement system, more than 1 in 4 teachers who are truly average in performance will be erroneously identified for special treatment, and more than 1 in 4 teachers who differ from average performance by 3 months of student learning in math or 4 months in reading will be overlooked.
>
> (Schochet and Chiang, 2010, p. 35)

The authors also noted that because student-level variables could account for nearly 90% of students' achievement, more data can make only modest improvements to these error rates. They estimated error rates would still be 12% with *10 years of data*!

Finally, VAM data do not arrive in time for principals to use the information in valuable ways for a teacher to change their practice for that given year or group of students (Goldring et al., 2015). When teachers do receive their VAM scores, the scores themselves do not tell a teacher what was taught well or how (Amrein-Beardsley & Collins, 2012), this is, in part, because of the low correlations between VAMs and observational data (which we discuss below). Furthermore, the high complexity of the statistical modeling used for VAMs reduces the effectiveness of their interpretation and use (American Statistical Association, 2014).

Despite the extensive effort it takes to apply VAMs, few teachers actually teach in tested grades and subject areas and individual VAMs are only assigned to anywhere between 22 and 30% of teachers (Collins & Amrein-Beardsley, 2014; Whitehurst et al., 2014). Teachers without individual value-added scores were sometimes assigned a school value-added score—an approach recommended by Schochet and Chiang (2010) in order to reduce error rates. As noted earlier, principals struggle to use school-level VAMs to make sense of teacher effectiveness (Donaldson & Woulfin, 2018). Further, the application of such scores tends to negatively impact good teachers in bad schools, and positively impact bad teachers in good schools (Whitehurst et al., 2014). One unintended consequence of this pattern is that it encourages good teachers to leave, and to avoid seeking employment in a low-performing school.

Together, these findings point to many limitations for using VAM for summative evaluations, and renders it nearly useless in a formative capacity. Likewise, observational measures can only do so much and their use in high-stakes teacher-evaluation models is constrained by low reliability. Because of these issues, RTTT advocated the use of multiple-measure teacher-evaluation systems. However, when we examine these measures together, new issues arise. We turn to those issues now.

Measures of Teacher Effectiveness are Weakly Correlated

Most measures of teacher effectiveness are weakly related—including those measuring correlations between teacher and teaching effects and students' attitudes and behaviors (Blazar & Kraft, 2017) and those measuring teacher quality and student attendance and student achievement (Gershenson, 2016). Although principals' ratings—both overall and specifically in teachers' abilities to improve mathematics and reading—are a significant predictor of teachers' actual student-achievement gains (Jacob & Lefgren, 2006), correlations range from .09–.73, but more often fall between .20–.40 (Jacob & Lefgren, 2006; Wilkerson, Manatt, Rogers, & Maughan, 2000). More recent research affirms these trends with correlations ranging from .168–.40 (Briggs & Dadey, 2017; Grossman, Cohen, Ronfeldt, & Brown, 2014; Harris, Ingle, & Rutledge, 2014; Morgan, Hodge, Trepinski, & Anderson, 2014). Similarly, correlations between observation scores and value-added scores from the notable Measures of Effective Teaching project range from 0.12 and 0.34 (Bill & Melinda Gates Foundation, 2012). And there are wide differences depending on the state test used to determine student-achievement gains or value-added measures (Polikoff, 2014).

Correlations Between Teacher Effectiveness Measures Vary

Furthermore, the correlations between observational measures and teachers' student-achievement outcomes are not stable—principals' ratings of teachers and teachers' student-achievement gains varies by subject area—for example stronger correlations have been documented in math as opposed to reading (Briggs & Dadey, 2017; Harris et al., 2014; Wilkerson et al., 2000).

This finding suggests that principals may struggle, in particular, with identifying those practices that yield student-achievement growth outcomes in reading for two reasons. First, in the study conducted by Wilkerson et al.

(2000), there was a strong and significant correlation between a parallel rating scale that students completed (parallel to the one that principals completed for their formative ratings) and teachers' student-achievement gains ($r = .75$). In other words, students, instead of principals, seemed to be able to better identify teachers who achieved greater reading gains. It is unclear why this is. One possibility is perhaps the fact that students see teachers on multiple occasions and this provides them with an advantage for tapping into the skills that are particularly predictive of teachers' achievement outcomes in reading. Second, these findings came after principals had already received two years of staff development in supervision, suggesting that either the staff development was ineffective in supporting principals in this particular task, or identifying effective teaching is particularly challenging for principals (Wilkerson et al., 2000).

So how can we make sense of the well-documented pattern that what teachers do in the classroom has little or no relationship with the student-learning gains they achieve? Some states responded to these concerns by encouraging and monitoring the alignment between teachers' ratings in achievement gains and observational scores. Yet, Berliner (2018b) argues that these low correlations merely demonstrate unique contributions to understanding teacher effectiveness. We believe that the variations observed by subject may be a function of evidence that teacher effects are greater in mathematics than in reading (Nye, Konstantopoulos, & Hedges, 2004), thus, we would expect to see higher correlations between measures of teachers' practices and teachers' student-achievement gains in mathematics as opposed to reading. Also, recall in Chapter 2, we pointed out the Rubie-Davies' experiment had more impact in math than reading. Regardless, the low correlations between teaching practices and student-achievement outcomes make it difficult for teachers to understand what they may or may not have done differently to acquire better or worse achievement gains, and the same holds true for principals when providing feedback to teachers. The correlations may also be restricted by the quality (and noise created) of the tools used to observe teachers.

The other, and harsher, criticism—and the most compelling to us—is, as we have pointed out, that the dimensions of teaching most related to student achievement were inadequately measured (Good & Lavigne, 2018; Lavigne & Good, 2015). Thus, in addition to measurement error and low reliability, there may be issues in validity, especially if one treats student achievement as a validity criterion for teaching practices, and vice versa, as opposed to unique measures of teacher effectiveness (Berliner, 2018b).

Principals Vary in Their Ability to Identify Effectiveness

Many will argue that they know a good teacher when they see one. Is there any truth to this claim when we apply it to modern-day teacher-evaluation models? Perhaps not. The ability of principals to correctly identify teacher effectiveness (as measured by student-achievement gains) varies, but it varies in random, or perhaps complex, ways. For example, Kimball and Milanowski (2009) used data from 39 and 59 evaluators respectively across two different years, indicating significant variation in the relationship between school leaders' ratings of teachers and teachers' student-achievement outcomes, with a significant number of negative correlations. Principals who were "accurate evaluators" (average $r = .68$ between their ratings and teachers' student-achievement gains) and "inaccurate evaluators" (average $r = -.37$) did not differ with reference to their will, skill, or context. The same authors suggested that perhaps, in the absence of a structured evaluation system, principals were relying on gut-level decisions to rate teachers instead of systematic methods (Kimball & Milanowski, 2009). Alternatively, principals' ratings may be a function of complex factors (some of which are introduced below).

Identifying Teacher Effectiveness Is Not Equal for All Teachers

It was known prior to RTTT that the extent to which principals' ratings of teachers predicted teachers' actual effectiveness varied. Principals were more successful in correctly identifying top teachers (as measured by value-added scores) and bottom teachers than they were in identifying teachers who were average (Jacob & Lefgren, 2006). So, it is challenging to differentiate between teachers who are average and on the cusps of ineffective and effective. This alone raises some concerns as principals' ratings of teachers were not great predictors of student-achievement gains for most teachers—the 60–80% of teachers who fall in the middle. Accuracy in identifying teacher effectiveness also varied by subject area. Principals were less likely to identify top teachers in reading (52% of the time) as opposed to mathematics (69% of the time). Similarly, principals struggled more with identifying teachers in the middle in reading (accurate 49% of the time) than in mathematics (54% of the time; Jacob & Lefgren, 2006). Had policymakers read these findings, it would have raised concerns about the use of high-stakes teacher evaluation, as they would have seen that some teachers would be at greater risk of misclassification than others. An inability to accurately identify which teachers are on the cusp of needing improvement and those who are on the cusp of highly effective might translate into an *almost* highly-effective teacher receiving relatively low ratings and hence significant coaching and professional development, while a teacher who really needs that type of support might receive none.

Has RTTT Improved Teaching and Learning?

Since much of what we summarized above does not allow us to connect changes in principal practice to changes in teacher practice and subsequent student outcomes, we take a few pages to summarize two large initiatives that do so.

Impact of Providing Feedback to Teachers and Principals

The first is a study conducted by the U.S. Department of Education's Institute of Education Sciences on the implementation of teacher and principal performance measures. Notably, although conducted at the time of RTTT and similar to RTTT initiatives, no stakes were attached to performance evaluations (Garet et al., 2017).

The study was conducted in 2012–2013 and 2014–2015 and included a selected sample of schools in eight districts. Schools were offered support in developing and using three measures: classroom-practice measure (observation rubric with feedback sessions; conducted four times a year), student-growth measure (value-added scores provided to teachers and their principals; once a year), and a principal-leadership measure (measure of leadership with feedback; conducted twice a year). Within each district, schools were randomly assigned to the treatment group (the measures described above) or not (the control group) (Garet al., 2017).

Districts were allowed to use one of two classroom-observation instruments—the Classroom Assessment Scoring System (CLASS) or the Danielson Framework for Teaching (FFT)—both measures used in the Measures of Effective Teaching project. Individual value-added scores were averaged across two years in reading/English language arts and mathematics for teachers in Grades 4–8. The VAL-ED, a survey about principals' practices, was provided to teachers to rate their principals (Garet et al., 2017).

Study Findings

The treatment group implemented the treatment with adequate fidelity—3.7 and 3.9 observations in Years 1 and 2, and 98% teachers received printed value-added scores in Year 2 (only 39% accessed the reports when they were disseminated online in Year 1). Teachers in the treatment group received more feedback sessions, with their ratings and a written justification, and more verbal feedback than those in the control group (the duration of the oral feedback was longer for the treatment group as opposed to the control group). Teachers in the treatment group also reported that the feedback they received was more useful (65%), and more specific about what constitutes high-quality teaching (79%), than the feedback currently offered in their district. However, nearly all teachers received classroom scores in the top two performance levels; and low reliabilities within dimensions (e.g., positive climate, language modeling, instructional learning format) across two years of observation limited the extent to which classroom measures provided information about areas for instructional improvement (reliabilities on the CLASS ranged from .35–.43, whereas on the FFT they ranged from .18–.30). Impact on teachers' classroom practice and student achievement was positive, but limited. Treatment teachers were no more likely than control teachers to report wanting to improve in or attend professional development in CLASS or FFT areas. Yet, differences in the ratings of lessons in both treatment and control groups indicated that the intervention had a positive impact on teachers' classroom practice on the CLASS—moving teachers from the 50th to 57th percentile. The intervention had a positive impact on students' achievement in mathematics in Year 1—the equivalent of four weeks of learning. In Year 2, the impact was the same, but not statistically significant. No differences were noted in reading/English language arts (Garet et al., 2017).

In sum, despite intensive efforts to provide teachers with more and better feedback, and teachers perceiving that feedback to be more useful, only modest gains were observed in teachers' practices—only on one observation instrument and in one area of student growth—mathematics. Since districts were not randomly assigned to the CLASS or FFT, it is difficult to reach causal conclusions. Despite this, the CLASS and FFT varied significantly in their measurement properties, which means that when districts choose an instrument, they have to weigh various tradeoffs (e.g., reliability, specificity, ability to foster improvement, validity). Furthermore, since the study only used VAMs, outcomes only apply to teachers in tested grades and areas (Grades 4–8 in ELA and mathematics). We also have limited information about why teachers in the treatment group perceived feedback to be useful, yet did not indicate higher levels of interest in improving their instructional practices or in attending professional development related to CLASS or FFT areas (Garet et al., 2017).

Intensive Partnerships for Effective Teaching

We now turn to a second initiative—the Bill and Melinda Gates Foundation's Intensive Partnerships for Effective Teaching (IP)—created in 2009. The project examined the effectiveness of teacher-evaluation systems and human-relation reforms in three school districts and four charter management organizations (CMOs) over a six-year period (the evaluation began in July 2010 and ended in 2016). The RAND Corporation and its partner, the American Institutes for Research (AIR), were selected by the foundation to evaluate their intensive and expensive effort. The IP initiative was designed to improve student outcomes, including improved test scores, high school graduation rates, and college attendance, especially for low-income minority (LIM students), by increasing their access to effective teaching. According to the final report, Stecher et al. (2018), the project included three major dimensions:

- Improving staff actions including:
  - Revise hiring practices to obtain teachers likely to be effective
  - Reform tenure and dismissal policies to retain more-effective teachers and to remove ineffective ones

- Adjust placement and transfer to give students with the greatest needs access to the most-effective teachers.
- Identify teacher weaknesses and overcome them through effectiveness-linked professional development (PD).
- Employ compensation and career ladders (CLs) as incentives for retaining the most effective teachers.

The funding was extensive and totaled more than 200 million in individual awards that ranged in size from 3.8 to 81 million dollars (awards were largely based on enrollments). The three school districts ranged in size from 27,000 to 185,000 students and at least 55% of students in each district were eligible for free or reduced-cost lunches. Further, at least 51% of students were Black, Hispanic, or American Indian. The CMOs ranged from 2,500 to 7,500 students: at least 80% were from minority populations and at least 70% of the students were eligible for free or reduced lunches.

Selecting Schools for the Intensive Partnership

The selection process was not detailed in the 2015–2016 report but we were able to obtain this information from the 2013–2014 project (see Stecher et al., 2016 for the 2013–14 project).

As noted, the Gates Foundation selectively screened districts based on enrollment (25,000–250,000) and student background (at least 40% of students had to be eligible for free or reduced-cost lunches). Further, state policy played a role in site participation (e.g., eliminating states with low thresholds for awarding tenure). This process identified 70 potential districts and these districts were further reduced on the basis of staff knowledge of each district and the district's commitment to improvement efforts. Eventually, about 24 districts were contacted to assess their interest in the initiative and to learn about district leaders' demonstrated ability to work effectively with key stakeholders. Further, they wanted a continuing commitment from the community and district leaders that reform effort would continue once foundation funding was eliminated. An analysis of these visits (i.e., perceived district capacity and commitment) resulted in a formal request for proposals from ten districts.

Each site received help from the foundation in developing their proposals, including technical assistance and support from a consulting firm that helped districts to analyze their data and to develop their plan. The potential sites had three collaborative meetings to share plans and progress. During these meetings "… sites pushed each other to improve their plans" (Stecher et al., 2016, p. 7). Final decisions about award winners were based upon the plan, the level of collaboration among local stakeholders, and a site's perceived ability to accomplish its stated goals. Further, the foundation ensured that they funded sites that differed in size and demographics so that results could be applied to a full range of school districts.

In many ways, the process that the Gates Foundation followed in selecting schools was very similar to procedures were used in RTTT to select state awardees (see our description in Chapter 2, p. 113). That is, interest in change, and capacity for change were part of the process but neither Gates nor the Federal Government based awards upon demonstrated performance, whether in terms of student graduation rates, student achievement, or ability to retain highly effective teachers. In the end, the selection committee for the Gates Foundation chose sites that had a strong commitment to raising student achievement and a willingness to change how teachers were being recruited, evaluated, and rewarded. Brian Stecher, who was the lead author on the report describes "the sites as 'fertile ground' for the initiative—positively inclined but diverse" (personal communication, July 3, 2018).

How Was the Program Implemented?

Unfortunately, the final (evaluation) report includes little information about how school districts implemented the teacher-effectiveness project. What we can conclude is that the teacher-effectiveness systems reflected what was being implemented in RTTT states, as would be expected since the three selected school districts were located in RTTT states. Thus, the following describes the teacher-evaluation systems:

- *Multiple-measure*: a teacher's final, summative evaluation score was based on multiple measures of effectiveness.
- *Product-process*: most weight was attributed to two measures of a teacher's effectiveness—practices (process) and student-achievement gains (product):
  - *Content neutral measures of process*: most observation rubrics used to assess the effectiveness of a teacher's practice did not attend to content and were, or were based on, structured, high-inference rubrics (such as the Danielson Framework for Teaching, see The Danielson Group, 2013).
  - *Growth measures of product*: Student growth percentiles (SGPs) and teacher- and/or school-level value-added measures (VAMs) were typically used to calculate a teacher's effect on student achievement.
- *Additional artifacts*: most sites used feedback from student surveys and/ or peer observations of instructional practice as measures of teacher effectiveness.

In the report, the authors indicate that they cannot quantify the dosage (their word) to describe the type of PD that was provided or the specific improvement plans that were developed. For example, there is no systematic evidence of the type of feedback that the evaluator (almost always an administrator) provided to teachers or about the teacher actions and classroom activities that should be adopted. Equally missing is any specific information about how much of the advice teachers acted upon and what teachers (or observers) thought about those attempts at improving instruction, and other changes in the distributions of teacher-evaluation ratings (through classroom observation and student-achievement outcomes), and there is no record of any other actions that were taken to improve teaching. Thus, despite this project providing arguably the best evidence of whether or not RTTT efforts were a success, we cannot come to any conclusions about whether or not it changed actual, observed practice in measurable ways and we are unable to conclude how gains, if observed, in student-achievement outcomes were acquired. Did teachers use the information provided to them? Is there any record that teacher actions changed as a result of feedback? For example, did teachers improve in classroom management or ask more questions that required higher-order thinking skills to more students? The basic answer is that we have no evidence. In many ways, the project is a black box study, but, at a minimum, it suggests that the lack of impact is not the fault of the evaluators.

As in earlier reforms, apparently policymakers thought quick changes to teaching could be achieved through RTTT—and that anyone could do the job. In other words, if principals identified poor teachers, the problem could be quickly resolved.

Teachers' Perceptions of Program Implementation

There were some efforts (self-reports) to assess teacher beliefs about the quality of information that they received and whether or not they tried to implement the feedback. Teachers generally reported that the feedback was useful and, across the multiple sites, the range of teachers that agreed strongly, or somewhat, that feedback was useful varied from 67 to 87%. The percentage of teachers reporting that they had made changes on the basis of feedback varied from 78 to 92%. But no data were collected to describe what teachers changed or why, nor were there observations to document the changes that teachers described they made.

With regard to the evaluations, only about half the teachers felt that their evaluations accurately reflected the quality of their teaching. Teachers had more favorable views on the validity of observational data as opposed to student-achievement data (as noted in other studies). Approximately 60–90% of teachers felt there were enough observations to provide an accurate understanding of their teaching effectiveness. In most study sites, 75% of teachers reported that those who observed them were qualified to comment upon their teaching. Yet, to reiterate (for emphasis), there is no information about the specific comments that were made or even any information about how long debriefing conferences lasted. To further complicate matters, the professional development (PD) that was provided was dependent upon individual principals and we do not know how alike PD was within or across sites.

Did Observations Represent Typical Lessons and Teaching?

The data are mixed on this point. For example, 65–88% of teachers reported that they did extra preparation for the lessons that were observed. Still, most teachers reported that they taught in the same general way when they were observed as they did when not being observed. So one inference from this is that the observed lesson was more polished or more practiced but it was representative of their normal approach to teaching. However, the evaluation report noted that some teachers "… mentioned side effects, such as a perceived need to 'play it safe' and avoid taking risk or exploring new instructional approaches" (Stecher et al., 2016, p. 111). But even if we conclude that the observations were representative of typical teaching, we do not know *what* constituted typical teaching. Hence, with this massive investment in evaluating teaching we have virtually no data to describe the independent variable(s). There is no evidence that teachers taught differently after the project began, and thus, an evaluation designed to improve teaching ironically provided little information about what was done to improve teaching.

What Impact Did the Program Have on the Distributions of Teacher Effectiveness?

What the study did collect data on was how the districts evaluated teachers. For example: How many teachers did each site expect to be rated as ineffective? How did sites determine cut-off scores for effectiveness ratings? Did the distribution of teacher-effectiveness ratings change over time? If so, what were the possible causes of these changes and related evidence? At the start of data collection—in 2012–2013—no more than 5% of teachers received the lowest teacher-evaluation rating (similar to the data we presented earlier in this chapter, p. 101). It was common that 2% of teachers (or less) were rated with the lowest teacher-evaluation rating. There were no expectations placed on sites about how many teachers should be rated ineffective and, at the start of the project, only one site indicated the expected percentage of teachers that would be rated ineffective—15%. Notably, only 1% of teachers actually received this designation in the first year.

Most sites used pilot data to determine cut-off points for their designated performance levels. One site also utilized external experts and the teachers' union, which resulted in nearly 15% of teachers being rated in the lowest two ratings in the first year. When teachers asked whether or not the teacher-evaluation systems differentiated between effective and ineffective teachers, 40–50% of teachers in the district sites agreed, as did 50–75% in the CMO sites. So, did the distributions of teacher-effectiveness ratings change over time?

Most sites observed an increase in the percentage of teachers rated as effective or highly effective over time. So, did teaching improve? Perhaps. One explanation for the increased ratings was because of changes in how student achievement was calculated, specifically the introduction of student-learning objectives (SLOs) in the 2014–2015 year, which resulted in higher scores, not lower because teachers could adjust the SLOs (with principal approval) mid-year to reflect areas in which they were acquiring significant success. The one site that set cut-off scores in consultation with experts and the union saw drastic changes across a period of five years. Notably, though, when 15% of teachers were rated with the lowest two ratings in the first year, no stakes were attached to the ratings. It is possible that the introduction of high-stakes teacher evaluation made principals more reluctant to give low ratings (see Kraft & Gilmour, 2017). Unfortunately, we do not have data on whether or not individual teachers who remained at the sites improved in their ratings from one year to the next, but, even if we did, and the numbers suggested improvement, given the limitations we already discussed it may be difficult to attribute increases in teacher-evaluation scores to actual improvements in instructional practice (given the low reliabilities of observation instruments, it is even difficult to make this claim in the Garet et al., 2017 study).

What Impact Did the Program Have on Student Outcomes?

As noted earlier, in assessing teacher and student outcomes, the sites used different weights, but, in all cases, student achievement and teacher evaluation were the largest component. The evaluation report provided a comprehensive analysis based on performance across all sites, school districts, CMOs, and even by individual site. The comparison group included schools of comparable size and demographics but who did not receive any special funding or programmatic instruction in effective teaching. However, as the evaluators note, most comparison school districts were attempting to improve teaching and student achievement, but we have no knowledge of the specific ways in which they were trying to bring about improvements in teaching and learning. The interested reader can find detailed reporting from Stecher et al. (2018). But for our purposes it is sufficient to note that IP schools in comparison with control schools did not reflect:

- Any improved achievement;
- Any improved graduation rates;
- Any clear evidence that LIM students received better teaching;
- Any evidence that districts were able to retain more-effective teachers; and
- Any evidence that districts were able to reduce less-effective teachers.

In summary, the evaluation report bluntly concluded, "the results imply that, across the board, no site was more effective than any of the others, either in implementing the reforms or in achieving positive outcomes" (Stecher et al., 2016, p. 496). Further, in concluding their report, the researchers noted that:

> a favorite saying in the educational measurement community is that one does not fatten a hog by weighing it. The IP initiative might have failed to achieve its goals because it succeeded more at measuring teacher effectiveness than at using the information to improve student outcomes.
>
> (Stecher et al., 2016, p. 504)

Together, these two studies indicate that even with extensive support, resources, and measurement with regard to fidelity, it is impossible or nearly impossible to achieve gains in teaching and learning using teacher evaluation, whether or not stakes are attached to teacher-evaluation scores. When gains were observed, it was only on one instrument, in one subject area, and these findings only apply to a relatively small subset of teachers who teach in tested grades and subject areas. Furthermore, it is not clear if these gains can be sustained.

Did Principals and Teachers Believe RTTT Was a Success?

Now we turn to principals and teachers—how did they perceive RTTT-inspired teacher evaluation?

Principals' Perceptions

Pitfalls of RTTT

Paufler (2018) conducted a study of 273 principals in a large, urban district that evaluated teachers based on professional practice (25%), instructional practice (25%), and value-added scores (50%). Paufler found that principals were concerned about the negative impact of a new teacher-evaluation system on morale. For example 88.6% of principals felt that the new teacher-evaluation system provided a culture of intimidation in the district. Paufler noted that one respondent indicated that: "all that matters [in this district] are the test results. Everything is about numbers." Another noted that "teachers with high professional standards are not valued. There is not a sense of teamwork" (Paufler, 2018, p. 8) Open-ended responses linked the heavy emphasis on students' tests scores with negative feelings and practices within and among teachers.

Another notable concern of principals was their lack of autonomy in making staffing decisions and evaluating teachers. Furthermore, principals noted feeling pressure to make decisions that they did not agree with or to fill particular quotas regardless of their distributions in teacher effectiveness. For example, nearly half the principals reported being told which teachers to place on an improvement plan or that more teachers should be recommended for review. A little less than half (40%) were told to give lower scores on observation and evaluations of teachers and nearly 40% were told what percentage of teachers should be on improvement plans, terminated, or recommended for nonrenewal (Paufler, 2018).

Finally, principals perceived that the new teacher-evaluation models devalued them as professionals, so much so that principals were actively looking for (or considering) positions outside the district or outside K-12 education altogether. More than half (61%) were looking for jobs outside the district, and 77% reported they would leave if they could find another job. Even their current employment felt relatively unpredictable with 41% unsure if they would be employed in the district in the next five years (Paufler, 2018).

Other unintended consequences included gaming the system. Donaldson and Woulfin (2018) reported that one principal indicated teachers wanting to exercise choice in which classes were observed in order to increase their chances of receiving a certain rating (e.g., having principals observe an advanced placement class).

Furthermore, policymakers ignored that principals, particularly those in secondary schools, must provide feedback to teachers in content areas outside of their expertise. This resulted in the unintended consequence of principals providing feedback almost entirely focused on pedagogy (Kraft & Gilmour, 2016). It seems unrealistic that principals could provide accurate and helpful content-specific feedback in all areas, yet, ignoring this barrier to feedback likely has real consequences for teachers and students as core content knowledge is important for teachers to develop (Hill et al., 2008).

Principals were well aware of the costs that came with RTTT—longer hours on the job, delegating tasks (e.g., discipline) to others, who may or may not be well-equipped to carry out such tasks, lack of balance, and small returns (Lavigne & Chamberlain, 2017). A principal in one study noted:

> The time I can spend on other very important duties is limited … It leaves little time to spend in classrooms of teachers you are not evaluating for the current year. It leaves little time to spend with students at lunch and recess. It leaves little time to improving instruction by planning valuable workshops, inservices, and professional reading.
>
> (Lavigne & Chamberlain, 2017, p. 194)

The value of teacher-evaluation reform efforts was particularly small for rural, small, or under-resourced schools in two ways. First, such schools are often unable to tap into the strategic retention assumptions made by RTTT (Grissom & Bartanen, 2018). These schools have a difficult time attracting and retaining teachers and having an unfilled position as a result of removing an ineffective teacher may be more costly than retaining him/her. Second, principals in these schools are responsible for addressing more roles than in other schools, and often do not have additional administrators for support (Lavigne & Chamberlain, 2017).

Promises of RTTT

There were some benefits. Principals did note value in placing a greater emphasis on instructional leadership (Lavigne, 2018), and creating a shared language to describe teacher effectiveness (Kraft & Gilmour, 2016; Stecher et al., 2018). Principals perceived that new teacher-evaluation models provided specific assessments to be used for evaluating teachers which helped reduce the subjectivity of the evaluation process. They felt that the greater level of specificity provided in these frameworks facilitated their feedback conversations with teachers. They also perceived that teacher development was inherently supported by increasing teachers' levels of control in the evaluation process and by making evaluation more regular—shifting the "gotcha" culture to a culture of systematic monitoring and support (Kraft & Gilmour, 2016). In another study, 61% of principals felt that improvement plans were effective in correcting poor performance. This was due, in part, to their belief that the extent to which teachers could or would improve was dependent on teachers' ownership of improvement plans (Range et al., 2011).

Teachers' Perceptions

VAMs

One barrier to improving teaching and learning pertains to the reliability and validity of the measures used to assess a teacher's effectiveness. The use of VAMs is relatively new and hotly debated, and VAMs have received significant attention in research. For example, teachers noted concerns about the fairness of using value-added data in evaluations, particularly if the scores were capturing factors outside a teachers' control (Hewitt, 2015; Jiang, Sporte, & Luppescu, 2015). In another study, teachers felt that VAM scores were biased: that some teachers would receive higher or lower VAM scores than others as a function of the schools in which they were employed or students they served. Nearly 60% felt the scores were not credible. Other concerns about the use of value-added measures included: their inability to capture the complexity of teaching, that they may reflect, to some degree, the students in the classroom and contextual factors (such as mobility), student absences, and that the tests used to calculate VAM scores are problematic (Hewitt, 2015, pp. 22–25). Teachers were also asked about the perceived effects they felt VAM would have on a number of outcomes. A majority—73%—felt that the use of VAMs would not result in a more equitable distribution of good educators, 74% felt it would discourage teachers from working with certain students, 70% felt that it would cause teachers to leave certain schools, and 76% believed that it would make it difficult to recruit teachers into the profession. Fewer, but still more than half, felt that the use of VAMs in teacher evaluations would not improve teaching (64%), learning (64%), or raise student achievement test scores (56%). Teachers also felt that the use of VAMs in evaluations would not improve the quality of educators (67%), would not make teaching a stronger profession (69%), and would harm students (57%) (Hewitt, 2015). Many of these findings affirm what we report throughout this book. When teachers were asked about the unintended consequences of the use of VAMs in teacher evaluations, teachers reported that: they felt pressure to teach to the test; they were concerned the stress and anxiety over test scores have hurt teacher morale and damaged teacher collaboration; and the use of VAMs has increased competition, since a teacher's value-added is relative to the value-added of teachers who teach similar students (Hewitt, 2015). Teachers have also reported concerns that VAMs have a negative impact on instruction because an excessive amount of time is spent preparing for the standardized tests used to calculate VAMs (Network for Public Education, 2016).

Pressley, Roehrig, and Turner (2018) examined teachers' perceptions of VAM to improve their instructional practice in Florida, a state that, at the time, was utilizing teacher evaluations that were 50% composed of VAMs and 50% of observational scores. Part of the challenge, regarding the extent to which teachers could use their VAMs to improve their instruction, was their lack of access to their VAMs, alongside a general lack of knowledge about how VAMs were calculated. Relatedly, teachers did not feel it was an accurate portrayal of their teaching effectiveness because the scores did not account for factors outside of their control (although the state model did control for some student-level variables). Overall, they did not feel VAMs provided information they could use to improve their practice. Instead teachers focused on test preparation: mandated test preparation included a 90-page test preparation booklet of scripted lessons and example tests.

Observations

In their interviews with Florida teachers, teachers indicated that they did make modifications to their instructional practice, particularly when administrators were infrequently in their classrooms; for example, sometimes teachers would mention the lesson's objective throughout the lesson and not just at the beginning. Some teachers only made changes for the observation in order to "get a specific box checked during an observation" (Pressley et al., 2018, p. 34). Teachers who had administrators frequently in their classrooms had greater confidence that their admnistrators had a good understanding of their teaching effectiveness. It also gave teachers immediate opportunities to demonstrate growth.

Feedback

Cherasaro et al. (2016) attempted to fill in some of the gaps we noted in the Gates IP study. For example, did teachers report that they used the feedback they received? We do not have direct observations, but according to teachers' reports in this study, a little more than half did (60%). There were four ways that teachers responded to the feedback they received—trying new instructional strategies (70%), seeking advice from an instructional leader (63%), trying new classroom management strategies (62%), and seeking professional development opportunities (60%). It is unclear, though, why 40% of teachers did not. Perhaps teachers did not have enough resources to leverage the feedback they received in productive ways, as only 62% indicated they had access to professional development, 61% planning time to implement new strategies, and 60% support from an instructional leader. Learning from other teachers was rare—only 33% agreed or strongly agreed that they had access to observing an expert teacher model feedback.

Findings from principals' and teachers' perceptions point to the many challenges and few benefits of RTTT. As noted throughout this chapter, RTTT was costly in terms of both money and time yet principals and teachers perceived small returns from these efforts.

Race to the Top: Returning to Its Underlying Assumptions

In concluding our evaluation of the RTTT effectiveness, we examine its two central assumptions:

Assumption 1

Teacher-evaluation reform can improve teaching and learning by changing overall teacher effectiveness: poor teachers will be remediated or removed (and replaced by more effective teachers).

This assumption rests on the belief that principals were failing to identify enough bad teachers and that a more "rigorous" teacher-evaluation system would encourage a more balanced distribution of teacher effectiveness (see references to *The Widget Effect* and *Waiting for Superman* elsewhere in this book (p. 153 and p. 31)) in that it would identify a greater number of ineffective teachers. With more ineffective teachers identified by principals because of more stringent evaluation practices, more ineffective teachers would voluntarily leave, be counseled out, or removed by their principals. The intent was that these vacancies would be filled by teachers who were more effective, and the effectiveness of the teacher population would increase in whole.

We then unpack the evidence related to RTTT's second assumption.

Assumption 2

Teacher-evaluation reform can improve teaching and learning by requiring principals to spend more time in classrooms and in providing teachers with useful feedback.

In order to determine *the amount of change* RTTT did or did not produce, we establish what was known relative to these two assumptions *prior to* and *then following* RTTT. We conclude whether or not RTTT was a success. In doing so, we discuss additional factors. For example, Assumption 1 requires that observational measures and student-achievement measures reliably identify teacher effectiveness, and that principals can engage in strategic retention, attrition, and recruitment practices. It also requires that an effective and adequate pool of teachers be equally available to all schools. However, as we demonstrate in Chapter 1 and Chapter 5, this is not the case. Assumption 2 rests on various factors: the effectiveness of principals in conducting classroom observations, the validity, reliability, and usefulness of classroom observation instruments, the quality of principals' feedback to teachers, and the extent to which feedback, from principals, can improve teaching and learning.

Both assumptions require that teaching be stable. In order for teacher-evaluation reform to change the overall effectiveness of teachers through personnel decisions, an evaluation of a teacher in a single year must be a reasonable indicator of that teacher's effectiveness in subsequent years. Thus, teachers who are removed are indeed, ineffective (and would be so should they remain in teaching), and those chosen to replace them, based on their prior evaluation scores, will be more effective in the upcoming year. Similarly, in order for teacher-evaluation reform to improve teaching and learning, teacher practice must be stable in order for observations of teacher practice to be representative measures of a teacher's "true" practice and so that suggestions and feedback are relevant and can appropriately inform future practice.

Did RTTT Change the Distribution of Teacher Effectiveness?

How Principals Rate Teachers

Although *The Widget Effect* asserted that less than 1% of teachers were rated as ineffective, receiving significant attention and alarm nationally, there was very little peer-reviewed research that provided conclusive evidence of the baseline of teacher-effectiveness ratings prior to RTTT. However, in one study of 13 elementary principals and their 202 teachers, Jacob and Lefgren (2006) found that most teachers were rated high from 1998 to 2003. The overall distribution of principals' ratings of teachers demonstrated a positive skew—an average rating of 8.1 (out of 10) and only 10% of teachers received scores below a 6. Despite this, principals generally used

5–6 point ranges (on a 10-point scale) when assigning ratings to their teachers. This suggests that prior to RTTT, principals utilized a fairly decent range when assigning ratings, even though their ratings often did not used the entire scale. As noted earlier, RTTT involved vast amounts of time and resources to identify poor teachers. Yet, the distribution of teacher-effectiveness ratings has not changed (Kraft & Gilmour, 2017) .[7]

Did RTTT Increase the Time Principals Spent Observing and Providing Teachers with Feedback?

How Principals Spend their Time on Instructional Leadership

How much time have principals typically spent on teacher supervision and evaluation? Lavigne and Good (2015) provided a broad summary of the expectations for principals (their tasks and roles), looking at what they *should* do, as well as how principals typically spend their time, that is, what they *actually* do. In their review of literature, the authors concluded that the amount of time principals spent on teacher supervision and evaluation was both limited and relatively stable across a 40-year period.

Lavigne and Good (2015) noted that these observational studies of how principals spent their time illuminated how difficult a principalship is—a natural characteristic of the principal's job—and a theme we will return to in Chapter 5. Notably, principals were often observed multitasking (e.g., taking a phone call while preparing for a staff meeting), engaging in several activities simultaneously (activities that were oftentimes interrupted or were a result of interruptions) (Martin & Willower, 1981). We can extrapolate from these findings that any time that principals spend on instructional leadership is likely interrupted, often. Furthermore, even almost 40 years ago, principals worked long weeks, 49.7 and 53.2 hours a week for elementary and secondary principals, respectively (Kmetz & Willower, 1982; Martin & Willower, 1981).

Despite working long hours, elementary principals only spent 2.5% of their time observing teachers. Instead, these principals spent their time in meetings (10.3% of their time) and organizational management, which accounted for nearly 40% of their time (Kmetz & Willower, 1982). Secondary principals did not fare much better, and spent only 2.4% of their time observing teachers (Martin & Willower, 1981).

Roughly 30 years after the studies by Martin and Willower (1981) and Kmetz and Willower (1982) were conducted, principals continued to struggle to find the time to supervise and evaluate teachers, an issue reported by 50% of principals (Kersten & Israel, 2005). Horng, Klasik, and Loeb (2010) found that principals spent little time on what they described as day-to-day instruction, which included supervising and evaluating teachers. Elementary principals, who clocked in the greatest amount of time, only spent 9.26% of their time on such tasks. Instead, nearly half their time was spent on management and organization, very much how principals were spending their time in the 1980s.

Grissom, Loeb, and Master (2013) studied how 125 elementary, middle, and high school principals allocated their time before RTTT and then after. Data collected in 2008 show that most of principals' instructional time was spent on informal walk-throughs (as opposed to formal evaluations), coaching, professional development, and developing the educational program. Overall, instructional tasks equated to 11.7% of their time for high school principals, 17.0% for middle school principals, and 16.4% for elementary school principals. The ranges were fairly wide, though, indicating that some principals spent as little as 1.1% of their time on instructional tasks whereas other principals spent as much as 30.3%! The ranges indicate that some principals spent *no time* conducting informal walk-throughs (or formal evaluations), coaching, engaging in professional development, or developing the educational program. As described earlier, principals still spent a relatively small amount of time on instructional leadership under RTTT, and perhaps even less considering they had more paperwork to complete (Flores & Derrington, 2017; Grissom et al., 2013)

Our analysis suggests that: 1) most principals were not well-prepared to enact teacher evaluation under RTTT, and 2) the time demands under RTTT would require most to radically alter how they spent their professional time. Although some principals were already spending significant time supervising and evaluating teachers, most were not—and would now have to figure out how to do so. In short, principals' ratings of teacher effectiveness did not change in substantial ways, nor did the time that they allocated to observing and providing teachers with feedback. Research studies that included the analysis of student achievement outcomes mirrors these findings and extends them by concluding that RTTT resulted in no changes to teaching and learning.

Conclusion

RTTT promised quick and sweeping success: These promises were not fulfilled. The reform had exaggerated the problems that schools faced, and whatever capacity the reform had to improve teaching and learning was heavily restricted because policymakers ignored the fact that principals would not have time to conduct all the observations expected of them (plus pre- and post-observations), to make reliable, summative evaluations of teachers, and to cope with the increased documentation. Policymakers also ignored the fact that not all districts and schools would have the same capacity to leverage strategic retention in the ways desired under RTTT. Thus, few teachers are rated as ineffective—then and now. Investment in teacher-evaluation systems has resulted in little change (Kraft & Gilmour, 2017).

Like the reforms that came before it, RTTT failed. It failed to change the distribution in teacher-effectiveness ratings in ways that led to improvements in teaching and learning. It failed to increase the time that principals spend observing and providing teachers with feedback in ways that can be linked to improvements in teaching and learning. The measures most commonly used in high-stakes teacher evaluations have limitations. Observational measures often lack reliability, and, even when reliability is achieved, it can be misleading and fail to account for the importance of context. Poor performance on standardized achievement outcomes is better explained by poverty than teachers. As Berliner (2018a) notes, "neither approach works well" (p. 3).[8]

This simple, but costly, reform effort ignored the lack of stability in teacher effectiveness and the low correlations between measures of teacher effectiveness, and ignored that these considerations alone would render RTTT useless. It suggests that policymakers were not following, or learning from, previous reforms, as this information was readily available (see Chapter 2). Policymakers' focus on quantity (of observations and feedback) as opposed to quality (of instruments and feedback) reduced the potential for RTTT to improve teaching and learning. Furthermore, had policy focused on quality, it would have been crucial to establish the quality of feedback principals currently provided to teachers (and how it could be improved). Even though many teachers valued the feedback they received (Stecher et al., 2018), we do not know if teachers actually changed their practice as a result of such feedback. Nor do we know what changes teachers made, if any; but we do know that teaching process in the context of high-stakes evaluation did not improve student achievement.

Policy into Practice

Policymakers often assume that policies are implemented in similar ways in different schools and settings and, thus, can achieve similar outcomes—improved teaching and learning. Beyond the conditions above that would promote differences when policy is put into practice, principals enact policies as a function of their individual beliefs, characteristics, perceptions, and attitudes (Lavigne, 2018). For example, Kerrins and Cushing (2000) examined the processes behind principals' assessments of instructional practice and how such processes might differ between novice and expert principals. Experts (principals with five or more years of experience and nominated by colleagues as excellent school leaders), when observing instructional practice, view the big picture when they interpret teacher behaviors and actions. They make note of lesson coherence and consider a teacher's ability to self-evaluate and reflect. When they provide comments to improve the lesson, they draw from evidence extracted from the lesson. Novices (most of whom were experienced teachers in this particular study) focus only on documenting and narrating what happens in the lesson—as opposed to also interpreting what they were observing. They are less likely to consider the lesson as a whole or its coherence (Kerrins & Cushing, 2000).

Expertise may guide how principals interact with teacher evaluation and supervision as well as their perceptions. For example, principals do not perceive all aspects of effective teaching as equally important, particularly when it pertains to concerns about teacher ineffectiveness. Principals are mostly likely to attribute teacher ineffectiveness to: classroom management skills, lesson implementation skills, and rapport with students, as opposed to lesson planning and content knowledge. In other words, principals perceive lesson planning and content knowledge as less-problematic deficiencies (and it may be that principals are less equipped to identify content errors). These perceived threats to teacher effectiveness were relatively consistent, regardless of administrator age, gender, educational attainment, or teaching or administrative experience. These findings suggest that principals may respond to teachers' areas of weaknesses as a function of their own perceptions about how problematic a given area of weakness is to a teacher's overall effectiveness (Torff & Sessions, 2005).

When adapting teacher-evaluation systems, principals may introduce other artifacts to guide the classroom observation and post-observation conferences or to map new teacher-evaluation systems onto existing ones in order to reduce teachers' cognitive loads. Principals may do this with relational trust in mind, and with a view to balancing tenure, expectations, and social position in the school when choosing the artifacts to guide each teacher's evaluation (Halverson & Clifford, 2006). Likewise, principals may adapt their practice and approaches depending on whether they are working with novice or experienced teachers. When principals work with novice teachers, they may focus on pedagogical issues and student understanding. They may also tailor their approach to supporting novice teacher growth and development by co-analyzing teachers' data and working with teachers on their portfolios (Youngs, 2007). Principals adapt teacher evaluation to accommodate teacher needs. For example, nearly 81% of principals indicate that they use developmental , while 62% indicate that they provide differentiated support. This comes in the form of goal setting to provide teachers autonomy and for mapping out professional development plans. It also comes in the form of more frequent supervision for non-tenured teachers (Range et al., 2011).

Finally, principals apply teacher-evaluation models as a function of their beliefs. For example, when applying new teacher-evaluation models to their own school context, principals who felt that teacher evaluation should focus on helping teachers improve their practice (75% of principals in this study) as opposed to those who recognized it as a system for dismissing educators, implemented the teacher-evaluation model in ways that likely yielded different experiences for teachers. Those who used evaluation as a process for removing ineffective teachers spent little time on evaluation, as opposed to their colleagues who leveraged the system for improving practice and that spent time on providing direct feedback and encouraging teacher self-reflection (Kraft & Gilmour, 2016).

Principals Do not Treat All Sources of Teacher Effectiveness Data Equally

Principals tend to rely heavily on observational data when making personnel decisions. Despite the multiple measures of teacher effectiveness promoted under RTTT, principals rely primarily on observational data when making human capital decisions. Principals utilize these measures more because they are perceived to be timely, transparent, and specific, as opposed to value-added data. They perceive value-added data as arriving too late in the school year to inform personnel decisions such as contract renewal or even hiring. Principals also perceive that value-added data lack utility—they could not connect what teachers actually *do* in a classroom to value-added data outcomes in meaningful ways, reducing a principal's ability to make interpretations about the "how" and "why," and thus reach conclusions about the possible causes of a teacher's effectiveness (or lack of effectiveness). Finally, many principals do not understand how value-added scores are calculated, do not trust the data, and therefore feel uncomfortable about using the data to inform personnel decisions (Goldring et al., 2015).

Even within a single school, principals may apply evaluation standards in different ways. The way that principals weigh different evaluation criteria vary by teacher role as well as by the personnel decision being made. For example, a teacher's ability to manage student behavior and engagement is weighted heavily for all personnel decisions, but a teacher's personal organization and planning is particularly salient in dismissal decisions. Furthermore, principals make distinctions between skills that are foundational for all teachers, as opposed to those they anticipate seeing in only expert teachers and that would be expected for promotion (Master, 2014). We have learned from earlier research that principals apply evaluation systems to meet the needs of their particular context (school). These findings suggest that principals make further adaptations to account for teachers' expertise or particular personnel decisions (Master, 2014). Future research needs to clarify how principals make these adaptations and to explore if those adaptations are more effective or less effective.

Appendix A: Student Learning Growth Measures: Value-added vs. Student Growth Percentiles.

Value-Added Models

Value-added models seek to capture the "value" a teacher adds to their students' learning outcomes. According to Walsh and Isenberg (2015) it is calculated by predicting:

the standardized test score performance that each student would have obtained with the average teacher and then compare the average performance of a given teacher's students to the average of the predicted scores. The difference between the two scores— how the students actually performed with a teacher and how they would have performed with the average teacher—is attributed to the teacher as his or her value added to students' test score performance.

(Walsh and Isenberg, 2015, p. 53)

These models can account for student-background characteristics as well as prior achievement.

Student-Growth Percentiles

Student-growth percentiles (SGP) (Betebenner, 2011) indicate "how a student's achievement at the end of the year compares with that of the other students who started the year at the same level" (RAND, 2012). A teacher's SGP is the median SGP for his or her students.

Notes

1 The states included in the analysis, in no particular order, were: Hawaii, Pennsylvania, New Jersey, Rhode Island, Delaware, Georgia, Indiana, Florida, Idaho, North Carolina, Michigan, Maryland, Washington, Ohio, Connecticut, Colorado, Massachusetts, New York, Louisiana, Arizona, Kansas, Tennessee, Oregon, and New Mexico.

2 Notably, these rates are similar to those found in other professions. Berliner (2018a) notes that licenses have been revoked from 1% of physicians and 1% of lawyers in 2016.

3 We do not believe that New Mexico actually has more ineffective teachers than most states. Instead we believe the variation in the percentage of teachers who are rated ineffective has less to do with their true effectiveness and more with how policy is put into practice. For example, in some places the belief that too many teachers were being rated effective meant that principals were encouraged to rate more or a specific percentage of teachers as ineffective. Teachers who were previously rated in the top category "4" might expect to only achieve a "3" in the new system.

4 Principals' effectiveness was determined by supervisors' ratings as well as results from a teacher survey assessing their principal's leadership.

5 This also required even more time, but principals' calendars were already full.

6 This is one example that illustrates that policymakers often propose reforms that are easier said than done.

7 The authors present data from *The Widget Effect* to make this claim.

8 Although elsewhere he stated, and we agree, that observational data have considerable potential for stimulating conversations about possible ways for improving teaching.

References

American Statistical Association. (2014, April 8). *ASA statement on using value-added models for educational assessment*. Washington, D.C.: Author.

Amrein-Beardsley, A., & Collins, C. (2012). The SAS Education Value-Added Assessment System (SAS EVAAS) in the Houston Independent School District (HISD): Intended and unintended consequences. *Education Policy Analysis Archives, 20*, 1–12.

Berliner, D. C. (2008). Research policy, and practice: The great disconnect. In S. D. Lapan & M. T. Quartaroli (Eds.), *Research essentials: An introduction to designs and practices* (pp. 295–326). San Francisco, CA: Jossey-Bass.

Berliner, D. C. (2018a). Between Scylla and Charybdis: Reflections on problems associated with the evaluation of teachers in an era of metrification. *Education Policy Analysis Archives, 26*(54), 1–29.

Berliner, D. C. (2018b). Comments on four papers. In The problematic relationship of research to practice. Symposium presented at the Annual American Psychological Association. San Francisco, CA.

Betebenner, D. W. (2011). *A technical overview of the student growth percentile methodology: Student growth percentiles and percentile growth projections/trajectories*. Dover, NH: National Center for the Improvement of Educational Assessment.

Bill & Melinda Gates Foundation. (2012). Gathering feedback for teaching: Combining high- quality observations with student surveys and achievement gains. Retrieved from http://www.metproject.org/downloads/MET_Gathering_Feedback_Practioner_Brief.pdf.

Blazar, D., & Kraft, M. A. (2017). Teaching and teacher effects on students' attitudes and behaviors. *Educational Evaluation Policy Analysis, 39*(1), 146–170.

Braun, H. I. (2005). *Using student progress to evaluate teachers: A primer on value-added models*. Princeton, NJ: Educational Testing Service.

Briggs, D. C., & Dadey, N. (2017). Principal holistic judgments and high-stakes evaluations of teachers. *Educational Assessment, Evaluation and Accountability, 29*, 155–178.

Cannata, M., Rubin, M., Goldring, E., Grissom, J. A., Neumerski, C. M., Drake, T. A., & Schuermann, P. (2017). Using teacher effectiveness data for information-rich hiring. *Educational Administration Quarterly, 53*(2), 180–222.

Cherasaro, T. L., Brodersen, R. M., Reale, M. L., & Yanoski, D. C. (2016). Teachers' responses to feedback from evaluators: What feedback characteristics matter?. Washington, DC: Regional Educational Laboratory Central. Retrieved from https://ies.ed.gov/ncee/edlabs/projects/project.asp?projectID=4489.

Chetty, R., Friedman, J. N., & Rockoff, J. E. (2014a). Measuring the impacts of teachers I: evaluating bias in teacher value-added estimates. *American Economic Review, 104*, 2593–2632.

Chetty, R., Friedman, J. N., & Rockoff, J. E. (2014b). Measuring the impacts of teachers II: Teacher value-added and student outcomes in adulthood. *The American Economic Review, 104*(90), 2633–2679.

Collins, C., & Amrein-Beardsley, A. (2014). Putting growth and value-added models on the map: A national overview. *Teachers College Record, 116*(1), 1–32.

Corcoran, S. P. (2010). Can teachers be evaluated by their students' test scores? Should they be? The use of value-added measures of teacher effectiveness in policy and practice. Providence, RI: Annenberg Institute for School Reform. Retrieved from http://www.annenberginstitute.org/products/Corcoran.php.

Darling-Hammond, L., Amrein-Beardsley, A., Haertel, E., & Rothstein, J. (2012). Evaluating teacher evaluation. *Phi Delta Kappan*, *93*(6), 8–15.

Donaldson, M. L., & Woulfin, S. (2018). From tinkering to going "rouge": How principals use agency when enacting new teacher evaluation systems. *Educational Evaluation and Policy Analysis*, *40*(4), 531–556.

Flores, M. A., & Derrington, M. L. (2017). School principals' views of teacher evaluation policy: Lessons learned from two empirical studies. *International Journal of Leadership in Education*, *20*(4), 416–431.

Garet, M. S., Wayne, A. J., Brown, S., Rickels, J., Song, M., & Manzeske, D. (2017). The impact of providing performance feedback to teachers and principals (NCEE 2018-4001). Washington, DC: National Center for Education Evaluation and Regional Assistance, Institute of Education Sciences, U.S. Department of Education. Retrieved from https://ies.ed.gov/ncee/pubs/20184001/pdf/20184001.pdf.

Gershenson, S. (2016). Linking teacher quality, student attendance, and student achievement. *Education Finance and Policy*, *11*(2), 125–149.

Goldring, E. B., Grissom, J. A., Rubin, M., Neumerski, C. M., Cannata, M., Drake, T., & Schuermann, P. (2015). Make room value added: Principals' human capital decisions and the emergence of teacher observation data. *Educational Researcher*, *44*(2), 96–104.

Good, T. L., & Lavigne, A. L. (2018). *Looking in classrooms* (11th ed.). New York, NY: Routledge.

Grissom, J. A., & Bartanen, B. (2018). Strategic retention: Principal effectiveness and teacher turnover in multiple-measure teacher evaluation systems. *American Educational Research Journal*. Advance online publication.

Grissom, J. A., Loeb, S., & Master, B. (2013). Effective instructional time use for school leaders: Longitudinal evidence from observations of principals. *Educational Researcher*, *42*, 433–444.

Grossman, P., Cohen, J., Ronfeldt, M., & Brown, L. (2014). The test matters: The relationship between classroom observation scores and teacher value-added on multiple types of assessment. *Educational Researcher*, *43*(6), 293–303.

Halverson, R. R., & Clifford, M. A. (2006). Evaluation in the wild: A distributed cognition perspective on teacher assessment. *Educational Administration Quarterly*, *42*(4), 578–619.

Hanushek, E. A. (2009). Teacher deselection. In Goldhaber, D. & Hannaway, J. (Eds.), *Creating a new teaching profession* (pp. 165–180). Washington, D.C.: Urban Institute Press.

Hanushek, E. A., & Rivkin, S. (2010). Generalizations about using value-added measures of teacher quality. *American Economic Review*, *100*, 267–271.

Harris, D. N., Ingle, W. K., & Rutledge, S. A. (2014). How teacher evaluation methods matter for accountability: Ratings by principals and teacher value-added measures. *American Educational Research Journal*, *51*(1), 73–112.

Herlihy, C., Karger, E., Pollard, C., Hill, H. C., Kraft, M. A., Williams, M., & Howard, S. (2014). State and local efforts to increase the validity and reliability of scores from teacher evaluation systems. *Teachers College Record*, *116*(1), 1–28.

Hewitt, K. K. (2015). Value-added measures: Undermined intentions and exacerbated inequities. *Education Policy Analysis Archives, 23*(76), 1–49.

Hill, H. C., Blunk, M. L., Charalambous, C. Y., Lewis, J. M., Phelps, G. C., Sleep, L., & Ball, D. L. (2008). Mathematical knowledge for teaching the mathematical quality of instruction: An exploratory study. *Cognition and Instruction, 26*(4), 430–511.

Hill, H. C., Charalambous, C. Y., & Kraft, M. A. (2012). When interrater-reliability is not enough: Teacher observation systems and a case for the generalizability theory. *Educational Researcher, 41,* 56–64.

Hill, H. C., Kapitula, L., & Umland, K. (2011). A validity argument approach to evaluating teacher value-added scores. *American Educational Research Journal, 48*(3), 794–831.

Ho, A. D., & Kane, T. J. (2013). *The reliability of classroom observations by school personnel.* Seattle, WA: Bill & Melinda Gates Foundation.

Horng, E., Klasik, D., & Loeb, S. (2010). Principal's time use and school effectiveness. *American Journal of Education, 116*(4), 491–523.

Illinois State Board of Education. (2017). Illinois state report card: Teacher evaluation. Retrieved from https://www.illinoisreportcard.com/State.aspx?source=teachers&source2=teacherevaluation&Stateid=IL.

Jacob, B., & Lefgren, L. (2006). When principals rate teachers: The best and the worst stand out. *Education Next, 6*(2), 59–64.

Jiang, J. Y., Sporte, S. E., & Luppescu, S. (2015). Teacher perspectives on evaluation reform: Chicago's REACH students. *Educational Researcher, 44*(2), 105–116.

Kane, T. J., & Staiger, D. O. (2008). *Estimating teacher impacts on student achievement: An experimental evaluation* (No. w14607). Cambridge, MA: National Bureau of Economic Research.

Kane, T. J., & Staiger, D. O. (2012). *Gathering feedback for teaching: Combining high-quality observations with student surveys and achievement gains.* Seattle, WA: Bill & Melinda Gates Foundation.

Kane, T. J., Taylor, E. S., Tyler, J. H., & Wooten, A. L. (2011). Identifying effective classroom practices using achievement data. *Journal of Human Resources, 46*(3), 587–613.

Kerrins, J. A., & Cushing, K. S. (2000). Taking a second look: Expert and novice differences when observing the same classroom teaching segment a second time. *Journal of Personnel Evaluation in Education, 14*(1), 5–24.

Kersten, T. A., & Israel, M. S. (2005). Teacher evaluation: Principals' insights and suggestions for improvement. *Planning and Changing, 36*(1–2), 47–67.

Kimball, S. M., & Milanowski, A. (2009). Examining teacher evaluation validity and leadership decision making within a standards-based evaluation system. *Educational Administration Quarterly, 45*(1), 34–70.

Kmetz, J., & Willower, D. (1982). Elementary school principals' work behavior. *Educational Administration Quarterly, 18*(4), 62–78.

Kraft, M. A., & Gilmour, A. F. (2016). Can principals promote teacher development as evaluators? A case study of principals' views and experiences. *Educational Administration Quarterly, 52*(5), 711–753.

Kraft, M. A., & Gilmour, A. F. (2017). Revisiting The Widget Effect: Teacher evaluation reforms and the distribution of teacher effectiveness. *Educational Researcher, 46*(5), 234–249.

Lash, A., Tran, L., & Huang, M. (2016). Examining the validity of ratings from a classroom observation instrument for use in a district's teacher evaluation system. Retrieved from https://relwest.wested.org/system/resources/217/REL_ 2016135.pdf?1464716784.

Lavigne, A. L. (2018). Examining individual- and school-level predictors of principal adaptation to teacher evaluation reform in the United States: A two-year perspective. *Educational Management, Administration and Leadership*. Advanced online publication. Retrieved from https://doi.org/10.1177/1741143218807491.

Lavigne, A. L., & Chamberlain, R. W. (2017). Teacher evaluation in Illinois: School leaders' perceptions and practices. *Educational Assessment, Evaluation and Accountability, 29*, 179–209.

Lavigne, A. L., & Good, T. L. (2014). *Teacher and student evaluation: Moving beyond the failure of school reform.* New York, NY: Routledge.

Lavigne, A. L., & Good, T. L. (2015). *Improving teaching through observation and feedback: Going beyond state and federal mandates.* New York, NY: Routledge.

Loeb, S., Kalogrides, D., & Béteille, T. (2012). Effective schools: Teacher hiring, assignment, development, and retention. *Education Finance and Policy, 7*(3), 269–304.

Martin, W. J., & Willower, D. J. (1981). The managerial behavior of high school principals. *Educational Administration Quarterly, 17*(1), 69–60.

Master, B. (2014). Staffing for success: Linking teacher evaluation and school personnel management in practice. *Educational Evaluation and Policy Analysis, 36*(2), 207–227.

McCaffrey, D. F., Lockwood, J. R., Koretz, D., Louis, T. A., & Hamilton, L. (2004). Models for value-added modeling of teacher effects. *Journal of Educational and Behavioral Statistics, 29*(1), 67.

Michigan State Board of Education. (2017). Statewide educator effectiveness snapshot: Teacher effectiveness. Retrieved from https://www.mischooldata.org/Dis trictSchoolProfiles2/StaffingInformation/NewEducatorEffectiveness/EducatorEffec tiveness.aspx?Common_Locations=1-A,0,0,0&Common_LocationIncludeCompa rison=False&Portal_InquiryDisplayType=Snapshot&Common_SchoolYear=-9& Common_StaffGroup=Teacher.

Morgan, G. B., Hodge, K. J., Trepinksi, T. M., & Anderson, L. W. (2014). The stability of teacher performance and effectiveness: Implications for policies concerning teacher evaluation. *Education Policy Analysis Archives, 22*(95). Retrieved from http://dx.doi.org/10.14507/epaa.v22n95.2014.

National Council on Teacher Quality. (2015). State of the states: Evaluating teaching, leading, and learning. Retrieved from https://www.nctq.org/dmsView/StateofSta tes2015.

Network for Public Education. (2016). Teachers talk back: Educators on the impact of teacher evaluation. Retrieved from http://networkforpubliceducation.org.

New Jersey State Board of Education. (2017). 2015–2016 educator evaluation implementation report. Retrieved from https://www.state.nj.us/education/AchieveNJ/ resources/201516EducatorEvaluationImplementationReport.pdf.

Nye, B., Konstantopoulos, S., & Hedges, L. V. (2004). How large are teacher effects?. *Educational Evaluation and Policy Analysis, 26*, 237–257.

Papay, J. P. (2011). Different tests, different answers: The stability of teacher value-added estimates across outcome measures. *American Educational Research Journal, 48*(1), 163–193.

Paufler, N. A. (2018). Declining morale, diminishing autonomy, and decreasing value: Principal reflections on a high-stakes teacher evaluation system. *International Journal of Education Policy & Leadership, 13*(8), 1–13.

Paufler, N. A., & Amrein-Beardsley, A. (2014). The random assignment of students into elementary classrooms: Implications for value-added analyses and interpretations. *American Educational Research Journal, 51*(2), 328–362.

Polikoff, M. S. (2014). Does the test matter?: Evaluating teachers when tests differ in their sensitivity to instruction. In T. J. Kane, K. A. Kerr, & R. C. Pianta (Eds.), *Designing teacher evaluation systems: New guidance from the Measure of Effective Teaching Project* (pp. 278–303). New York, NY: John Wiley.

Pressley, T., Roehrig, A. D., & Turner, J. E. (2018). Elementary teachers' perceptions of a reformed teacher-evaluation system. *Teacher Educator, 53*(1), 21–43.

PRNewswire-USNewswire. (2011, June 28). Charlotte Danielson's Framework for Teaching sees record growth as states and districts redefine teacher evaluation. Retrieved from https://www.prnewswire.com/news-releases/charlotte-danielsons-framework-for-teaching-sees-record-growth-as-states-and-districts-redefine-teacher-evaluation-124646653.html.

RAND. (2012). Student growth percentiles 101: Using relative ranks in student test scores to help measure teaching effectiveness. Retrieved from https://www.rand.org/pubs/corporate_pubs/CP693z5-2012-09.html.

Range, B. G., Scherz, S., Holt, C. R., & Young, S. (2011). Supervision and evaluation: The Wyoming perspective. *Educational Assessment, Evaluation and Accountability, 23*, 243–265.

Rothstein, J. (2010). Teacher quality in educational production: Tracking, decay, and student achievement. *Quarterly Journal of Economics, 125*(1), 175–214.

Sartain, L., Stoelinga, S. R., & Brown, E. R. (2011, November). Rethinking teacher evaluation in Chicago: Lessons learned from classroom observations, principal-teacher conferences, and district implementation (Research Report). Chicago, IL: Consortium on Chicago School Research at the University of Chicago. Retrieved from http://ccsr.uchicago.edu/sites/default/files/publications/Teacher%20Eval%20Report%20FINAL.pdf.

Schochet, P. Z., & Chiang, H. S. (2010). Error rates in measuring teacher and student performance based on student test score gains. Washington, D.C.: IES National Center for Education Evaluation and Regional Assistance. Retrieved from https://ies.ed.gov/ncee/pubs/20104004/pdf/20104004.pdf.

Stecher, B. M., Garet, M. S., Hamilton, L. S., Steiner, E. D., Robyn, A., Poirier, J., … de los Reyes, B. (2016). Improving teaching effectiveness: Implementation. The intensive partnerships for effective teaching through 2013–2014. Retrieved from https://www.rand.org/pubs/research_reports/RR1295.html.

StecherB. M., Holtzman, D. J., Garet, M. S., Hamilton, L. S., Engberg, J., Steiner, E. D., … Chambers, J. (2018). Improving teaching effectiveness. Final report. The intensive partnerships for effective teaching through 2015–2016. Retrieved from https://www.rand.org/content/dam/rand/pubs/research_reports/RR2200/RR2242/RAND_RR2242.pdf.

The Danielson Group. (2013). The Danielson Framework for Teaching. Retrieved from https://www.danielsongroup.org/framework/.

Torff, B., & Sessions, D. N. (2005). Principals' perceptions of the causes of teacher ineffectiveness. *Journal of Educational Psychology, 97*(4), 530–537.

Van der Lans, R. M., van de Grift, W. J. C. M., van Veen, K., & Fokkens-Bruinsma, M. (2016). Once is not enough: Establishing reliability criteria for feedback and evaluation decisions based on classroom observations. *Studies in Educational Evaluation, 50*, 88–95.

Walsh, E., & Isenberg, E. (2015). How does value added compare to student growth percentiles?. *Statistics and Public Policy, 2*(1), 1–13.

Walsh, K., Joseph, N., Lakis, K., & Lubell, S. (2017). Running in place: How new teacher evaluations fail to live up to promises. Washington, D.C.: National Council on Teacher Quality. Retrieved from https://www.nctq.org/dmsView/Final_Evaluation_Paper.

Weisberg, D., Sexton, S., Mulhern, J., & Keeling, D. (2009). The widget effect: Our national failure to acknowledge and act on difference in teacher effectiveness. Brooklyn, NY: The New Teachers Project. Retrieved from http://widgeteffect.org/downloads/TheWidgetEffect.pdf.

Whitehurst, G. J., Chingos, M. M., & Lindquist, K. M. (2014). Evaluating teachers with classroom observations: Lessons learned in four districts. Retrieved from https://www.brookings.edu/wp-content/uploads/2016/06/Evaluating-Teachers-with-Classroom-Observations.pdf.

Wilkerson, D. J., Manatt, R. P., Rogers, M. A., & Maughan, R. (2000). Validation of student, principal, and self-ratings of 360° Feedback® for teacher evaluation. *Journal of Personnel Evaluation in Education, 14*(2), 179–192.

Wright, R. (2012). Recent teacher policy changes in Tennessee: Teacher evaluations. Retrieved from http://www.comptroller.tn.gov/Repository/RE/Teacher%20Evaluations.pdf.

Youngs, P. (2007). How elementary principals' beliefs and actions influence new teachers' experiences. *Educational Administration Quarterly, 43*(1), 101–137.

5

LEARNING FROM FAILURE

Introduction

Chapter 4 demonstrated that there is no evidence that principal practice, teaching, and student learning improved as a result of RTTT. Despite the vast resources invested in it, RTTT failed. In understanding this failure, there is much to address and various factors to consider. As we assess what can be learned from this flawed reform, we start with a discussion of policymakers' failure to account for many variables, including: the variability of teaching, the complexity of teaching and leadership, the existing knowledge about teacher effectiveness, and the extent to which principals were prepared to enact new teacher-evaluation models. Following our assessment, we address the key question: What now? This chapter provides suggestions for current principals and teachers (and those who prepare them) for improving teaching and learning through observation and feedback. Then we suggest ways for enhancing classroom research to better inform teacher supervision and professional development. Finally, we ask society to support their teachers and schools by recognizing what teachers can and cannot do. We end by advocating for increased efforts to implement programs that have shown great promise, particularly high-quality early education for *all children*.

What Went Wrong

Why didn't RTTT succeed? Here we address the most significant factors as to why RTTT failed to improve teaching and learning. Our analysis is focused on RTTT, but many of these factors have also contributed to the failure of previous reforms and should be addressed if future reforms are to be more successful. We first start with the principals—those most immediately impacted by RTTT. Principals were tasked with the responsibility of administering new teacher-evaluation models under RTTT.

Principals Were Not Prepared Well for What Policymakers Wanted

The primary activity of schools is teaching and learning, Yet, if we look back at the history of the principalship, as we did in Chapter 4, we see that principals have always spent remarkably little time observing and providing teachers with feedback. In the 1980s, principals spent 2.4–2.5% of their time observing teachers (Kmetz & Willower, 1982; Martin & Willower, 1981). Nearly 30 years later, principals spent from 9.26–17% of their time supervising and evaluating teachers (Grissom, Loeb, & Master, 2013; Horng, Klasik, & Loeb, 2010). Despite this increase, the time principals spend on such tasks is small relative to other duties, even after RTTT.

Limited time spent on observing and providing teachers with feedback does not necessarily suggest that principals were ineffective in doing their job prior to RTTT, both more recently and in the early years of it. After all, historically, the role of the principal was that of general management and was concerned mostly with budgets, transportation, safety, parents, and the community. However, the very limited evidence that existed prior to RTTT does raise concern, if indeed instructional supervision is to be the major responsibility of principals (see Short, 1995 for a review of the literature on instructional leadership and specifically conferences with teachers).

In their study of six school districts in the 1980s and 1990s, Frase and Streshly (1994) found that principals rarely visited teachers (and 4,728 observations that should have taken place based on district or state policy, did not), and, when they did, they seldom provided helpful suggestions and often overlooked problematic practices. Instead, principals engaged in conversations ("chitchat") that were often unrelated to teaching and they sometimes provided inaccurate feedback. In some cases, teachers did not have lesson plans, engage students, or enact instructional practices that went beyond drill and practice, and merely provided opportunities for low-level cognition. Despite these obvious teacher problems, when principals provided those teachers with feedback, the teachers were told they were doing great. Researchers noted that teachers' professional growth plans often did not align with the professional development opportunities offered them. One teacher had expressed an interest in increasing students' time on task, but instead the principal recommended that the teacher further her expertise in the state curriculum assessment skills. Further, a substantial percentage of teachers were not even evaluated by their principals. Such problematic practices led the authors to provide a scathing review of principals as instructional leaders and the disappointing state of teacher evaluation at the time:

> The contention that evaluation and supervision is the primary process in today's schools by which instructional excellence is achieved

and maintained (Pajak, 1990) is wishful thinking. Rather this characterization is dead wrong. Teacher evaluation has lost or never had a purpose.

(Frase and Streshly, 1994, p. 55)

We could attribute these ineffective practices to a number of factors. For example, because teacher supervision was seen as relatively insignificant to other demands placed on principals, perhaps principals had little time to practice and refine supervision and evaluation skills. Relatedly, perhaps principal-preparation programs spent little time preparing principals to do these tasks well. To examine this latter hypothesis, Hess and Kelley (2007) reviewed 210 syllabi across 31 principal-preparation programs and found that preparation programs did little to address educational reforms and that they were failing to effectively prepare principals who could improve student achievement.

Principals' beliefs about their preparation in instructional leadership paints a mixed report. On the one hand, studies indicate that principals feel underprepared to be successful in today's schools, with 67% of principals indicating that their graduate program was out of touch with the realities of today's schools. Much of their dissatisfaction came from the feeling that principal-preparation programs do not help principals to develop practical skills for dealing with day-to-day tasks and decisions (Farkas, Johnson, & Duffet, 2003). This finding confirms other research, which suggests the courses and content offered to aspiring principals is dated and irrelevant, and principal-preparation programs range from "inadequate to appalling, even at some of the country's leading universities" (Levine, 2005, p. 23). However, more recent research indicates that perhaps principal-preparation programs are improving. Today's principals feel prepared for the tasks required of them under recent reforms: interpreting school data, assessing student achievement, engaging in data-driven decision-making, and improving instruction (Hernandez, Roberts, & Menchaca, 2012; Styron & LeMire, 2009).

Although it is difficult to reach conclusions with such limited evidence, it may well be that principals who graduated from their preparation programs some time ago were not as well prepared to enact new teacher-evaluation models as more recent graduates. It is unclear if the great experience of veteran principals helps to close this possible gap. However, Frase and Streshly's (1994) data suggest that principals did not develop these skills through experience.

Leading is Complex and Difficult

Beyond specific preparation in fulfilling supervision and evaluation roles under RTTT, policymakers ignored the reality of the principalship—a role that is complex, difficult, and evolving. In an earlier text, we noted that the expectations about what good principals are expected to do are varied and often change without compelling justification (Lavigne & Good, 2015).

Once principals were expected to be effective "building managers." Being a principal was a full-time job and we noted this traditional job was complete with varied tasks (e.g., budgets, facilities management, buses, funding, substitute teachers). Today, principals are expected to do all that and more. They are expected to be exceptional instructional leaders—a role emphasis that seems to have returned from the 1980s (Edmonds, 1982). They are also expected to ensure that all students learn and that the school environment is safe. The demands coping with student behavior issues have increased, as have the demands for responding to accountability measures (DiPaola & Tschannen-Moran, 2003). This, coupled with the growing expectations to use technology to enhance teaching and learning as well as to communicate with parents and the community, while sustaining the cultures of an increasingly linguistically and culturally diverse student body, is daunting—and the demands for principals to do even more continues now in this post-RTTT period.

Principals Were Not Well Prepared to be Instructional Leaders

When RTTT was conceived, several clear facts were known about principals' capacity for instructional leadership. Extant data showed that the role of the principal was basically that of a building manager, with diverse tasks that required long hours to do everything well. A principal's focus would be fragmented with frequent interruptions. Most principal-preparation programs had typically prepared principals as building managers, not instructional leaders. Research (as rare as it was) suggested that when principals did observe and evaluate teachers, they did it poorly. Within this context, some principal-preparation programs had started to emphasize instructional leadership, but many had not. Thus, when RTTT requirements were drafted, it should have been clear that many principals would need extensive training in order to be instructional leaders. Further, had principals been actively invited to share their perspectives, many principals would have pointed out the impossibility of RTTT, or at a minimum, would have indicated the significant amount and type of help they would have needed to implement the expectations of RTTT well. Apparently many policymakers did not read the literature, talk to principals, or conduct pilot work.

Given all of the responsibilities listed above, it is not surprising that a principal's day is fragmented (Sebastian, Camburn, & Spillane, 2018). We have known this for a long time. Martin and Willower (1981), summarizing their findings from observation of five high school principals over a period of 25 days, noted that 82% of all observed activities of principals ranged from one to four minutes in length and "50% of all observed activities were either interrupted or were interruptions" (p. 74). Martinko and Gardner (1990) observed similar patterns—40% of principals' activities were unscheduled and ended up consuming nearly 30% of principals' time. Clearly, large amounts of a principal's time are characterized by "fire-fighting" and "brief encounters" (Spillane & Hunt, 2010, p. 294), things that are not within a principal's control. Research by cognitive psychologists illustrates that the sheer nature of a principal's work severely restrains their ability to attend to tasks meaningfully and productively. Research has long shown that we can attend to only so many things at a given time and that divided attention undermines short-term memory processing (Craik, Govoni, Naveh-Benjamin, & Anderson, 1996; Naveh-Benjamin, Craik, Guez, & Dori, 1998). Because of this, time management and work-life balance are two of the top six biggest challenges principals face (*Education Week*, 2018).

This is not to say that principals cannot be good instructional leaders, but that policy is often disconnected from the "real work" of principals. This is coupled with the expectations of policymakers that principals can and should do it all. Peck, Reitzug, and West (2013), in their historical analysis of policy, found that over time policymakers have framed principals as individuals who are central to school improvement, delegate leadership to others, and also accept individual responsibility for school results (particularly in the context of No Child Left Behind). Peck et al. (2013) go on to note:

> Offering perspective from the White House, a report from a Wallace Foundation-led school leadership conference quoted U.S. Secretary of Education Arne Duncan stating, "if at the end of the day, our 95,000 schools each had a great principal, this thing [school improvement] would take care of itself" (Wallace Foundation, 2010, p. 21). Adding to this sense that principals can make a significant difference in school achievement, studies have emerged demonstrating that focusing on principals is also cost-effective as compared to reform efforts targeting other K-12 stakeholders such as teachers (Butrymowicz, 2011). Apparently, not only is principal reform a silver bullet, but it is also a cheap one. However, creating a context in which we expect 95,000 principals to be superheroes is destined to lead to disappointment. As Superman, Spiderman and Wonder Woman would tell you, only a select few can be imbued with extraordinary powers.
>
> (Peck et al., 2013, p. 64)

Unfortunately, unrealistic expectations and demands of principals under-estimates the complex (and also limited) role that principals play. When these demands exceed the time principals have available—something that we have documented excessively—job stress increases (Flores & Derrington, 2017). Coupled with limited control, principals experience diminishing motivation and growth, jeopardizing their success and desire to remain in the job (Ford, Lavigne, Gilbert, & Si, 2018).

Principals Lack Time and Resources

Today, there is wide consensus from professional organizations (National Association of Elementary School Principals, 2001; National Association of Secondary School Principals, 2001) and researchers (Goldring, Porter, Murphy, Elliott, & Cravens, 2009; Leithwood, Harris, & Hopkins, 2008; Robinson, 2010; Robinson, Lloyd, & Rowe, 2008) that effective instructional leadership is vital to teaching and learning. So, even before RTTT, there was growing pressure for principals to spend more time on instructional-leadership tasks. This is also clearly reflected in the National Policy Board for Educational Administration's (2015) Professional Standards for Educational Leaders (formerly known as the Interstate School Leaders Licensure Consortium standards), which underscores a principal's role in implementing coherent and effective systems of curriculum and instruction, and supporting teachers through professional development, collegial feedback, and collective learning, innovation, and improvement. However, the Institute for Educational Leadership (IEL) (2000) indicates why putting instructional leadership first is a challenge:

> Principalship as it is currently constructed—a middle management position overloaded with responsibilities for basic building operations—fails to meet this fundamental priority ... The demands placed on principals have changed, but the profession has not changed to meet those demands and tension is starting to show.
> (Institute for Educational Leadership, 2000, p. 3)

The increased time to evaluate and supervise teachers, as required by RTTT *failed* to take into consideration that, even in the previous, less-demanding evaluation models that existed prior to RTTT, principals struggled to find the time to evaluate and supervise teachers (Donaldson, 2013; Frase & Streshly, 1994; Kersten & Israel, 2005). Further, we have known for some time that principals work long hours—approximately 59 hours a week (Lavigne, Shakman, Zweig, & Greller, 2016)—and bring home work to complete during the evening and on weekends (Davis & Hensley, 1999; Lavigne, 2018). We wonder how RTTT policymakers believed principals would find the time to do more?[1] What resulted was what we might have expected—principals writing evaluations of teachers and making high-stakes decisions on a Sunday evening at 11:00 pm after already clocking in nearly 60 hours. The implications of this increased workload were both real and unfair for principals, as noted in this quote from a principal implementing a new teacher-evaluation model:

> It has taken a lot of time outside of working hours. I mean weekends and nights and breaks. You've got to find the hours somewhere, and it's hard to do. We don't like it to take away from the school day (Flores & Derrington, 2017, p. 425).

As noted in Chapter 4, contrary to the intent of the reform, principals were actually spending *less* time in classrooms. Instead, the increased time allocated to instructional-leadership tasks was actually spent on writing teacher evaluations and recording and documenting observational data (Flores & Derrington, 2017). Carefully conducted and relatively inexpensive pilot studies could have identified this problem before full implementation. But, as we have seen in past reforms, policymakers do not take the time to learn from earlier reform failures or take the time to carefully plan the new reform (Lavigne & Good, 2014, 2015).

Unfortunately, principals had to cope with these increased time demands with limited support. If we look back 15 years, we find that only 29–46% of principals felt they had adequate support and resources to fulfil instructional leadership responsibilities, however 52–57% of principals felt well supported in administrative and management responsibilities (DiPaola & Tschannen-Moran, 2003). These trends have not changed. One form of support that principals receive is supervision.[2] In one study of 175 principals, nearly half of principals were supervised by their superintendents, but only 18% of superintendents focused on instructional leadership to any great extent. Those that were supervised by someone other than the superintendent benefited from a greater focus on instructional leadership—28% of principals reported that *these* supervisors focused on instructional leadership to a great extent (Johnston, Kaufman, & Thompson, 2016). Notably, though, no matter whether supervision is done by others, focus is not on instruction. Principals in smaller or mid-sized districts—districts that often experience the time "squeeze" caused by RTTT the most (Lavigne & Chamberlain, 2017)—received the least amount of support from their supervisor on instruction, and were offered fewer opportunities to be mentored by a supervisor or attend professional development opportunities with instructional leadership as the focus (Johnston et al., 2016).

Increased time demands, lack of support and resources, and unrealistic expectations driven by high-stakes teacher evaluations has resulted in principals feeling devalued as professionals. In Paufler's (2018) study of principals' perspectives of high-stakes teacher evaluations that were based, in part, on valued-added measures, one principal summarized how the district:

> prompts a negative environment with all employees—administrators and teachers [and] promotes an unsustainable model of change that is only sustainable by employing a modernized version of the 1900s factory model of education. Administrators are cheap and unimportant raw materials that are chewed up and spit [sic] out without any care or concern for their personal well-being. [This district] has lost countless dedicated employees who admirably and effectively served impoverished communities. Talent leaves when it is not valued, but more importantly we have lost all [our] sense of

humanity in the name of ambiguous measures of student gains [as per EVAAS®] that no one truly understands.

(Paufler, 2018, p. 10)

Tragically, policymakers' recommendations are ecologically invalid, ineffective, and flawed when they are not grounded in these realities of the principalship. Had policymakers incorporated what was already known about principals' capacity to fulfill the expectations of high-stakes teacher evaluation, perhaps they would have realized that principals would need much preparation and support to do this job well. This fundamental error was costly not only to principals, but also to teachers and their students.

Teaching is Complex and Difficult

Now let's consider teachers who were expected under RTTT to demonstrate notable improvements in their teaching and in their students' learning. As they did for principals, RTTT policymakers failed to acknowledge the difficult and complex nature of teaching. Instead, they attempted to reduce teaching to fast and simple measures[3] of teaching effectiveness, thus masking what researchers who study teaching have known for some time—teaching is "unforgivingly complex" (Cochran-Smith, 2003, p. 4). They also failed to recognize that teaching is difficult and challenging. Sinnema, Meyer, and Aitken (2017) note that:

> ... complexity arises from the fact that teachers typically work simultaneously with many and diverse students. It also arises from the multiple, wide-ranging, changing, and sometimes competing aims and objectives that frame the work of teachers—some of those objectives are immediate, some short term, and some much longer term. Furthermore, teaching involves multiple unknowns, including students' responses and the uniqueness of each and every teaching situation.
>
> (Sinnema et al., 2017, p. 15)

These unknowns create a job that is characterized by "chronic uncertainty" (Labaree, 2000, p. 231). A child gets sick in class, a fire alarm goes off amidst an "ah-ha" moment, or just as a reluctant student started to participate for the first time in a week. This is not to say that good teaching is a function of luck, or that its complexity negates any possibility for improvement or evaluation. Marilyn Cochran-Smith (2003) notes:

> As teachers—and teacher educators—we must be held accountable for our work. But measures of this work cannot be determined by narrow conceptions of teaching quality and student learning that

144

focus exclusively on test scores and ignore the incredible complexity of teaching and learning and the institutional realities inherent in the accountability context.

(Cochran-Smith, 2003, p. 4)

Nor does the complexity of teaching justify *not* measuring it, but it does call for the need to develop better measures for describing teachers and supporting teachers' development over time. Unfortunately, classroom instruments commonly used for high-stakes evaluation are instruments that focus only on general aspects of teaching and largely (and intentionally) ignore context. Principals need some measurement tools that allow them to consider teaching generally, but they also need to collect data that captures the different conditions in which teachers teach, even within the same school. We address the issue of bringing classroom context into classroom supervision later in the chapter (see p. 162).

Teacher Practice and Effectiveness Varies, and Often Should

Under RTTT, policymakers assumed that teacher effectiveness was stable (and so they provided principals with observational tools that assumed that teachers were stable and that context was not important). This is not the case. Classroom researchers have shown that teacher effects over multiple years vary and that teacher actions even vary from lesson to lesson (recall the evidence we reviewed in Chapter 2). Too often, citizens, policymakers, and researchers who do not conduct research on classroom effectiveness (and who apparently do not read this literature) see teaching as stable. Those who do conduct classroom research know how varied teaching can be and how even subtle factors can alter instructional plans dramatically.

Good and Lavigne (2015a) noted that, even in other professions, performance is rarely stable. They analyzed the stability of football team rankings within a one-week period and over time. From preseason to week 12, 8 of the top 25 teams were no longer ranked, and 8 new teams appeared in week 12 that had not appeared on the top-25 list during the preseason. Even teams that were relatively strong in the preseason (ranked #4, #9, #11, #12) dropped out of the top-25 by week 12. But one could argue that gameday conditions vary substantially and, thus, so should athletic performance.

However, even under highly stable athletic conditions, performance is still not stable. Good (2014) examined the performance of the top ten bowlers in the United States in 2008–2009. As opposed to football, the conditions of bowling are very stable. The lane remains the same in most instances—60 feet long, 42 inches wide. The pin weight, material, and location of pins is consistent. Bowlers' performance is scored with 100% reliability—no need to pause the game so that referees can review a play on camera—that may

145

or may not have been captured at a good angle. He found that *six of the top ten* ranked bowlers in the United States in 2008–2009 were not even ranked in the *top 40* in 2010–2011! Thus, even in the best case scenario, where conditions are relatively stable, performance is not.

Given the variations in performance in other professions, should we expect anything different from teachers? Should we expect day-to-day variation? Lesson to lesson? We might hope teachers would be stable in their end-of-year effects on students (a demonstration that students had learned during the year). Yet, even this varies substantially. Recall in Chapter 2 we noted that when Good and Grouws (1977) went to identify teachers who were consistently in the top or bottom of effectiveness over a period of three years, less than 25% qualified as stable. Surely there are reasons beyond the control of the teacher that may impact their effectiveness (for example, this year they receive 12 students who have not been in their school before and they also have 3 more special education students). It would seem that changing conditions (cohort effects, student demographics, teacher shortages) might impinge upon teacher effectiveness from year to year.

But doesn't good teaching mean that teachers should teach similarly from lesson to lesson and from day to day? The answer to that question is no. Why? Think about the conditions of teaching. Across multiple lessons, equipment (and the functionality of such equipment) could vary, interruptions, preparation time allocated to the teacher, and class composition (Kennedy, 2010). The teacher may have 20 students enrolled in the class, but on a given day the teacher may have only 14 students. This one factor alone will have impact on the teacher because a greater amount of material will need to be reviewed in the following lesson when the six students return, and, of course, this is likely to be on six different days. So lesson plans constantly need to be revised.

Students get sick in classrooms and lawnmowers can roar incessantly outside the class window, but these events cannot be anticipated. These and countless other unplanned activities can disrupt lessons and require changes in lesson plans. Berliner (2018) put it this way:

> We know, and the world does not that, in any one year, if we have in our classrooms more boys than girls; an extra special education student or two; an extra English language learner or two; or, if we experience a school shooting; or have a student or teacher death occur; or have just one extra crazy parent; or go through a change in the school principal; or experience a higher than normal move-in of new kids; or deal with a new testing requirement; and so forth and so on, we can expect effects on teachers productivity and classroom achievement.
>
> (Berliner, 2018, pp. 8–9)

We have established that the conditions of teaching vary and, understandably, that this may cause variation in teacher practice from year to year and even from lesson to lesson. And, indeed we have known for some time that teachers' instructional practice *does* vary by student composition (Brophy, 1973; Rosenshine, 1970) and even within a year, when the student composition remains the same (Emmer, Evertson, & Brophy, 1979; Rosenshine, 1970). Patrick, Mantzicopolous, and French (2018) have documented that teacher and class actions vary from lesson to lesson in mathematics and reading. When reliability is discussed, typically the emphasis is on the extent to which two or more observers report observing essentially the same events. When something happens, do different observers code it in the same or dissimilar ways? The essence of reliability is that observers are consistent in what they report.

Patrick et al. (2018) addressed a different question. They wanted to know if teachers taught in the same way from one lesson to the next. To do this, they video-recorded 3 lessons each from 20 teachers and had those videotapes rated by 3 different observers. They found that rater error was very small (only 8% of the variation). More importantly, variance from teacher to teacher contributed about a third (37%) of the variance in instructional scores and differences from lesson to lesson within a single teacher explained about 30% of the variation. In other words, teachers' own lessons vary almost as much as they vary against those of other teachers in both reading and mathematics.

This becomes even more complex as teaching fluctuates during a lesson. Gaertner and Brunner (2018) argued that two structural components of teaching occur in any lesson. The first is the deep structure of teaching (Klieme, Pauli, & Reusser, 2009, p. 139), which consists of non-visible activities and the learning process itself. The second is the visible structure of a lesson—the actual activities that occur or methods that deliver instruction (e.g., discussions, presentations, group work, individual work). They argued that the surface features of teaching—how the teaching is choreographed and delivered—can vary widely even within a lesson, but that the deep structure of instruction can be relatively stable.

Are these fluctuations reflected in other measures of effective teaching, like student evaluations? Gaertner and Brunner (2018) studied the degree of stability in student evaluations of teachers and whether or not stability is moderated by time between assessments, subjects taught by teachers, and students' grade levels. Using data from 1,328 teachers and 41,978 students' ratings of their teachers across two occasions, the authors found that time, subject, and grade level only affected teachers' ratings to a small degree, with grade level having the most significant effect. Across the 16 constructs, stability of instructional practices varied from $r = .46$ to $r = .82$. Certain teaching practices showed large variations in the students' ratings, for example: managing homework, formal structure, enthusiasm, and achievement expectations. These findings underscore the adaptability of teaching and, as has been found by a larger of body of research relating to the stability of teachers' practices, some variables of teacher effectiveness are more stable than others.

Should teaching fluctuate? Beyond the stability of the particular practice or variable being measured, there are other reasons why teaching should fluctuate. Brophy (1979), in reflecting on his review of extant research on teaching, commented that "the influence of context is being recognized as more and more important. Thus, there do not appear to be any universal teaching competencies ... that are appropriate in any and all circumstances" (p. 5). We also recognize that different contexts warrant different approaches to teaching, as has been noted for some time (see Chapter 2; Sigurdson, Olson, & Mason, 1994). Likewise, emerging research (e.g., Cohen & Grossman, 2016; Gutiérrez, 2002; Loeb, Soland, & Fox, 2014) and theory (e.g., Gay, 2010; Ladson-Billings, 2006) suggest that certain students may benefit more than others from teachers who possess a specialized set of skills, experiences, and practices. Teachers should, and do, adapt and modify their instruction to meet the needs of their students in both important and effective ways. This may happen when a teacher selects an alternative way to explain a concept if students struggle, or a teacher delays planned instruction to entertain a discussion that was initiated by students. Furthermore, we know that teachers may modify their instructional practice and do so in measurable ways through coaching, training, professional development, and professional learning communities (e.g., Franke, Carpenter, Levi, & Fennema, 2001; Rubie-Davies, 2014; and reviews by Borko, 2004; Good and Lavigne, 2018).

Taken together, we can conclude from the literature on the stability of teacher effectiveness that:

- The *conditions of teaching vary* from year to year, from fall to spring, and even from lesson to lesson.
- Teachers' *instructional practices vary* from year to year, from fall to spring, from lesson to lesson, and even within a lesson.
- Some instructional practices vary more than others (e.g., achievement expectations and formal structure varies widely from class to class taught by the same teacher).
- There are appropriate instructional reasons for teachers to vary their practices.
- Variation in instructional practice within a teacher is often as great as the variation between teachers.

What does this variation in teaching imply for high-stakes evaluation? It means that serious measurement problems are often overlooked. Recall that in the value-added paradigms, the core goal for researchers is to relate typical or representative teacher behaviors to student achievement. If we observe a teacher on one occasion but then we find that the teacher teaches differently the next time, which score do we believe? We don't know. If teachers teach in different ways then it takes a lot of observations to describe *typical* behavior. Because of the extent to which instructional practices vary, some aspects of teaching may be reasonably captured in fewer observations than others, but many are not. The point here is that principals are given estimates of typical behavior that are not, in fact, typical.

The Measures of Effective Teaching (MET) project was able to acquire a reliability of .65 with four observations using four different raters (Ho & Kane, 2013). They call for averaging scores over multiple observations to capture a teacher's effectiveness. This may be the most appropriate for evaluation, but we encourage readers to consider how the information will be used to support a teacher's growth. For example, and as we note below, observing the range of a teacher's practice might be more informative than seeking the "average," as a principal might be able to leverage a teacher's strength as well as address areas for improvement. Further, oftentimes general, high-inference instruments (like those primarily used in teacher evaluations) seek to capture the experience of the average student in the class or the experience of most students in the class, ignoring students on the margin that might be a useful focus for a teacher's improvement efforts. We also caution readers that a direct application of the MET project findings will likely not yield the same results, as the MET project differed from real schools in a number of ways (e.g., observers were rigorously trained, no stakes were attached to ratings), as noted in Chapter 4. Thus, in most situations, principals' ratings will have less reliability than those of the MET study.

Unfortunately, in many cases, principals are left with very confusing and possibly misleading recommendations for collecting and using observational data. And, unfortunately, they are offered no advice on how to deal with this situation. Furthermore, if teachers vary within themselves almost as much as they vary from their colleagues down the hallway, it becomes very difficult, perhaps impossible, to know whether summative teacher-evaluation scores are true representations of differences between teachers, and this renders high-stakes teacher-evaluation observation data useless. Unfortunately, policymakers wrongly assumed that teaching would be stable, and hence that the observation scores obtained would be representative of the teachers' typical behavior—but they are not. We provide a few thoughts about how to deal with this exceedingly difficult situation later (p. 162).

We recognize that we continue to re-emphasize that policymakers (and even some RTTT researchers who implemented reform efforts) were largely uninformed by the rich literature that was readily available, but that they ignored. We cannot overstress that we have known both that teachers vary in their behavior and that different teaching is required in different situations. And we have known this for a long time. It is time for policy-makers to read and to learn from the research on teaching.

High Stakes Undermines Teaching and Learning

Race to the Top failed because policymakers ignored what had been learned from previous reforms. Using lessons from high-stakes testing, a number of scholars foreshadowed RTTT's poor prognosis at a 2012 conference, which later appeared in print in a *Teachers College Record* special issue, *High-Stakes Teacher Evaluation: High Cost—Big Losses* (Lavigne, Good, & Marx, 2014). The issue established that RTTT lacked adequate evidence and research, and presented compelling concerns about relying on student-achievement outcomes to hire, fire, and grant teachers tenure. In the fore-word to the special issue Ravitch (2014) notes:

> The entire construct of test-based accountability rests on a sim-plistic, naive belief in the scientific validity of standardized testing. But the tests are cultural products, not scientific instruments. The construction of the questions is not standardized, neither are the answers. Sometimes the questions are ambiguous, some-times the answers are wrong. The scoring of constructed responses is rife with potential error. There is random error, statistical error, human error. And yet federal policy decrees that these frail instruments can accurately determine the quality of students, teachers, principals, and schools.
>
> (Ravitch, 2014, p. 4)

A number of concerns were raised about relying on student-achievement outcomes to make personnel decisions. These included that students are not randomly assigned to teachers (another reason why the MET findings lack utility) and that teacher effectiveness varies, which may increase the mis-identification of ineffective and effective teachers. Furthermore, there were concerns that an overemphasis on testing would narrow the curriculum, promote unethical behavior, and reduce teacher morale. These concerns were appropriate, but not new. Berliner and Biddle (1995) note that policy has placed, and continues to place, too much emphasis on standardized testing.

However, new concerns were raised at this conference as well. For example, Herlihy et al. (2014) raised the concern that districts were not providing sufficient training for principals, something that foreshadowed the problems with effectively using observations to improve teaching. Lavigne (2014) raised the concern that high-stakes teacher evaluation might actually drive new teachers out and even discourage high school graduates from entering the profession. Other negative predictions have also been confirmed. We noted in Chapter 1 that today few parents want their children to enter teaching. Further, in a study of the supply of new teachers from 2002–2016, Kraft, Brunner, Dougherty, and Schwegman (2018) examined the number of teacher licenses granted by states from year to year. In states that adopted high-stakes teacher evaluation, fewer licenses were granted—a decrease of about 17%.

Kraft et al. (2018) also noted that there was no evidence that reforms strengthened the qualifications of prospective teachers. Further, increased standards for teachers did nothing to attract teachers into teaching areas where they were needed. In summary, the authors conclude that high-stakes testing lowered the teacher applicant pool by 20% and did not encourage highly qualified candidates to seek teaching careers, nor was it successful in finding teachers in areas of critical shortage. These declines point to a flawed reform policy. Coupled with the negative media depictions and patterns we described in Chapter 1, both teachers and the profession of teaching need more support now than ever.

Of course, this should come as no surprise, as many of the lessons from the high-stakes testing era provided adequate warning signs that RTTT, and especially high-stakes teacher evaluation, may do more harm than good. For example, Nichols (2018) continues to remind us that high-stakes testing did not improve student achievement, increase graduation rates, or provide more or more-qualified teachers to the field. Race to the Top did not do good, but it did do much harm.

Nichols' work carefully documents several negative and unintended outcomes of high-stakes testing and notes that some of these complaints have been known for some time (Nichols, 2018). High-stakes testing has:

1   influenced instructional practices by watering-down and disconnecting instructional goals (e.g., Au & Gourd, 2013; Polesel, Rice, & Dulfer, 2013);
2   undermined how teachers relate to their students, as teachers diverted resources to students on the "bubble" (e.g., Booher-Jennings, 2005; Nichols & Valenzuela, 2013);
3   increased cheating on and gaming of educational tests and process (e.g., Figlio & Getzler, 2006);
4   increased bad instructional practice in special education classrooms (e.g., Nichols & Castro-Villarreal, 2016);
5   eroded teacher morale and sense of professionalism, especially among new teachers (e.g., Pedulla et al., 2003);
6   reduced teacher motivation and work satisfaction (e.g., Finnigan & Gross, 2007; Valli & Buese, 2007);
7   stratified the teacher force so that better teachers (as perceived by principals) were assigned to grades that were being assessed (Cohen-Vogel, 2011; Fuller & Ladd, 2012).

Principals suffered, too. Using data from the Principal Follow-Up Survey of the Schools and Staffing Survey, Mitani (2018) demonstrated that No Child Left Behind sanctions were associated with higher levels of both job stress and turnover of principals. Together, these findings show that high-stakes reforms were tremendously costly (in terms of money and time) and have failed to increase student achievement and graduation rates, but have had costly and identifiable negative consequences.

Negative outcomes have been observed in other countries as well, when tests have high stakes for teachers' evaluations. Smith and Kubacka (2017) examined data from the Teaching and Learning International Survey (TALIS). This survey was administered to 85,400 teachers in lower secondary education (and their principals) in 33 countries. The authors explored the role of testing in high-stakes teacher-evaluation systems in TALIS countries, its prevalence relative to other measures, and its relative importance in teachers' perceived feedback.

They found that student test scores were the most common component used in teacher appraisals—97% of teachers' evaluations included student achievement as a component, just a notch above observation (96%). Nearly 79% of teachers in the sample had high stakes attached to their evaluations, and 75% of teachers in the sample worked in a school that attached high stakes specifically to *student test scores*. When principals provided feedback to teachers, student performance was the most emphasized component. Unfortunately, when principals did this, *teachers perceived the feedback to be less useful*. When the stakes of teacher evaluation are high and based on student achievement, it results in principals providing feedback to teachers that undermines teacher growth—43% of teachers felt that evaluations had little impact on their instruction and 50% felt that the task was merely administrative (Smith & Kubacka, 2017).

Why might that be? When we turn back to US-based research, we find, as we might have predicted from NCLB findings, that high-stakes evaluations drive teachers to focus on immediate ways to boost their scores, as opposed to deeper, more sustainable changes to their instructional practice. Ford (2018) provides one example from a teacher participant, when they were asked how they used the data from the teacher evaluation process in their teaching:

> P: The scores ... OK. My first one [lesson observation], at the beginning of the year, I think it was like in September, I made all 3s. So I want to know what things I could improve in. So I looked at some of the easier ones for me to increase my score. [Effective proficient rating].

Principals were aware of this as well. One principal noted: "Teacher energy is focused on the appraisal system rather than on student learning" (Flores & Derrington, 2017, p. 424). This was particularly the case if teachers perceived the system to be bureaucratic with no real implications for their teaching and student learning. Unfortunately, many of the unintended effects of an overemphasis on student achievement outcomes undermine exactly what RTTT was intended to do—improve teaching and learning.

Misguided Expectations for Distributions of Teacher Effectiveness

As argued in Chapter 1, concerns about bad teachers have been a dominant underlying theme in the policy efforts related to highly qualified teachers and has continued under high-stakes teacher evaluation (Goldstein, 2015; Kumashiro, 2012). Lavigne (2018) and Lavigne and Good (2015) pointed to the coincidence that, in the same year that RTTT was announced, *The Widget Effect* (Weisberg, Sexton, Mulhern, & Keeling, 2009)—was released. This report garnered significant interest (according to Google Scholar, as of October 2018 it had acquired 923 academic citations, and in public media likely even more) and was even referenced by Arne Duncan, the Secretary of Education at the time (Gabriel, 2010). The most cited finding from the report was that fewer than 1% of teachers were being rated as unsatisfactory—in other words nearly 99% of teachers were satisfactory (or higher). Furthermore, the report indicated that, despite nearly all teachers being rated as satisfactory, 81% of administrators could identify a teacher in their school that was ineffective. This led policymakers to conclude that perhaps principals were failing to rate teachers as ineffective (for various reasons), and that teacher evaluation, as whole, needed to be fixed.

It is unclear what percentage of "bad" teachers policymakers believed were being protected by the system, but the following quote from Arne Duncan's address at the fourth annual IES research conference in 2009 provides some insight:

> In California, they have 300,000 teachers. If you took the top 10 percent, they have 30,000 of the best teachers in the world. If you took the bottom 10 percent, they have 30,000 teachers that should probably find another profession, yet no one in California can tell you which teacher is in which category. Something is wrong with that picture.
>
> (Duncan, 2009)

Perhaps it is difficult to count the number of "bad" teachers. Yet, ironically, the distributions of teacher-evaluation ratings has remained relatively stable across time, even considering that policymakers hoped that using rating scales with multiple points (as opposed to binary assignments) would result in a more even distribution—or at least in more teachers rated poorly. In 1994, Frase and Streshly (1994) found that 89% of teachers were rated as standard or superior and only .3% below standard or unsatisfactory.

Yet, interestingly Duncan (2009) suggested that *10%* of teachers might be eligible for removal. We wonder, where did this figure come from? The figure is not based on any evidence or any reasonable rationale for it. This figure seems odd since historically (Frase & Streshly, 1994; Langlois & Colarusso, 1988), and across time, only 1–3% of teachers have been rated as ineffective (Illinois State Board of Education, 2017; Kraft & Gilmour, 2017; Michigan State Board of Education, 2017; New Jersey State Board of Education, 2017; Weisberg et al., 2009). Even with teacher-evaluation systems that should be better at detecting effective and ineffective teachers, there has been little or no change in the percentages of teachers rated as effective and ineffective (Stecher et al., 2018). This raises the question: How many ineffective teachers are there? Given that all of these studies pull from ratings of direct supervisors, Berliner (2018) notes that it is difficult to draw conclusions about base rates of teacher effectiveness (as rated by someone or multiple individuals outside of the school or district), yet many politicians and citizens assume that only 1% of teachers being rated as ineffective is impossible, despite the consistent trends mentioned above. Some research has pointed to evidence that principals can identify many more teachers as ineffective than are actually rated thus in their summative ratings (see Kraft & Gilmour, 2017). But, as Berliner notes, perhaps instead of thinking of principals as protecting bad teachers, perhaps, the rate of *really bad teachers* is actually this low.

We agree with Holmes and colleagues (Holmes, Berliner, Koerner, Piepgrass, & Valcarcel, 2018) that it is *not* the case that there are no bad teachers. Clearly there are teachers who should be removed or counseled into a different profession before even entering the classroom. These teachers can pose a real threat to students' physical, social, or psychological health. However, policymakers equating bad teacher = low student-achievement gains is flawed, narrow, and will not capture bad teachers as described above. Instead Holmes and colleagues propose the following definition of a bad teacher:

> … one who, for whatever reason, either cannot teach the intended curriculum (e.g., because of recurring inadequate preparation for their classes, lack of knowledge of the subject area, problems of classroom control, extensive absences) or is harmful cognitively, physically, or socially to students or their families (e.g., displays of prejudice, punishes excessively, criticizes in demeaning ways, or is uncommunicative or disrespectful of parents or colleagues).
>
> (Holmes et al., 2018, p. 3)

However, the challenge still remains of how best to identify these teachers, and then what steps should be taken once such teachers are identified. Are they immediately removed from the classroom? Clearly, some scenarios would warrant this—for example, if there is a risk of physical and emotional harm. In other scenarios, remediation may be recommended, but is it effective?

Perhaps more importantly, the ability for schools to hire effective teachers varies substantially, and our efforts might be better used to establish resources and supports to reduce this inequity. For example, School A, an affluent school, may receive nearly 300 applications for a given teacher opening, whereas School B, a less affluent school, may struggle to fill a position, even just a week before school starts. Clearly this, alone, is hugely problematic and may yield wide gaps in the effectiveness of teachers in different schools. It also changes how principals spend their time. Teachers who struggle require significant support from principals in improving their instructional practice, even more so if they qualify for dismissal.

In our example, the principal at School A could enter a year of teacher supervision and evaluation with the preconceived notion that most of the teachers are the cream of the crop. On top of that, School A likely has better retention rates, which means a smaller case load of evaluations for that year. The principal at School B likely has many new teachers, making the time demands of teacher supervision and evaluation challenging. This equates to less time that the principal at School B can spend in the classroom providing feedback. Moreover, the principal at School B, wouldn't have had the opportunity to choose the best teacher out of 300 for the vacancy, which may leave School B susceptible to hiring teachers who, on average, are less effective (through no fault of the principal). At the end of the year, the principals at School A and School B will have spent their time supervising and evaluating teachers quite differently. Further, it was irresponsible of policymakers not to consider that many principals would be adversely impacted by their reforms. We conclude that the policymakers' focus on filling an ineffectiveness "quota" that has limited evidence distracted them from the inequities—perhaps yielding even greater variation in the opportunities for students to have access to effective teachers.

Appropriate Reliability Cannot Be Achieved to Justify High-Stakes Teacher Evaluation

In Chapter 4, we pointed to some of the limitations of observational and student-achievement measures for determining teacher effectiveness. Standards for reliability are increased when high-stakes are attached. Clearly, we want to be sure we are dismissing a teacher who is truly ineffective and rewarding a teacher who is truly effective, otherwise we are doing significant harm. We provided evidence that, in order to achieve adequate reliability for high stakes (on the low end, 90%), a teacher would need to be observed nearly ten times in a given year (Van der Lans, van de Grift, van Veen, & Fokkens-Bruinsma, 2016). If principals struggled to conduct three observations, clearly ten is completely outside of the realm of possibility—but what is the cost if teachers were the observers? Berliner (2018) notes:

> If trained raters who are also practicing teachers would observe two teachers a day, the costs might be around $500 per observation, about $1,000 per day ... we would likely require about nine observations, at about $500 per day, or $4,500, to get that piece of information reliably. On the other hand, if we intend to use one observer on one occasion to gather information, as we so often do, we can do so at much less cost and meet our obligation to evaluate teachers, *even if a good deal of what was coded and rated and judged is unreliable.*
>
> (Berliner, 2018, p. 15)

Unfortunately, student achievement measures do not fare much better. Recall that in Chapter 4, we presented data that demonstrated that, even with ten years' worth of individual value-added data, we would be incorrectly classifying the performance of 12% of teachers (Schochet & Chiang, 2010). Clearly, error is inherent in all measures, but when the stakes are high, what percent of the time are you willing to be wrong? 1%? 5%? 10%? Given what we know, it is likely current high-stakes teacher-evaluation models are producing error rates much greater than this.

Unhappily, we have seen that high-stakes evaluation was both costly and ineffective. This story includes many reasons for what went wrong, including: policymakers that did not bother to read or understand previous literature on teaching and supervision as well as evaluation combined with their willingness to ask principals to perform roles for which they were untrained. Instruments for classroom observation were insensitive to context. Those involved in schools sometimes distorted achievement data by cheating. Unfortunately, this is *déjà vu*—we have been here before, and inevitably we find our way back to policymakers, and sometimes educators, underestimating the complexity of teaching, supervising, and learning in modern schools. We need to recognize our collective failure. Now is the time to plan and devise better models and methods.

What Now? Prioritize Teacher Growth and Development

School reform is incredibly complex, and multiple layers have to be addressed if we want schools to educate students successfully. A key focus of this book is to use lessons learned from high-stakes teacher evaluation to support *teachers' growth and development*. We acknowledge that shifts in teacher-evaluation practice are already happening. For example, in Chapter 4, we described that value-added measures, as an indicator of teacher effectiveness, had received substantial criticism, and we looked at why this was the case. These value-added measures had led to more than 12 lawsuits, related to teacher-evaluation systems, being filed by the American Federation of Teachers and the National Education Association between 2011 and 2015 (Loewus, 2017). Under the Every Student Succeeds Act (ESSA), states are no longer required to include student achievement as a significant measure, as was required under RTTT. For some states, this has given an opportunity to pull away from using student-growth measures, however, even in recent years, there has been significant legislative activity around teacher evaluation. In 2017, at least 20 bills were enacted in 16 states with regard to the purpose, design, and use of teacher evaluations (Education Commission of the States, 2018). Alaska, Arkansas, Kansas, Kentucky, North Carolina, and Oklahoma have dropped the requirements for student-growth measures in evaluations, allowing districts to decide how to assess teachers. Even New Mexico, which had set student growth at 50% of a teacher's evaluation, is now only allocating 35% to student growth (Loewus, 2017). Thus, the current evaluation climate suggests that some states are making changes to teacher-evaluation systems that align, to some extent, with the lessons we have learned from RTTT. For example, that the state of New Mexico is now placing less reliance on standardized testing is likely a good policy action.[4] However, our opinion rests, in part, on the usefulness of measures used to account for the other 65% of a teacher's evaluation.

To capitalize on this shift in teacher evaluation, we first discuss how principals and teachers (and the programs that prepare them) can put *improving* teaching and learning first. We also provide a framework and suggestions for enhancing teachers' capacity for improving their own teaching and learning. Our comments include suggestions for individual teachers and for groups of teachers. We then provide suggestions for those who are conducting classroom research, or are in school-university research partnerships, to better inform professional development efforts as well as to improve the capacity of schools and districts to engage in data-driven decision-making. In alignment with these shifts, we place our greatest emphasis on observing, and using observational data to improve practice. Finally, we note how schools and society can support these efforts. We underscore that society needs to recognize that teachers can only do so much and we advocate for high-quality early-education experiences for all.

Principal Preparation and Practice

There is mixed evidence on how effective today's principal-preparation programs are at preparing aspiring leaders to be exemplary instructional leaders. Some data suggest that principals feel adequately prepared to interpret school data, assess student achievement, and engage in data-driven decision-making and leadership as it relates to curriculum and instruction (Hernandez et al., 2012; Styron & LeMire, 2009). However, it is possible that these findings hold true and yet the preparation of principals in instructional leadership still lags relative to other areas. The 2017 INSPIRE-Graduate survey was completed by 834 recent graduates of principal-preparation programs from 23 University Council for Educational Administration member institutions. Recent graduates rated instructional leadership as one of the weakest areas (out of seven),[5] on average, of principal-preparation programs, with a mean of 4.2 in quality on a 5-point scale (Pounder, Groth, Korach, Rorrer, & Young, 2018). The same trends were true in the 2016 INSPIRE-Graduate survey data, which included 1,110 respondents across 29 institutions and 38 preparation programs (Pounder et al., 2016). There was notable variation, suggesting that some programs have responded to recent trends and prioritize instructional leadership in their coursework. Still it appears that some, if not many, programs still need to better prepare principals so that they can provide instructional leadership.

With this in mind, we focus our efforts, for the remainder of the chapter, on ways that principal-preparation programs, districts, and the principals themselves can enhance instructional leadership generally and also respond to the limitations of high-stakes teacher evaluation we have raised throughout the book. Here we present just a few ways that principal-preparation programs and districts can support principals in building their instructional-leadership capacity.

To enhance teaching and learning, one must know which teaching practices are consistently linked to student-achievement outcomes, yet few principal-preparation programs include this as part of their curriculum (Darling-Hammond, LaPointe, Meyerson, Orr, & Cohen, 2007) and current principals feel only partially knowledgeable about these practices (Lavigne & Chamberlain, 2017), such as those we mention in Chapter 2 (Good & Lavigne, 2018). This offers rich opportunities for principal-preparation programs and districts to enhance current and prospective principals' knowledge base. Principals-in-training need coursework that allows them to have an understanding of how research on effective teaching practice was obtained. This coursework should involve principals in discussion and debate about the meaning of the findings, and if and how the findings might apply to other contexts. Other coursework might focus on improving instruction through the use of observation and feedback that focus on applying the knowledge gained from the initial course to practice. Here the focus would be on observing what matters (teaching practices that have consistently been linked to student-achievement outcomes), how, when, and what to observe, and providing effective feedback—content that we explore momentarily. As part of the course, prospective principals could engage in an observation cycle (pre-observation conference, observation, post-observation conference), or a mock observation cycle, to refine their observation and feedback skills. We recommend that prospective principals practice providing feedback to novice and veteran teachers, and teachers who exhibit exemplary, average, *and* ineffective teaching practices. Observing how an experienced and effective instructional leader plans for and enacts a year's worth of teacher (and staff) evaluations would provide valuable insight about how principals effectively manage the logistical issues of teacher supervision and evaluation. And, indeed, this is what principals war (Lavigne & Chamberlain, 2017).

Districts can play an important role in building the instructional-le' er-ship capacity of their principals once they leave principal-preparatio' pro-grams. In alignment with our first suggestion, professional developm .at can be focused on enhancing principals' knowledge base of effective ins' .ctional practices and observing and providing useful feedback. It is also mportant that principals have continued support in this aspect of .structional leadership.

A recent RAND report (mentioned earlier in this r .apter, p. 159) summarized the findings from 175 principals and assis .at principals on the support that districts offer for instructional leade .aip. When princi-pals and assistant principals were supervised by ' .ir superintendents, only 18% focused on instructional leadership to .ny real extent. This offers a great opportunity either to utilize s .aeone other than the superintendent (e.g., other central office le' ers in curriculum and instruction), who will tend to focus more or .aaching or learning, or to enhance the ways that superintendents sup/ ise principals. Principals in larger districts received greater support ir .astructional leadership. They had more opportunities for profession' development that focused on teaching and learning, greater super ,ory communication with their supervisors, and that communicatior ad a greater focus on instruction. Often, larger districts have the ca city to hire specialized supervisory staff to support instructional lead .hip (Johnston et al., 2016).

How can districts leverage the .incipal supervisor in ways that enhance teaching and learning? One ' ɔject examined just that—the Principal Supervisor Initiative (PSI). The .our-year, $24 million dollar project engaged six urban school districts tc transform the principal supervisor's role into one that focused primaril, on helping principals improve instruction in schools. In a report prepared for the Wallace Foundation, Goldring et al. (2018) explored the effectiveness of the initiative. The initiative focused on accomplishing the following five goals:

1   Revise the principal supervisor's job description to focus on instruc-tional leadership.
2   Reduce the principal supervisor's principal supervision load; change how principals are assigned to supervisors.
3   Train principal supervisors.
4   Develop systems to identify and train new principal supervisors.
5   Strengthen central office to support and sustain changes outlined in #1–4.

In achieving these goals, districts were able to reduce the caseload of principal supervisors down to 12 from a previous average of 17. Supervisors were strategically assigned to networks, so that support could be targeted and network-specific. Principal supervisors were trained in effective instructional practices, observing classrooms to identify instructional quality, determining and making decisions on protocols and procedures for classroom walk-throughs, improving student growth and achievement, and coaching principals on providing teachers with actionable feedback. With decreased caseloads and increased training, principal supervisors were able to spend 3–5 hours a month conducting site visits with each principal to provide support, coaching, and feedback. These are just a few suggestions, but ones that can shift the focus more to teaching and learning in the preparation and practice of principals.

Now, we shift to specific suggestions. We recognize that principals must balance conflicting goals—supporting professional growth and providing summative evaluation judgments. In essence, they are both the coach and the judge, which makes both tasks inherently difficult and leads to formative aspects (supervision) being subsumed under summative ones (evaluation) as noted by Flores and Derrington (2017). We agree with principals that promoting teacher growth as the main purpose of evaluation has value (Flores & Derrington, 2017). One way to improve principals' instructional-leadership repertoire and teachers' abilities to reflect on their practice is to challenge and expand the typical ways that teachers are observed.

Supplementing Existing Observation Instruments

Perhaps you are a principal who is using an instrument designed to capture generally effective instructional practices (which are often required by the district). Can you supplement this instrument in important ways to capture different or better information about a teacher's practice? We believe that checklists, even simple ones, can add important value, supplementing information obtained on the observation instruments. Checklists can be created quickly to help collect data on concerns a teacher or student teacher may have (e.g., cognitive level of questions being presented, feedback provided to students). Checklists have been included in other fields, including medicine and aviation, and there is evidence that they are inexpensive, easy to use, and are important (e.g. save lives!). Further, unlike high-inference measures, they provide direct points for possible intervention. Table 5.1 presents a general form that could be used in isolation, but may be most effective when paired with existing high-inference instruments. And, of course, principals or observers could adapt one in various ways, including, for example, designing one that allows for follow-up on the previous conference to determine if recommended procedures were implemented.

Table 5.1 The ALL GOOD Checklist

---

1. Did the lesson begin smoothly and on time?

2. Was there a clear statement of what would be learned that day and why that would be of value?

3. Were there moments when students were required to think or explain their reasoning?

4. Was the class generally free of distractions and misbehavior?

5. Did a range of students have the chance to participate during the lesson?

6. Did the students know what they were to do during the lesson?

7. Was there any evidence that students did or learned what was expected?

8. Was the classroom climate supportive of students' participation, such that students were encouraged to share their opinion without undue concern about possible failure?

9. When the class ended, did the teacher know how much students had learned in the lesson?

10. At the end of the lesson did students know how to prepare for the next class?

11. During the lesson, were any content errors made by the teacher or by students that were not corrected by the teacher?

12. When errors did occur did teachers treat them as normal and something to learn from?

13. Was there a sense of "we-ness" in the class, meaning that students listened to one another and sometimes commented upon what other students had suggested?

Note: This checklist does not yield a score. Rather the checklist provides a focal point for teachers and supervisors to begin a shared conversation. However, it does touch upon many things known about teacher actions that influence student achievement (see Chapter 2).

The ALL GOOD Checklist: General Considerations

Before presenting the checklist, we provide some general considerations—time, participation, focus on comprehension, and end of lesson. This checklist is informed, in part, by the 15 teaching variables that have been consistently related to student achievement over time (see Chapter 2). First, studies have shown that teachers vary widely in how much *class time* they use actually advancing content topics. Teachers who start class on time, and who move smoothly through transitions, provide much more time for students to learn than do teachers who manage time poorly. Second, students can learn, even if they do not ask or answer questions" some students are less verbal, even though they may be active listeners, and thus they participate though in a less obvious way. Still consideration of student participation is important for two reasons. First, as noted in Chapter 2, some teachers communicate low expectations to students by not calling on them often or by asking unchallenging questions. Second, if teachers hear from only a few students, it is difficult to assess students' overall level of comprehension and to plan subsequent lessons. Third, considerable theory and research shows that students learn best when their instruction addresses both procedural (facts, concepts, skills, and definitions) and conceptual knowledge (understanding, explanations, valuing) (Hiebert & Grouws, 2007). Although opportunities for both procedural and conceptual learning do not need to be included in every successful lesson, the absence of any attention to "why" or "how" this applies can be an indication of teachers' low expectations for the learning potential of the class as a whole.

Fourth, when lessons are ending, student learning can be extended in several ways. For example: "Before tomorrow's lesson, take a couple of minutes and write down in two to three sentences your summary of what you learned in today's lesson. Let's see how your summary compares to your classmates'." Or: "When you look at tomorrow's assignment, bring to class one or two questions about what you want to learn." Or, if you prefer :" Think about how we can use what we learned today."

The ALL GOOD Checklist can provide information about the considerations we have listed above. It has not been assumed that *all* these questions will be answered with a yes when good teaching occurs. As we have said, it is simply a checklist to think about how the lesson went, and ways in which it could be improved. In some classrooms, some questions may not be relevant.

Observer Comments:

1   What could have made the lesson more interesting? More effective?
2   Were there strategies, actions, materials that could be shared with other teachers?

Planning Observations Strategically

Principals are busy and have limited time to observe teachers. We offer some thoughts about how to use time strategically. We believe there is value in visiting a teacher multiple times. Since teaching practices vary by student composition and in secondary settings, principals might consider observing the same lesson for two different classes or groups of students. In elementary settings, since teachers typically remain with the same group of students throughout the day and teaching practices vary by content, principals might consider observing two different content areas. We also believe there is value in making sequential visits to the class. Visiting the same class on consecutive days allows observers to see the flow across lessons. Were the gains and momentum of the previous lesson maintained? Were any misunderstandings from the past lesson corrected?

LESSONS THAT BEGIN AND END UNITS OF INSTRUCTION

Given that we know that teacher practice varies from lesson to lesson, one way to consider how coherent instruction is provided over time is to compare how units begin and end. For example:

- How do teachers structure the unit for students? (Were comments made about the previous unit, how this unit builds on it, and where we are headed?)
- What concepts did the teacher include in the unit and why?
- What are the major learning goals and why are they important? How can they be applied?
- How will students' learning be assessed?

Observing toward the end of the unit allows for the examination of flow and coherence of instruction. Appropriate end-of-unit questions are:

- Were review activities consistent with initial expectations and objectives?
- How are students told to prepare for the end-of-unit assessment?

DAY AFTER UNIT TESTING

The principal or observer could obtain a copy of the assessment and a brief summary of student performance from the teacher. This would allow for a meaningful comparison between how the unit was structured and how it was evaluated.

- Was the assessment representative of important objectives announced in the introductory lesson of the unit?
- Was the assessment consistent with what was emphasized in the review?
- Did the teacher identify and reteach the concepts that proved to be the most difficult?

Principals have limited time for observing, so instead of seeing the day-after analysis as an observation, it could rather be part of a conference conversation. Actually seeing the lesson would provide more information about the extent to which teachers retaught important information (if needed). But, still much could be achieved if only a conference took place.

Other Suggestions for Selecting Lessons to Observe

Although we tend to think of representative lessons as providing the most information, we have seen that the range of lessons that teachers provide is so wide that often it is hard to call any lesson representative. Hence, even though you may randomly visit classrooms, what is observed may not be a typical or representative lesson, even if that is what is requested. Especially with teachers that have been teaching for a couple of years, it seems important that they should have a role in selecting a lesson that they think is good teaching or a lesson that they have had problems teaching in the past, where they would like feedback in order to improve the lesson. Higher-performing teachers are most likely to seek advice from their colleagues, thus it is important for principals to foster that expectation (Rosenholtz, Bassler, & Hoover-Dempsey, 1986; Spillane, Shirrell, & Adhikari, 2018). Such lessons and conversations about them make it more likely, but will not guarantee, that the observed teaching improves. Using deliberately selected lessons allows for more focused conversations: Why is this a good lesson? What constitutes good teaching? Is it comparatively easy to teach (for example, does the classroom activity almost guarantee student involvement)? What makes this content or objective difficult to teach? Allowing teachers or student teachers to pick a problematic lesson enables you to be a coach and a mentor, as the teacher is not asking for evaluation but is seeking ways to make a lesson better. Even the best teachers have lessons that they are still developing and this gives them the chance to obtain helpful (and welcome) feedback. Allowing teachers to select a lesson they feel is representative of some of their best teaching, provides teachers with opportunities to have it confirmed that they are teaching effectively. Conferences that support teachers can be as important as those that identify problematic behavior. After all, retaining good teachers is important.

Providing Useful Feedback

When teachers do not perceive feedback to be useful, they are less satisfied with their work (Smith & Kubacka, 2017). This is significant, as many dissatisfied teachers will eventually leave the profession. Further, teacher turnover harms student achievement, particularly in high-needs schools (Rondfelt, Loeb, & Wyckoff, 2013). Useful feedback supports the effort to retain teachers. Further, teachers who find feedback to be useful are more likely to pursue professional development (PD) following post-appraisal feedback (Delvaux et al., 2013).

In their review of international trends, Smith and Kubacka (2017) noted that high-stakes teacher evaluation has blurred the lines between supervision and evaluation, and one unintended consequence (as noted on p. 122) is feedback practices that overemphasize test scores and offer little support for improving teaching and learning. In the United States, one positive outcome from high-stakes teacher evaluation was that, in some studies, teachers reported that the feedback they received was helpful—90% of teachers in Chicago Public Schools indicated that, under the new teacher-evaluation model, they received specific suggestions and guidance on how to improve (Jiang, Sporte, & Luppescu, 2015). Furthermore, a recent report from RAND (Prado Tuma, Hamilton & Tsai, 2018) suggests that when teachers received regular feedback they believed it to be helpful for improving their instructional practice: that is, teachers had positive perceptions of both informal and formal feedback.

Their national study, the American Teacher Panel, was comprised of a randomly selected, nationally representative sample of 1,825 public school teachers in the United States during the 2015–2016 school year.

An interesting finding from the American Teacher Panel was that more teachers found feedback from other teachers (86%) and from mentors and coaches (82%) to be the most useful, followed by informal student feedback (77%), school leaders (73%), parent feedback (62%), and student surveys (62%). So, recent data suggest that teachers believe that principals provide good feedback, yet, as we learned in Chapter 4 (p. 109, 120, 122), few teachers felt that this would actually result in improved practices. Furthermore, teachers feel the feedback they receive from teachers, mentors, and coaches is more useful than the feedback they receive from principals. Yet, in the United States, nearly 85% of teachers receive feedback from principals (OECD, 2014a).

We imagine there are a number of possible explanations for these findings. First, we can only expect principals to do so much. Current demands may place constraints on the time they are able to allocate to providing high quality feedback. Further, as mentioned earlier, principals are limited in their content expertise and likely cannot, or only rarely, offer teachers content-based feedback. Thus, it makes sense that peers, especially peers who are intentionally selected by the teacher as peer observers, can offer useful feedback. Outside the US, peers are leveraged in the observation and feedback process much more, with 42% of teachers receiving feedback from peers compared with 27% in the United States (OECD, 2014a). We return to this opportunity below.

For principals who continue to carry the responsibility of providing feedback, we offer a few modest guidelines. Referring to from various research-based work (Baumeister, Bratslavsky, Finkenauer, & Vohs, 2001; Brinko, 1990; Kluger & DeNisi, 1998; Friedkin & Slater, 1994; Hattie & Timperley; 2007; McDonald & Boud, 2003; Nicol & MacFarlane-Dick, 2006; Taras, 2001, 2002, 2003), when providing feedback to teachers and student teachers, feedback should be provided in a timely manner and should:

- *Clarify performance expectations*: This helps refine understanding of effective teaching.
- *Facilitate reflection*: This offers the teacher an opportunity to think about the "what," "why," and "how" of teaching.
- *Deliver accurate information*: This reflects what actually happened during the observed lesson.[6]
- *Promote improvement*: This provides specific suggestions for a reasonable number of "next steps" that can be implemented in the next lesson; feedback is explicitly linked to growth opportunities (e.g., professional developing, observing a peers' practice).
- *Provide clear information*: This information should be concise and focus on a reasonable amount (taking into account cognitive load).

- *Establish a balanced account of performance*: This addresses both teacher strengths and areas for improvement.
- *Encourage dialogue related to teaching and learning*: This focuses on what teachers and students were doing.

Teacher Preparation and Practice

A growing body of literature indicates that principals influence student learning indirectly through teachers (Hallinger & Heck, 1998; Leithwood, Louis, Anderson, S., & Wahlstrom, K., 2004; Waters, Marzano, & McNulty, 2003; Witziers, Bosker, & Kruger, 2003). More recently a study conducted by Supovitz and colleagues of principals and teachers of Grades 1–8 affirmed these findings (Supovitz, Sirinides, & May, 2010). Specifically, they found that principal leadership is a positive and significant predictor of teachers' reported changes in instructional practice in both English Language Arts (ELA) and mathematics. In other words, principals' focus on developing missions and goals, creating a collaborative and trusting environment, and supporting instructional leadership, is related to teachers' reports of the degree of change in their instructional practice. Principal leadership also has an effect on peer influence (advice networks, instructional conversation, interaction around teaching and learning), which, in turn, is related to teachers' reported changes in practice. Importantly, in this particular study, in both ELA and mathematics peer influence was a stronger direct predictor of teachers' changes in practice than principal leadership. In mathematics, the effects of peer influence were nearly twice as large, suggesting that, for mathematics, perhaps teacher leaders are better sources of support and assistance than principals. These findings only come from one study, but they do overlap with concerns raised earlier about the extent to which principals can and should provide content-based feedback to teachers, and if so, in what areas teachers can benefit the most from being observed by a content-area specialist.

With this in mind, we turn to teachers and how principals and teacher-preparation programs can support teachers in improving their practice. We make an explicit effort to discuss why and how teachers can learn from one another. Earlier in the chapter, we agreed with scholars who criticized policymakers' efforts to promote a narrow, simplistic, and inaccurate perception of teaching, which inadvertently communicates the message that teaching is easy. Sinnema et al. (2017) call for a more nuanced approach, the Teaching for Better Learning model, to frame the work of improving teaching and learning. The model can be used by teachers and those who supervise teachers.

It considers teachers as active researchers who can use inquiry as a means to improve by tapping into five sets of resources. In the Teaching for Better Learning model, Sinnema et al. present five resources that teachers can draw from:

- *Education's body of knowledge*: This includes knowledge about all learners, the process of learning, society and culture, pedagogy, content, content-based pedagogy, curriculum, and assessment.
- *Competencies*: This resource includes relational, technical, cultural, and intellectual competencies.
- *Dispositions*: This includes a teacher's dispositions toward student learning, open-mindedness, agency.
- *Ethical principles*: This resource includes a teacher's commitment to society, the profession, the community, families, and students.
- *Social justice*: This resource includes a teacher's beliefs about and approach to challenging racism, inequity, injustices, and deficit thinking.

In no particular order, Sinnema et al. (2017) present six inquiries that can be used to guide a teacher's practice:

- *Learning priorities inquiry*: Here the basic inquiry is: "What is most important for students to learn?" This goes beyond what students *should* learn and encourages teachers to prioritize learning objectives in order to structure time well around prioritized learning outcomes.
- *Teaching strategies inquiry*: Here the basic inquiry is: "What teaching strategies could I try?" This is quickly followed by: "What evidence exists to support those strategies? What is the quality of that evidence?" This inquiry encourages teachers to make evidence-based decisions about the use of existing strategies and the incorporation of new ones.
- *Enactment of teaching strategies inquiry*: Here the basic inquiry is: "Did I enact those strategies well?" This inquiry is particularly challenging as it often requires teachers (or others) to reflect in the moment or immediately after the lesson—a luxury typically not provided to teachers in systematic ways.
- *Impact inquiry*: Here the basic inquiry is: "What happened?" followed by "Did I make enough of a difference for each learner?" Oftentimes this is: "Did the teaching strategy make a measurable difference in student-learning outcomes for all learners?" It is important, though, to be mindful that teachers may observe a measurable difference for all learners that is *not* significant. Here, teachers need to be mindful of "all learners" and also how a teacher intends to define "enough of difference."
- *Professional learning inquiry*: Here teachers reflect on the other inquiries and their thinking in relationship to those inquiries.
- *Education system inquiry*: This inquiry requires teachers to think critically about the broader context of schooling. In other words, "How does the broader context of schooling influence what is possible for me as a teacher?"

The expectation in this model is that teachers draw on their five resources when engaging in the above inquiries. For example, if one were to apply the first inquiry to the context of the five resources, it would translate to the following:

> Defensible decisions of learning priorities for each of my learners are made by: drawing on education's body of knowledge about all learners, learning, society and culture, content, pedagogy, content pedagogy, curriculum and assessment; using cultural, intellectual, critical, relational and technical competencies; demonstrating dispositions including open-mindedness, fallibility, discernment and agency; applying ethical principles and demonstrating commitment to learners, families, the profession and society; and demonstrating commitment to social justice by challenging racism, inequity, deficit thinking and injustice.

Although this does not make the work of the teacher easier, we believe this makes explicit the types of thinking that already inform many teachers' decision-making on a daily basis, albeit, perhaps implicit for a majority of the time as teachers grow.

Leveraging Communities of Practice

Teachers continually seek ways to improve their teaching to enhance student learning. Sometimes this occurs through personal self-reflection; at other times it occurs with others. Up to this point in the chapter, we have thought about the role of the principal in improving teaching and learning, yet teachers can engage in these activities collectively and through professional learning communities (PLCs).

In the last decade, PLCs have gained momentum because they offer a way for teachers to come together to look deeply at assessment and learning, and, collectively, to seek out ways to improve teaching and student outcomes. Smooth-running and effective PLCs help teachers establish shared values and visions and engage in reflective dialogue about teaching and learning. As noted earlier, leveraging peers to improve instructional practice has been a common method in many other countries. Notably, teachers who report participating in collaborative learning at least five times a year report greater self-efficacy (OECD, 2014a).

Teacher Teams

When successful, teacher teams promote professional belongingness, teachers' ongoing development, and collaboration and consistency across classrooms. By enhancing individual teachers' instruction and consistency across the school (Johnson, Reinhorn, & Simon, 2018), schools may observe increased student achievement (Bryk, Sebring, Allensworth, Luppescu, & Easton, 2010). In a qualitative study composed of interviews with 142 teachers, administrators, and staff in six successful, high-poverty, high-minority urban elementary and middle schools, Johnson et al. (2018) found that five of the schools relied on teacher teams as a mechanism for school improvement. Teams had substantial blocks of time weekly to meet as they focused on various concerns—curriculum, lesson plans, and student achievement— as well as the students as a cohort—their progress, group behavior and cohesion, and culture and climate.

Historically teachers' work has been isolated. Apart from interactions in the hallway or scheduled faculty and staff meetings, teachers may experience a whole day alone with their students, with little interruption or support. However, the climate is beginning to change. In a survey of over 9,000 teachers in Miami-Dade County, nearly 84% participated in a team/group with colleagues (Rondfeldt, Farmer, McQueen, & Grissom, 2015). Given these normative and historical experiences and current trends, how can a principal foster a climate to enact and sustain successful teacher teams?

Some suggestions include:

- Create protected and sustained time and space for required teacher team meetings (Charner-Laird et al., 2017; Johnson et al., 2018).
- Establish the areas of focus for the team—two appropriate and common areas are academic content (e.g., curriculum, lesson planning, assessments) and students (e.g., individual students, students as a cohort/grade, behavior, climate, culture).
- Identify teacher leaders as facilitators—teacher leaders may also meet weekly with the administrator to review progress of the teacher teams, set goals, and discuss challenges (Johnson et al., 2018).
- Provide ongoing and active support, including observing and participating in teams, and providing guidance and feedback (Edmonson, 2012).
- Establish a clear, meaningful purpose for teacher teams, one that is driven by the school's mission (Johnson et al., 2018).

What are some productive ways for teachers to use their time together? Some practices that teachers have noted include: sharing student work, sharing recordings of classroom instruction for discussion, unpacking research and talking about implications for instructional practice, and common planning. Teachers might use their teacher teams to share the responsibility for developing lesson plans that are divided among individual team members to construct, but then are shared and used by the entire team in practice. This "divide and conquer" approach is particularly useful for elementary teachers who, without shared lesson planning, may have to construct 20 lessons on their own for a given week. For those teams who choose to share lesson planning, have teacher teams identify examples of, or criteria for, shared lesson plans to support consistent high-quality lesson plans. Other tasks that teacher teams can tackle could include addressing concerns related to individual students to determine shared or unique struggles a student might be experiencing across content areas (Johnson et al., 2018).

How should teacher teams be organized? Teacher teams, often called professional learning communities, offer a means of responding to an accountability era that tends to discourage collaboration because of its focus on holding individual teachers accountable. In order for school leaders to meet the needs of accountability, while still supporting collaboration, administrators should think carefully about how to organize teacher teams in a way that makes sense for academic and student purposes. Grade level and content area are logical ways to organize teams, but perhaps there are more creative and innovative ways to think about supporting teacher development (as individuals and teams) and school improvement efforts simultaneously.

Lesson Study

Japanese lesson study offers a promising example of professional development that can occur within a learning community (Doig & Groves, 2011; Hamos et al., 2009). Gero (2015) proposes that lesson study helps target the 'script' that teachers develop of what teaching should be. In other words, teachers often share a common mental schema of teaching, and, more specifically, of how to plan and implement units and lessons. It also provides a mechanism by which gradual, incremental improvements in teaching can occur over time (as opposed to sweeping changes that policymakers often inappropriately expect). Lesson study seeks to disrupt the isolated nature that has historically defined teaching practice in the United States. It also requires American teachers to take a self-critical mindset and be comfortable with teaching in front of their peers.

In Japan, lesson study may be conducted once every one to three years, however, novice teachers are involved in conducting lesson study as much as three times a year. Furthermore, mentors play a crucial role in lesson study—these may be mentors who are formally assigned to new teachers, supervisors, or knowledgeable retried teachers or research professors from local universities (Chichibu, 2016). Japanese lesson study consists of five main components (Doig & Groves, 2011). We note each one and then describe it in detail.

Step 1: Goal Setting

In Step 1, goals are collaboratively established and time is spent on developing a deeper understanding of the specific content area. In Step 1, teachers can:

- Get to know one other;
- Establish lesson study rules, norms, and schedule;
- Identify long-term goals for students related to the relevant content area;
- Choose a specific goal to identify for the lesson study;
- Identify what the expected student learning outcome is for the goal.

Teachers may also choose to discuss students' strengths and areas for improvement as part of the goal-setting process. It may be useful for teachers to articulate and record how they arrived at the long-term goals and the specific goal for the lesson study. For example, the specific goal may arise from an identified problem—if so, evidence of the problem should be documented. In the United States, teachers may struggle with maintaining a focus on student learning (Fernandez, Cannon, & Sonal, 2003). Thus, the identified goal should have clear student-learning outcomes that are measurable.

Step 2: Research

In Step 2, teachers:

- Unpack the curriculum related to the identified goal; and
- Examine related research.

These activities may include the study of grade-level content, textbooks, scope and sequence of the curriculum, and standards. Research may reveal common misconceptions or difficulties students have in acquiring mastery of the specified goal, as well as effective instructional approaches. Teachers should also be able to identify trends in research-based practices as well as current research that may both challenge or affirm historical understandings (Hiebert & Stigler, 2000).

Step 3: Create

In Step 3, teachers create a lesson or unit that is based on the research conducted during the previous step. Teachers outline the unit to be designed or the lesson to fit within that unit. In doing so, teachers may want to consider the following questions:

- What is students' prior knowledge?
- How does the unit/lesson connect with previous or future instruction?
- What is/are the objective(s) for the lesson/unit?
- What will be taught? How?
- What resources will be needed for the lesson?

- How will students be engaged in the lesson?
- How will the teacher know the students have mastered the objective for the lesson/unit?

In this step, teachers might weigh, compare, and contrast different approaches to teaching the unit/lesson as well as brainstorm possible problems, barriers, or challenges that might occur during lesson delivery (and possible ways to counteract or prevent such issues). It is important that the lesson is a collaborative effort, so that all teachers take ownership for "authoring" the work. There should be a clear division of tasks, so that each teacher has a stake in the lesson/unit. Beside a strong focus on student learning, the collaborative nature of the lesson/unit planning is likely one of the most important components, because when lessons are collaborative it allows teachers to reflect more on the effectiveness of the lesson itself and less on the teacher's personal strengths (Gero, 2015). Teachers should be sure that student learning is what drives the lesson planning rather than get drawn in to planning entertaining or elaborate lessons.

Step 4: Teach

A teacher teaches the lesson from #3 (or from the unit) while others observe and gather data. Again, teachers will generally feel more comfortable about this when the lesson was truly a collaborative effort (Gero, 2015). Observers should agree beforehand about what they want to collect data on, keeping the previously outlined problem or objective in mind. Typically, lesson study is focused on improving the lesson, so data are often collected on how students are interacting with, engaging in, and understanding the content (as opposed to the teacher's actions).

Step 5: Reflect

Collectively the teachers reflect on the lesson (from #4) and make improvements. Critique is more effective when the lesson was planned in collaboration (Gero, 2015). Some questions that might guide this step include:

- Did the lesson achieve the desired outcomes?
- Did all students master the objective or just some?
- What factors supported or hindered student success?

For more detailed information on lesson study, as well as guiding templates and questions for each step, we direct readers to the Lesson Study Alliance (http://www.lsalliance.org).

Classroom Research: Improving Educational Policy and Teaching and Learning

We believe that classroom research offers many opportunities to extend learning from RTTT high-stakes teacher evaluation in various ways. We describe two general ways that classroom research can be leveraged to better support educational policy and schools in improving teaching and learning.

Cost-Benefit Analyses

Throughout the text we have noted how costly RTTT was, as were many of the reforms that came before it. We believe that if policymakers had understood existing research about teaching, supervision, and evaluation, RTTT high-stakes evaluations would have never emerged in the first place, or would at least have taken a very different course. We also argue that cost-benefit analyses relating to high-stakes teacher evaluations would have provided useful information for policymakers as well as schools, districts, and states. Unfortunately, RTTT policymakers, like those before them, were in too much of a rush: after all they thought they knew what they problem was and how to fix it.

Cost-benefit analyses have been advocated in education for some time (Levin, 1975). Yet, with the exception of preschool programming (see Barnett, 1993) many educational studies fail to include a cost-benefit analysis. Even in journals focused on education evaluation (where these types of analyses would be most appropriate), this has been rare. In their review of evaluation studies published between 1988 and 1992 in the *Journal of Educational Evaluation and Policy Analysis*, Monk and King found that only 14% had assessed cost (Monk & King, 1993). Unfortunately, these trends in educational research leave policymakers and district leaders to sort through findings from educational interventions that might have significant and meaningful effects on student learning, but without providing them with any tools to understand the financial value or cost the intervention would have for their school, teachers, and students. Hummel-Rossi and Ashdown (2002) provide a very detailed analysis of cost-benefit analyses in education (as well as in medicine and health). In the cost-effectiveness protocol for educational research, they suggest that educational researchers address ten different components (p. 20):

1 *Perspective*: Clearly articulated evaluation goals that have consensus.
2 *Cost-analysis*: Cost information and sources, hidden and obvious costs.
3 *Comparators*: Current practice and reasonable alternatives.
4 *Estimate program effects*: Experimental or quasi-experimental design that addresses hidden/qualitative outcomes, and positive/negative outcomes and is rigorous (e.g., good sampling, randomized control groups).

5 *Outcome measures*: Standardized achievement measures, effect sizes, and qualitative measures.

6 *Distributional consequences*: Costs and effects assigned to the appropriate parties; transparency and the stability of funding resources identified.

7 *Analysis of time effects*: Analysis of annualized costs accounting for inflation and discounted costs over time.

8 *Sensitivity analysis*: Exploration of variations in assumptions and parameters; and identification of impact on cost-effectiveness to determine robustness of conclusions.

9 *Decision rule*: Cost analysis used to inform decisions, but not the only factor/variable.

10 *Reporting of findings*: Technical report and findings published in an academic journal.

Applying these recommendations to educational studies would be particularly useful in formulating educational policy as well as to school and district leaders, as they expect to acheive more and more (often with fewer resources and funding) and to excel at data-driven decision-making.

Professional Development

Another opportunity for educational researchers is to examine how their current work can be extended into professional development opportunities. This is particularly useful for lines of inquiry that are progressive. Let's assume we have two variables. Variable X is a teaching practice and variable Y is a student-achievement outcome. When initially exploring a research question, oftentimes the first step is a correlational study: Is variable X related to variable Y? The subsequent study may then identify the independent and dependent variables, and the degree to which one explains the other: Does variable X predict variable Y? How much variance does variable X explain in variable Y? To determine causation, a quasi-experimental or experimental study might be conducted. We think it is valuable for researchers not to stop there, but to extend their work to determine: Can teachers be taught to do X well? Can professional development (PD) for teachers about X change teachers' practices in meaningful ways that cause a change in Y?[7] Examples of this type of research are noted in Chapter 2.

Citizens Advocating Schools and Teachers

Teachers can only do so much, and although the goal is to support teachers in being the most effective they can be, there is likely a ceiling effect in just how much effect a teacher can have on their students' outcomes. Have we reached this ceiling? We will not know unless we get behind teachers and schools. We believe that American citizens and policymakers can join this effort in two ways—making and supporting good investments in education, and valuing teachers and teaching.

Making and Supporting Good Investments

If we are to invest in education, what should we invest in and why? We could provide a number of possibilities, but given the evidence and the use of cost-effectiveness analyses, we describe one investment we think has the greatest value—early-childhood education.

The first few years of life are incredibly formative. Conditions, even in early childhood, have long-term consequences, with kindergarten and first grade being a pivotal time where socioeconomic status sorts students into unequal long-term pathways (Alexander, Entwisle, & Dauber, 1993; Entwisle, Alexander, & Olson, 2004). The effectiveness of early intervention, which seeks to identify and address development delays in children from birth to age three, demonstrates how formative the early years are. For example, well-designed early-childhood interventions have been found to generate a return of $1.80 to $17.07 for every dollar spent because they reduce future difficulties in academic achievement, behavior, educational attainment, labor market success, and delinquency and crime (Karoly, Kilburn, & Cannon, 2005). The early years are important.

Throughout this book we have noted the detrimental effects of poverty on education, as well as the inequities that continue in U.S. schools. Notably, the effects of these inequities begin early. In 2016, nearly 19% of children ages five and under lived below the poverty line (Child Trends, 2018a). Poverty and its effects in the early years are more important to future cognitive achievement outcomes than later poverty (Duncan, Yeung, Brooks-Gunn, & Smith, 1998). This is, in part, a function of access to fewer resources and opportunities. For example, children who live below the poverty line are less likely to be enrolled in early-childhood education than their more affluent peers. In 2012, 46% of three- to six-year-olds in poor families and 52% in low-income families were enrolled in center-based programs, compared to 72% of children in families with higher incomes (Child Trends, 2018b). These opportunity gaps result in children from poor homes being further behind their more affluent peers in kindergarten in reading and mathematics (Burkam, Ready, Lee, & LoGerfo, 2004). Thus, it is important to eliminate the opportunity gap, and to eliminate it early.

This has been recognized by some policymakers. State spending for preschool was $2.4 billion in 2002. In 2014, spending was nearly double—$5.6 billion (Barnett, Carolan, Squires, Clarke Brown, & Horowitz, 2015). In 1990, 1.2 million children were enrolled in public early-childhood programs. In 2013, this number rose to 2.6 million (Current Population Survey, 2015). Despite these efforts, we know that gaps still continue and only modest progress has been made in enrollment over the last six years. For example, increases occurred for access to full-day programming—54% of three- to five-year-olds were enrolled in full-day programs in 2016 compared to 47% in 2000, and these percentages are 81% and 60% for kindergarteners, respectively.

However despite this the percentage of students who enroll in early-education programs has not changed. In 2016, 42% of three-year-olds, 66% of four-year-olds, and 86% of five-year-olds were enrolled in early-childhood programs—percentages that are not significantly different from enrollment trends in 2000 (U.S Department of Education, National Center for Education Statistics, 2018). Notably, we fall far behind a number of other countries in enrollment in early-childhood care. Data from OECD (2015) indicates an average of 80% of three- and four-year-olds are enrolled in early-childhood care, whereas the United States is at 54%. This gap has been a problem, historically. Now is the time to see this gap as a challenge *and* as an opportunity. To make a valuable investment, citizens can expect a return of $8–$14 on every dollar we invest in early-childhood education (Duncan, Ludwig, & Magnuson, 2007).

Valuing Teachers and Teaching

In Chapter 1, we presented the disconnection between how much citizens believe teachers contribute to society, how important they are, and how little we pay them. We argued for teachers and also for teachers arguing for themselves. Clearly higher teacher pay is one solution, and provides a strong indicator of how much we value teachers. Additionally, countries where teachers feel valued tend to have higher student-achievement outcomes (OECD, 2014b). Teacher pay is not the only solution. The teachers working in schools that serve a larger percentage of students from poverty and a larger percentage of minority students, are faced with the most challenging working conditions—limited resources and support. Advocacy for more equitable distribution of resources and funding across schools is vital and demonstrates value for teachers by understanding their working conditions.

Conclusion

RTTT required principals to spend more time in classrooms observing and providing teachers with feedback. This did not happen. Instead, principals often spent more time completing teacher-evaluation paperwork and documentation than observing teachers. More "rigorous" teacher-evaluation models were designed to weed out the excessive number of "bad teachers" that policymakers believed to be in classrooms. Yet, the distribution of teacher-evaluation ratings has remained remarkably unchanged. With new teacher-evaluation models in nearly all states, and over $4 billion spent, this costly reform has not improved teaching and learning. RTTT failed.

In this chapter and others we pointed to many considerations why RTTT failed: lack of principal preparation, failure to understand the complexity of teaching, teacher effectiveness and practice, the use of observation instruments that did not adjust to context, weak correlations between teacher practice and student-learning outcomes, the unintended consequences of high-stakes, and misguided and exaggerated expectations for what teachers can accomplish. Utilizing the lessons we have presented throughout the text, we provided reasonable suggestions for principals, teachers, and those who prepare them, to regain a greater focus on supporting teacher growth and development, and ultimately improving teaching and learning. We also acknowledged the role that classroom researchers can play in enhancing educational policy and teaching and learning by including cost-benefit analyses in research as well as the effectiveness of professional development. Finally, we ended by thinking about the role that citizens can play moving forward by investing in and valuing education, teachers and teaching, including: investing in early-childhood education for all, increasing teacher pay, and reducing the opportunity gap, particularly across schools.

We end this book by returning to where we started: a paradox. Teachers are highly valued but poorly paid. If we do not value teachers who have the responsibility of educating 56.6 million children a year (NCES, 2018), what do we value? Now is the time to pay teachers for the important work they do. If we want students to consider and enter teaching as a career, to be effective teachers, and to remain in the profession, we need to support their success by supporting policies that provide resources that foster teacher collaboration, growth, development, and improvement.

Notes

1 It is likely that most policymakers did not even consider the immense burdens that their policy actions placed on principals.

2 There is limited research on principal supervisors, however Baker and Bloom (2017) point to principal supervisors as, historically, an area of weakness and an opportunity for improvement. They note that, "principal supervisors, many of whom have other high-stakes responsibilities ranging from the superintendency to positions in areas such as human resources and curriculum and instruction, have not been asked to make principal development a priority. Principals often only hear from their supervisors when there is a problem, complaint, or operational issue" (pp. 61–62). In their article, they describe the implementation of a coherent principal-supervision model to enhance principal supervision in the Long Beach Unified School District.

3 In a peer commentary on an article by Gargani and Strong (2015), Good and Lavigne (2015) cautioned about the use of fast, cheap, and oversimplified measures to capture teaching effectiveness, such as the six-item inventory used to identify effective teaching in one 20-minute lesson proposed by Gargani and Strong. Good and Lavigne noted that simple observational measures of teacher effectiveness often fail to acknowledge research on teacher effectiveness, as well as its complexity and nuance (e.g., importance of both alerting and accountability in good classroom management).

4 As noted in Chapter 4, VAMs are seriously flawed (see Braun, 2005; Rothstein, 2010). Low correlations between VAM scores and observational data make it difficult to pinpoint which practices yielded certain outcomes. In turn, principals and teachers indicate that these scores are rarely helpful in informing instructional practice (Goldring et al., 2015; Hewitt, 2015).

5 The other six areas are: ethics and professional norms, strategic leadership, operations and management, professional and organizational culture, supportive and equitable learning, and family and community engagement.

6 Although video-recordings may not always be feasible, results from the Best Foot Forward project indicated that having video-recorded observations (with principals' notes/questions embedded and viewable to the teacher in advance of the post-observation conference) can increase teachers' perceptions of fairness, while reducing teacher defensiveness because principals and teachers are less likely to disagree on what occurred during the lesson (Kane, Gehlbach, Greenberg, Quinn, & Thal, 2015). For more information and support on using videos for observation, see: https://cepr.harvard.edu/best-foot-forward-project.

7 We underscore the importance of high-quality PD and recommend readers review the characteristics of high quality PD described by Garet, Porter, Desimone, Birman, and Yoon, 2001.

References

Alexander, K. L., Entwisle, D. R., & Dauber, S. L. (1993). First-grade classroom behavior: Its short and long-term consequences for school performance. *Child Development*, 64, 801–814.

Au, W., & Gourd, K. (2013). Asinine assessment: Why high-stakes testing is bad for everyone, including English teachers. *English Journal*, 103(1), 14–19.

Baker, J. A., & Bloom, G. S. (2017). Growing support for principals: Principal supervisors collaborate and problem solve in learning communities. *Learning Professional*, 38(2), 61–65.

Barnett, S. W. (1993). Economic evaluation of home visiting programs. *The Future of Children*, 3, 93–112.

Barnett, W. S., Carolan, M. E., Squires, J. H., Clarke Brown, K., & Horowitz, M. (2015). *The state of preschool 2014: State preschool yearbook*. New Brunswick, NJ: National Institute for Early Education Research.

Baumeister, R. F., Bratslavsky, E., Finkenauer, C., & Vohs, K. D. (2001). Bad is stronger than good. *Review of General Psychology*, 5(4), 323–370.

Berliner, D. C. (2018). Comment on four papers by David C. Berliner. In The Problematic Relationship of Research to Practice. Symposium at Annual American Psychological Association Conference, San Francisco, CA.

Berliner, D. C., & Biddle, B. J. (1995). *The manufactured crisis: Myths, fraud, and the attack on America's public schools*. New York, NY: Basic Books.

Booher-Jennings, J. (2005). Below the bubble: "Educational triage" and the Texas accountability system. *American Educational Research Journal*, 42(2), 231–268.

Borko, H. (2004). Professional development and teacher learning: Mapping the terrain. *Educational Researcher*, 33(8), 3–15.

Braun, H. (2005). Value-added modeling: What does due diligence require? In R. Lissitz (Ed.), *Value-added models in education: Theory and applications* (pp. 19–39). Maple Grove, MN: JAM Press.

Brophy, J. (1973). Stability of teacher effectiveness. *American Educational Research Journal, 10*, 245–252.

Brophy, J. E. (1979). Teacher behavior and its effects. *Journal of Educational Psychology, 71*(6), 733–750.

Bryk, A., Sebring, P. B., Allensworth, E., Luppescu, S., & Easton, J. Q. (2010). *Organizing schools for improvement.* Chicago, IL: University of Chicago Press.

Burkam, D. T., Ready, D. D., Lee, V. E., & LoGerfo, L. F. (2004). Social-class differences in summer learning between kindergarten and first grade: Model specification and estimation. *Sociology of Education, 77*, 1–31.

Butrymowicz, S. (2011, October 20). Studies point to principal training as "cost effective" reform. HechingerEd Blog. Retrieved from http://hechingered.org/content/studiespoint-to-principal-training-as-cost-effective-reform_4410/.

Charner-Laird, M., Ng, M., Johnson, S. M., Kraft, M. K., Papay, J. P., & Reinhorn, S. K. (2017). Gauging goodness of fit: Teachers' expectations for their instructional teams in high-poverty schools. *American Journal of Education, 123*, 553–584.

Chichibu, T. (2016). Impact on lesson study for initial teacher training in Japan: Focus on mentor roles and kyouzai-kenkyuu. *International Journal for Lesson and Learning Studies, 5*(2), 155–168.

Child Trends Databank. (2018a). Children in poverty. Retrieved from https://www.childtrends.org/indicators/children-in-poverty.

Child Trends Databank. (2018b). Children in poverty. Retrieved from https://www.childtrends.org/?indicators=children-in-poverty.

Cochran-Smith, M. (2003). The unforgiving complexity of teaching: Avoiding simplicity in the age of accountability. *Journal of Teacher Education, 54*(3), 3–5.

Cohen, J., & Grossman, P. (2016). Respecting complexity in measures of teaching: Keeping students and schools in focus. *Teaching and Teacher Education, 55*, 308–317.

Cohen-Vogel, L. (2011). Staffing to the test: Are today's school personnel practices evidence based?. *Educational Evaluation and Policy Analysis, 33*(4), 483–505.

Craik, F. I. M., Govoni, R., Naveh-Benjamin, M., & Anderson, N. D. (1996). The effects of divided attention on encoding and retrieval processes in human memory. *Journal of Experimental Psychology General, 125*, 159–180.

Current Population Survey. (2015). School enrollment of the population 3 years old and over, by level and control of school, race, and Hispanic origin 1995 to 2013. Retrieved from http://www.census.gov/hhes/school/data/cps/historical/.

Darling-Hammond, L., LaPointe, M., Meyerson, D., Orr, M. T., & Cohen, C. (2007). *Preparing school leaders for a changing world: Lessons from exemplary leadership development programs.* Stanford, CA: Stanford University, Stanford Educational Leadership Institute.

Davis, S. H., & Hensley, P. A. (1999). The politics of principal evaluation. *Journal of Personnel Evaluation in Education, 13*(4), 383–403.

Delvaux, E., Vanhoof, J., Tuytens, M., Vekeman, E., Devos, G., & Van Petegem, P. (2013). How may teacher evaluation have an impact on professional development? A multilevel analysis. *Teaching and Teacher Education, 36*, 1–11.

DiPaola, M., & Tschannen-Moran, M. (2003). The principalship at a crossroads: A study of the conditions and concerns of principals. *NASSP, 87*(634), 43–63.

Doig, B., & Groves, S. (2011). Japanese lesson study: Teacher professional development through communities of inquiry. *Mathematics Teacher Education and Development, 13*(1), 77–93.

Donaldson, M. L. (2013). Principals' approaches to cultivating teacher effectiveness: Constraints and opportunities in hiring, assigning, evaluating, and developing teachers. *Educational Administration Quarterly, 49*(5), 838–882.

Duncan, A. (2009). Robust data gives us the roadmap to reform. Speech given at the fourth annual IES Research Conference. Retrieved from https://www2.ed.gov/news/speeches/2009/06/06082009.html.

Duncan, G. J., Ludwig, J., & Magnuson, K. A. (2007). Reducing poverty through preschool interventions. *Future of Children, 17*(2), 143–160.

Duncan, G. J., Yeung, W. J., Brooks-Gunn, J., & Smith, J. R. (1998). How much does childhood poverty affect the life chances of children?. *American Sociological Review, 63*(3), 406–423.

Edmonds, R. R. (1982). Programs of school improvement: An overview. *Educational Leadership, 40*, 4–11.

Edmondson, A. C. (2012). *Teaming: How organizations learn, innovate, and compete in the knowledge economy.* San Francisco, CA: Jossey-Bass.

Education Commission to the States. (2018). Policy snapshot: Teacher evaluations. Retrieved from https://www.ecs.org/wp-content/uploads/Teacher_Evaluations.pdf.

Education Week. (2018, November 7). Special report: Principals under pressure. Retrieved from https://www.edweek.org/ew/collections/principal-solutions/index.html?cmp=eml-eb-sr-prin18-10172018&M=58642032&U=2032901.

Emmer, E., Evertson, C., & Brophy, J. (1979). Stability of teacher effects in junior high classrooms. *American Educational Research Journal, 16*, 71–75.

Entwisle, D. R., Alexander, K. L., & Olson, L. S. (1997). *Children, schools and inequality.* Boulder, CO: Westview Press.

Farkas, S., Johnson, J., & Duffet, A. (2003). *Rolling up their sleeves: Superintendents and principals talk about what's needed to fix public schools.* New York, NY: Public Agenda.

Fernandez, C., Cannon, J., & Sonal, C. (2003). A US–Japan lesson study collaboration reveals critical lenses for examining practice. *Teaching and Teacher Education, 19*(2), 171–185.

Figlio, D., & Getzler, L. (2006). Accountability, ability and disability: Gaming the system?. In D. Jansen & T. Gronberg (Eds.), *Improving school accountability. Advances in applied microeconomics* (Vol. 14, pp. 35–49). Bingley, UK: Emerald Group.

Finnigan, K. S., & Gross, B. (2007). Do accountability policy sanctions influence teacher motivation? Lessons from Chicago's low-performing schools. *American Educational Research Journal, 44*(3), 594–629.

Flores, M. A., & Derrington, M. L. (2017). School principals' views of teacher evaluation policy: Lessons learned from two empirical studies. *International Journal of Leadership in Education, 20*(4), 416–431.

Ford, T. G. (2018). Pointing teachers in the wrong direction: Understanding Louisiana elementary teachers' use of Compass high-stakes teacher evaluation data. *Educational Assessment, Evaluation and Accountability, 30*, 251–283.

Ford, T. G., Lavigne, A. L., Gilbert, A. M., & Si, S. (2018). Applying motivational lenses to an understanding of district support for leader learning, development, and success in an accountability era: A review of the literature. Paper presented at the annual meeting of the University Council of Educational Administration, Houston, TX.

Franke, M. L., Carpenter, T. P., Levi, L., & Fennema, E. (2001). Capturing teachers' generative growth: A follow-up study of professional development in mathematics. *American Educational Research Journal, 38,* 653–689.

Frase, L. E., & Streshly, W. (1994). Lack of accuracy, feedback, and commitment in teacher evaluation. *Journal of Personnel Evaluation in Education, 1,* 47–57.

Friedkin, N. E., & Slater, M. R. (1994). School leadership and performance: A social network approach. *Sociology of Education, 67,* 139–157.

Fuller, S. C., & Ladd, H. F. (2012, April). School based accountability and the distribution of teacher quality among grades in elementary schools. CALDER Working Paper, No. 75.

Gabriel, T. (2010, September 1). A celebratory road trip for education secretary. *New York Times.* Retrieved from https://www.nytimes.com/2010/09/02/education/02duncan.html.

Gaertner, H., & Brunner, M. (2018). Once good teaching, always good teaching? The differential stability of student perceptions of teaching quality. *Educational Assessment, Evaluation and Accountability, 30,* 159–182.

Garet, M. S., Porter, A. C., Desimone, L., Birman, B. F., & Yoon, K. S. (2001). What makes professional development effective? Results from a national sample of teachers. *American Educational Research Journal, 38*(4), 915–945.

Gargani, J., & Strong, M. (2015). Can we identify a successful teacher better, faster, and cheaper? Evidence for innovating teacher observation systems. *Journal of Teacher Education, 65*(5), 389–401.

Gay, G. (2010). *Culturally responsive teaching: Theory, research, and practice* (2nd ed.). New York, NY: Teachers College Press.

Gero, G. (2015). The prospects of lesson study in the US: Teacher support and comfort within a district culture of control. *International Journal for Lesson and Learning Studies, 4*(1), 7–25.

Goldring, E. B., Grissom, J. A., Rubin, M., Rogers, L. K., Neel, M., & Clark, M. A. (2018). A new role emerges for principal supervisors: Evidence from six districts in the Principal Supervisor Initiative. New York, NY: Wallace Foundation. Retrieved from http://www.wallacefoundation.org/knowledge-center/Pages/A-New-Role-Emerges-for-Principal-Supervisors.aspx.

Goldring, E. B., Grissom, J. A., Rubin, M., Neumerski, C. M., Cannata, M., Drake, T., & Schuermann, P. (2015). Make room value added: Principals' human capital decisions and the emergence of teacher observation data. *Educational Researcher, 44*(2), 96–104.

Goldring, E., Porter, A. C., Murphy, J., Elliott, S., & Cravens, X. (2009). Assessing learning-centered leadership: Connections to research, professional standards, and current practices. *Leadership and Policy in Schools, 1,* 1–36.

Goldstein, D. (2015). *The teacher wars: A history of America's most embattled profession.* New York, NY: Doubleday.

Good, T. L. (2014). What do we know about how teachers influence student performance on standardized tests: And why do we know so little about other student outcomes. *Teachers College Record, 116*(1), 1–41.

Good, T. L., & Grouws, D. A. (1977). Teaching effects: A process-product study in fourth-grade mathematics classrooms. *Journal of Teacher Education, 28*(3), 49–54.

Good, T. L., & Lavigne, A. L. (2015a). Issues of teacher performance stability are not new: Limitations and possibilities. [Peer commentary on the paper, "The stability of teacher performance and effectiveness: Implications of policies concerning teacher evaluation" by G. B. Morgan, K. J. Hodge, T. M. Trepinksi, & L. W. Anderson]. *Education Policy Analysis Archives, 23*(2), 1–16.

Good, T. L., & Lavigne, A. L. (2015b). Rating teachers cheaper, faster, and better: Not so fast. [Peer commentary on the paper, "Can we identify a successful teacher better, faster, and cheaper? Evidence of innovating teacher observation systems" by J. Gargani & M. Strong]. *Journal of Teacher Education, 66*(3), 288–293.

Good, T. L., & Lavigne, A. L. (2018). *Looking in classrooms* (11th ed.). New York, NY: Routledge.

Grissom, J. A., & Bartanen, B. (2018). Strategic retention: Principal effectiveness and teacher turnover in multiple-measure teacher evaluation systems. *American Educational Research Journal.* Advance online publication.

Grissom, J. A., Loeb, S., & Master, B. (2013). Effective instructional time use for school leaders: Longitudinal evidence from observations of principals. *Educational Researcher, 42,* 433–444.

Gutiérrez, R. (2002). Beyond essentialism: The complexity of language in teaching mathematics to Latina/o students. *American Educational Research Journal, 39*(4), 1047–1088.

Hallinger, P., & Heck, R. H. (1998). Exploring the principal's contribution to school effectiveness: 1980–1995. *School Effectiveness and School Improvement, 9*(2), 157–191.

Hamos, J. E., Bergin, K. B., Maki, D. P., Perez, L. C., Prival, J.T., Rainey, D. Y. ... Vander Putten, E. (2009). Opening the classroom door: Professional learning communities in the math and science partnership program. *Science Educator, 18*(2), 14–24.

Hattie, J., & Timperley, H. (2007). The power of feedback. *Review of Educational Research, 77,* 81–112.

Herlihy, C., Karger, E., Pollard, C., Hill, H. C., Kraft, M. A., Williams, M., & Howard, S. (2014). State and local efforts to increase the validity and reliability of scores from teacher evaluation systems. *Teachers College Record, 116*(1), 1–28.

Hernandez, R., Roberts, M., & Menchaca, V. (2012). Redesigning a principal preparation program: A continuous improvement model. *International Journal of Educational Leadership Preparation, 7*(3), 1–12.

Hess, F. M., & Kelley, A. P. (2007). Learning to lead: What gets taught in principal preparation programs. *Teachers College Record, 109*(1), 221–243.

Hewitt, K. K. (2015). Value-added measures: Undermined intentions and exacerbated inequities. *Education Policy Analysis Archives, 23*(76), 1–50.

Hiebert, J., & Grouws, D. A. (2007). The effects of classroom mathematics teaching on students' learning. In F. K. Lester (Ed.), *Second handbook of research on mathematics teaching and learning* (pp. 371–404). Greenwich, CT: Information Age.

Hiebert, J., & Stigler, J. W. (2000). A proposal for improving classroom teaching: Lessons from the TIMSS video study. *The Elementary School Journal, 101*(1), 3–20.

Hill, H., Charalambous, C. Y., & Kraft, M. A. (2012). When interrater-reliability is not enough: Teacher observation systems and a case for the generalizability theory. *Educational Researcher, 41,* 56–64.

Ho, A. D., & Kane, T. J. (2013). The reliability of classroom observations by school personnel. Retrieved from http://www.danielsongroup.org/wp-content/uploads/2017/11/Reliabiilty_Observations_School_Personnel_Gates.pdf.

Holmes, J., Berliner, D. C., Koerner, M. E., Piepgrass, N., & Valcarcel, C. (2018). Is the teaching profession dominated by bad teachers? How would we know?. *Teachers College Record*, 1–4.

Horng, E., Klasik, D., & Loeb, S. (2010). Principal's time use and school effectiveness. *American Journal of Education*, 116(4), 491–523.

Hummel-Rossi, B., & Ashdown, J. (2002). The state of cost-benefit and cost-effectiveness analyses in education. *Review of Educational Research*, 72(1), 1–30.

Illinois State Board of Education. (2017). Illinois state report card. Retrieved from https://www.isbe.net/Documents/2018-State-Report.pdf.

Institute for Educational Leadership. (2000). *Leadership for student learning: Reinventing the principalship. A report of the task force on the principalship.* Washington, DC: Institute for Educational Leadership.

Jiang, J. Y., Sporte, S. E., & Luppescu, S. (2015). Teacher perspectives on evaluation reform: Chicago's REACH students. *Educational Researcher*, 44(2), 105–116.

Johnson, S. M., Reinhorn, S., & Simon, N. (2018). Ending isolation: The payoff of teacher teams in successful high-poverty urban schools. *Teachers College Record*, 120, 1–46.

Johnston, W. R., Kaufman, J. H., & Thompson, L. E. (2016). Support for instructional leadership. Supervision, mentoring, and professional development for U.S. school leaders: Findings from the American School Leader Panel. RAND Corporation. Retrieved from https://www.wallacefoundation.org/knowledge-center/Documents/Support-for-Instructional-Leadership.pdf.

Kane, T. J., Gehlbach, H., Greenberg, M., Quinn, D., & Thal, D. (2015). The Best Foot Forward project: Substituting teacher-collected video for in-person classroom observations. Retrieved from https://cepr.harvard.edu/files/cepr/files/l4a_best_foot_forward_research_brief1.pdf.

Kane, T. J., Staiger, D. O., McCaffrey, D., Cantrell, S., Archer, J., Buhayar, S., … Parker, D. (2012). *Gathering feedback for teaching: Combining high-quality observations with student surveys and achievement gains.* Seattle, WA: Bill & Melinda Gates Foundation.

Karoly, L. A., Kilburn, M. R., & Cannon, J. S. (2005). Early childhood interventions: Proven results, future promises. Santa Monica, CA: RAND Corporation.

Kennedy, M. M. (2010). Attribution error and the quest for teaching quality. *Educational Researcher*, 39, 591–598.

Kersten, T. A., & Israel, M. S. (2005). Teacher evaluation: Principals' insights and suggestions for improvement. *Planning and Changing*, 36(1–2), 47–67.

Klieme, E., Pauli, C., & Reusser, K. (2009). The Pythagoras study: Investigating effects of teaching and learning in Swiss and German mathematics classrooms. In T. Seidel & P. Najvar (Eds.), *The power of video studies in investigating teaching and learning in the classroom* (pp. 137–160). Münster, Germany: Waxmann.

Kluger, A. N., & DeNisi, A. S. (1998). Feedback interventions: Toward the understanding of a double-edged sword. *Current Directions in Psychological Science*, 7, 67–72.

Kmetz, J., & Willower, D. (1982). Elementary school principals' work behavior. *Educational Administration Quarterly*, 18(4), 62–78.

Kraft, M. A., & Gilmour, A. F. (2017). Revisiting The Widget Effect: Teacher evaluation reforms and the distribution of teacher effectiveness. *Educational Researcher*, 46(5), 234–249.

Kraft, M. A., Brunner, E. J., Dougherty, S. M., & Schwegman, D. (2018). Teacher accountability reforms and the supply of new teachers. Working Paper. Providence, RI: Brown University.

Kumashiro, K. (2012). *Bad teacher! How blaming teachers distorts the bigger picture.* New York, NY: Teachers College Press.

Labaree, D. (2000). On the nature of teaching and teacher education: Difficult practices that look easy. *Journal of Teacher Education, 51*(3), 228–233.

Labaree, D. (2010). *Someone has to fail.* Cambridge, MA: Harvard University Press.

Ladson-Billings, G. (2006). Yes, but how do we do it? Practicing culturally relevant pedagogy. In J. Landsman & C. W. Lewis (Eds.), *White teachers/diverse classrooms: A guide to building inclusive schools, promoting high expectations, and eliminating racism* (pp. 29–42). Sterling, VA: Stylus.

Langlois, D. E., & Colarusso, M. R. (1988). Improving teacher evaluation. *The Education Digest, 54,* 13–15.

Lavigne, A. L. (2014). Exploring the implications of high-stakes teacher evaluation on schools, teachers, and students. *Teachers College Record, 116*(1), 1–29.

Lavigne, A. L. (2018, August). Assessing the bridge between research and practice from the principal's point of view. Paper presented as part of the symposium, The problematic relationship of research to practice, at the Annual Convention of the American Psychological Association, San Francisco, CA.

Lavigne, A. L., & Chamberlain, R. (2017). Teacher evaluation in Illinois: School leaders' perceptions and practices. *Educational Assessment, Evaluation and Accountability, 29*(2), 179–209.

Lavigne, A. L., & Good, T. L. (2014). *Teacher and student evaluation: Moving beyond the failure of school reform.* New York, NY: Routledge.

Lavigne, A. L., & Good, T. L. (2015). *Improving teaching through observation and feedback: Going beyond state and federal mandates.* New York, NY: Routledge.

Lavigne, A. L., Good, T. L., & Marx, R. W. (Eds.). (2014). High-stakes teacher evaluation: High cost—big losses [Special issue]. *Teachers College Record, 116*(1), 1–29.

Lavigne, H. J., Shakman, K., Zweig, J., & Greller, S. L. (2016). *Principals' time, tasks, and professional development: An analysis of Schools and Staffing Survey data.* Washington, DC: Regional Educational Laboratory Northeast & Islands.

Lei, X., Li, H., & Leroux, A. J. (2018). Does a teacher's classroom observation rating vary across multiple classrooms?. *Educational Assessment, Evaluation and Accountability, 30*(1), 27–46.

Leithwood, K., Harris, A., & Hopkins, D. (2008). Seven strong claims about successful school leadership. *School Leadership & Management, 28*(1), 27–42.

Leithwood, K., Louis, K. S., Anderson, S., & Wahlstrom, K. (2004). *How leadership influences student learning.* New York, NY: Wallace Foundation.

Levin, H. M. (1975). Cost-effectiveness in evaluation research. In M. Guttentag & E. Struening (Eds.), *Handbook of educational research* (pp. 89–122). Thousand Oaks, CA: Sage Publications.

Levine, A. (2005). *Educating school leaders.* New York, NY: Teachers College, The Education Schools Project.

Loeb, S., Kalogrides, D., & Béteille, T. (2012). Effective schools: Teacher hiring, assignment, development, and retention. *Education Finance and Policy, 7*(3), 269–304.

Loeb, S., Soland, J., & Fox, L. (2014). Is a good teacher a good teacher for all? Comparing value added of teachers with their English Learners and Non-English Learners. *Educational Evaluation and Policy Analysis, 36*(4), 457–475.

Loewus, L. (2017). Are states changing course on teacher evaluation? Test-score growth plays lesser role in six states. *Education Week, 37*(13), 1–7.

McDonald, B., & Boud, D. (2003). The impact of self-assessment on achievement: The effects of self-assessment training on performance in external examinations. *Assessment in Education, 10,* 209–220.

Martin, W. J., & Willower, D. J. (1981). The managerial behavior of high school principals. *Educational Administration Quarterly, 17*(1), 69–90.

Martinko, M. J., & Gardner, W. L. (1990). Structured observation of managerial work: A replication and synthesis. *Journal of Management Studies, 27*(3), 329–357.

Michigan State Board of Education. (2017). Educator effectiveness snapshot 2017–2018. Retrieved from https://www.mischooldata.org/DistrictSchoolProfiles2/StaffingInformation/NewEducatorEffectiveness/EducatorEffectiveness.aspx.

Mitani, H. (2018). Principals' working conditions, job stress, and turnover behaviors under NCLB accountability pressure. *Educational Administration Quarterly, 54* (5), 822–862.

Monk, D. H., & King, J. A. (1993). Cost analysis as a tool for education reform. In S. L. Jacobson & R. Berne (Eds.), *Reforming education: The emerging systemic approach* (pp. 131–152). Thousand Oaks, CA: Corwin Press.

National Association of Elementary School Principals. (2001). Leading learning communities: Standards for what principals should know and be able to do. Alexandria, VA: National Association of Elementary School Principals. Retrieved from www.naesp.org/llc.pdf.

National Association of Secondary School Principals. (2001). NASSP Background [Online]. Retrieved from www.principals.org/about_us/02-01.html.

National Policy Board for Educational Administration (2015). Professional standards for educational leaders 2015. Reston, VA: National Policy Board for Educational Administration.

Naveh-Benjamin, M., Craik, F. I. M., Guez, J., & Dori, H. (1998). Effects of divided attention on encoding and retrieval processes in human memory: Further support for an asymmetry. *Journal of Experimental Psychological Learning, Memory, and Cognition, 24*(5), 1091–1104.

National Center for Education Statistics (NCES). (2018). Fast facts: Back to school statistics. Retrieved from https://nces.ed.gov/fastfacts/display.asp?id=372.

New Jersey State Board of Education. (2017). Educator evaluation implementation report. Retrieved from https://www.state.nj.us/education/AchieveNJ/resources/201516EducatorEvaluationImplementationReport.pdf.

Nichols, S. L. (2018). High-stakes testing: A tragic national policy. Paper presented as part of the symposium, The problematic relationship of research to practice, at the Annual Convention of the American Psychological Association, San Francisco, CA.

Nichols, S. L., & Castro-Villarreal, F. (Eds.). (2016). Accountability practices and special education services: Impact and implications. *Teachers College Record (Yearbook), 118*(14). Retrieved from http://www.tcrecord.org. ID Number: 21537.

Nichols, S. L., & Valenzuela, A. (2013, summer). Educational policy and youth: Effects of policy on practice. *Theory into Practice, Special Issue: Educational policy and the socialization of youth for the 21st century*, 52(3), 152–159.

Nicol, D. J., & Macfarlane-Dick, D. (2006). Formative assessment and self-regulated learning: A model and seven principles of good feedback practice. *Studies in Higher Education*, 31(2), 199–218.

OECD. (2014a). Results from TALIS 2013: United States of America. Retrieved from http://www.oecd.org/unitedstates/TALIS-2013-country-note-US.pdf.

OECD. (2014b). Teachers love their job but feel undervalued, unsupported and unrecognised. Retrieved from http://www.oecd.org/newsroom/teachers-lo ve-their-job-but-feel-undervalued-unsupported-and-unrecognised.htm.

Pajak, E. (1990). Identification of dimensions of supervisory practice in education: Reviewing the literature. Paper presented at the Annual Meeting of the American Educational Research Association, Boston, MA.

Patrick, H., Mantzicopoulos, P., & French, B. (2018). The utility and value of observation measures of instruction: Differences for research and practice. In The problematic relationship of research to practice. Symposium presented at the Annual American Psychological Association, San Francisco, CA.

Paufler, N. A. (2018). Declining morale, diminishing autonomy, and decreasing value: Principal reflections on a high-stakes teacher evaluation system. *International Journal of Education Policy & Leadership*, 13(8). Retrieved from http://journals. sfu.ca/ijepl/index.php/ijepl/article/view/813/187.

Peck, C., Reitzug, U. C., & West, D. L. (2013). Still waiting for "superprincipal": Examining U.S. policymaker expectations for school principals, 2001–2011. *NCPEA Education Leadership Review*, 14(1), 58–68.

Pedulla, J. J., Abrams, L. M., Madaus, G. F., Russell, M. K., Ramos, M. A., & Miao, J. (2003, March). Perceived effects of state-mandated testing programs on teaching and learning: Findings from a national survey of teachers. Boston, MA: Boston College, National Board on Educational Testing and Public Policy. Retrieved from http://www.bc.edu/research/nbetpp/statements/nbr2.pdf.

Polesel, J., Rice, S., & Dulfer, N. (2013). The impact of high-stakes testing on curriculum and pedagogy: a teacher perspective from Australia. *Journal of Education Policy*, 29(5), 1–18.

Pounder, D., Groth, C., Korach, S., Rorrer, A., & Young, M. D. (2018). *Findings from the 2017 Inspire Graduate (G) Survey*. Charlottesville, VA: UCEA.

Pounder, D., Ni, Y., Winn, K., Korach, S., Rorrer, A., & Young, M. D. (2016). *Findings from the 2016 Inspire-Graduate (G) Survey*. Charlottesville, VA: UCEA.

Prado Tuma, A., Hamilton, L. S., & Tsai, T. (2018). *A nationwide look at teacher perceptions of evaluation systems: Findings from the American Teacher Panel*. Santa Monica, CA: RAND Corporation. Retrieved from https://www.rand.org/p ubs/research_reports/RR2558.html.

Praetorius, A. K., Pauli, C., Reusser, K., Rakoczy, K., & Klieme, E. (2014). One lesson is all you need? Stability of instructional quality across lessons. *Learning and Instruction*, 31, 2–12.

Ravitch, D. (2014). Foreword. In A. L. Lavigne, T. L. Good, & R. W. Marx (Eds.), High-stakes teacher evaluation: High cost—big losses [Special issue]. *Teachers College Record*, 116(1), 1–4.

Robinson, V. J. (2010). From instructional leadership to leadership capabilities: Empirical findings and methodological challenges. *Leadership and Policy in Schools*, 9(1), 1–26.

Robinson, V. M. J., Lloyd, C. A., & Rowe, K. J. (2008). The impact of leadership on student outcomes: An analysis of the differential effects of leadership types. *Educational Administration Quarterly*, 44, 635–674.

Rondfeldt, M., Loeb, S., & Wyckoff, J. (2013). How teacher turnover harms student achievement. *American Educational Research Journal*, 50(1), 4–36.

Rondfeldt, M., Farmer, S. O., McQueen, K., & Grissom, J. A. (2015). Teacher collaboration in instructional teams and student achievement. *American Educational Research Journal*, 52(3), 475–514.

Rosenholtz, S. J., Bassler, O., & Hoover-Dempsey, K. (1986). Organizational conditions of teacher learning. *Teaching and Teacher Education*, 2(2), 91–104.

Rosenshine, B. (1970). The stability of teacher effects upon student achievement. *Review of Educational Research*, 40, 647–662.

Rothstein, J. (2010). Teacher quality in educational production: Tracking, decay, and student achievement. *Quarterly Journal of Economics*, 125(1), 175–214.

Rubie-Davies, C. (2014). *Becoming a high expectation teacher: Raising the bar*. New York, NY: Routledge.

Schochet, P. Z., & Chiang, H. S. (2012). What are error rates for classifying teacher and school performance using value-added models?. *Journal of Educational and Behavioral Statistics*, 38, 142–171.

Schuler, R. S. (1979). Managing stress means managing time. *Personnel Journal (Pre-1986)*, 58, 851–854.

Sebastian, J., Camburn, E. M., & Spillane, J. P. (2018). Portraits of principal practice: Time allocation and school principal work. *Educational Administration Quarterly*, 54(1), 47–84.

Short, E. C. (1995). A review of studies in the first 10 volumes of the Journal of Curriculum and Supervision. *Journal of Curriculum and Supervision*, 11(1), 87–105.

Sigurdson, S. E., Olson, A. T., & Mason, R. (1994). Problem solving and mathematics learning. *The Journal of Mathematical Behavior*, 13(4), 361–388.

Sinnema, C., Meyer, F., & Aitken, G. (2017). Capturing the complex, situated, and active nature of teaching through inquiry-oriented standards for teaching. *Journal of Teacher Education*, 68(1), 9–27.

Smith, W. C., & Kubacka, K. (2017). The emphasis of student test scores in teacher appraisal systems. *Education Policy Analysis Archives*, 25(86), 1–29.

Spillane, J. P., & Hunt, B. R. (2010). Days of their lives: A mixed-methods descriptive analysis of the men and women at work in the principal's office. *Journal of Curriculum Studies*, 42(3), 293–331.

Spillane, J. P., Shirrell, M., & Adhikari, S. (2018). Constructing "experts" among peers: Educational infrastructure, test data, and teachers' interactions about teaching. *Educational Evaluation and Policy Analysis*, 40(4), 586–612.

Stecher, B. M., Garet, M. S., Hamilton, L. S., Steiner, E. D., Robyn, A., Poirier, J., … de los Reyes, B. (2016). Improving teaching effectiveness: Implementation. The intensive partnerships for effective teaching through 2013–2014. Retrieved from https://www.rand.org/pubs/research_reports/RR1295.html.

Styron, R. A., & LeMire, S. D. (2009). Principal preparation programs: Perceptions of high school principals. *Journal of College Teacher and Learning*, 6(6), 51–61.

Supovitz, J., Sirinides, P., & May, H. (2009). How principals and peers influence teaching and learning. *Educational Administration Quarterly*, 46(1), 31–56.

Taras, M. (2001). The use of tutor feedback and student self-assessment in summative assessment tasks: Towards transparency for students and tutors. *Assessment and Evaluation in Higher Education*, 26(6), 605–614.

Taras, M. (2002). Using assessment for learning and learning from assessment. *Assessment and Evaluation in Higher Education*, 27(6), 501–510.

Taras, M. (2003). To feedback or not to feedback in student self-assessment. *Assessment and Evaluation in Higher Education*, 28(5), 549–565.

The Wallace Foundation. (2010). Education leadership: An agenda for school improvement. The Wallace Foundation. Retrieved from http://www.wallacefoundation.org/KnowledgeCenter/KnowledgeTopics/CurrentAreasofFocus/EducationLeadership/Pages/education-leadership-an-agenda-for-school-improvement.aspx.

Valli, L., & Buese, D. (2007). The changing roles of teachers in an era of high-stakes testing accountability. *American Educational Research Journal*, 44(3), 519–558.

van der Lans, R. M. (2018). On the "association between two things": The case of student surveys and classroom observations of teaching quality. *Educational Assessment, Evaluation and Accountability*, 30(4), 347–366.

van der Lans, R. M., van de Grift, W. J. C. M., van Veen, K., & Fokkens-Bruinsma, M. (2016). Once is not enough: Establishing reliability criteria for feedback and evaluative decisions using classroom observation. *Studies in Educational Evaluation*, 50, 88–95.

Waters, T., Marzano, R. J., & McNulty, B. (2003). *Balanced leadership: What 30 years of research tells us about the effect of leadership on student achievement*. Aurora, CO: Mid-Continent Research for Education and Learning.

Weisberg, D., Sexton, S., Mulhern, J., & Keeling, D. (2009). *The Widget Effect: Our national failure to acknowledge and act on difference in teacher effectiveness*. Brooklyn, NY: The New Teachers Project. Retrieved from http://widgeteffect.org/downloads/TheWidgetEffect.pdf.

Witziers, B., Bosker, R. J., & Kruger, M. L. (2003). Educational leadership and student achievement: The elusive search for an association. *Educational Administration Quarterly*, 39(3), 398–425.

INDEX

Page numbers in *italics* refer to figures, those in **bold** indicate tables.